Cambridge studies in medieval life and thought

Edited by WALTER ULLMANN, LITT.D., F.B.A.
Professor of Medieval History in the
University of Cambridge

Third series, vol. 15

FROM THE CIRCLE OF ALCUIN TO
THE SCHOOL OF AUXERRE

CAMBRIDGE STUDIES IN
MEDIEVAL LIFE AND THOUGHT

THIRD SERIES

FROM THE CIRCLE OF ALCUIN
TO THE SCHOOL OF AUXERRE

LOGIC, THEOLOGY AND PHILOSOPHY
IN THE EARLY MIDDLE AGES

JOHN MARENBON

Fellow of Trinity College, Cambridge

The King's Library

CAMBRIDGE UNIVERSITY PRESS

CAMBRIDGE

LONDON   NEW YORK   NEW ROCHELLE

MELBOURNE   SYDNEY

Published by the Press Syndicate of the University of Cambridge
The Pitt Building, Trumpington Street, Cambridge CB2 1RP
32 East 57th Street, New York, NY 10022, USA
296 Beaconsfield Parade, Middle Park, Melbourne 3206, Australia

© Cambridge University Press 1981

First published 1981

Printed in Great Britain by
Western Printing Services Ltd, Bristol

British Library Cataloguing in Publication Data

Marenbon, John
From the circle of Alcuin to the school of
Auxerre. – (Cambridge studies in medieval life
and thought: 3rd series; 15).
1. Middle Ages 2. Europe – Intellectual life
I. Title II. Series
189   CB351   80–41235
ISBN 0 521 23428 X

TO MY PARENTS

CONTENTS

ACKNOWLEDGEMENTS

I have been extremely fortunate in the help, support and encouragement I have received, both from individuals and institutions, in the course of the research and writing which have resulted in this book.

In Peter Dronke I had a liberal supervisor, who left me free to shape my work according to my own inclinations, whilst giving me much welcome encouragement and advice. Edouard Jeauneau, who supervised my work during six months spent in Paris, has been the kindest of advisers, and I have profited greatly from many enjoyable hours of conversation with him about John Scottus and his contemporaries. Dr Michael Lapidge and Professor David Luscombe, who examined my Cambridge Ph.D. thesis, contributed a number of valuable suggestions for changes which have been incorporated in this book. And I should like to express an especial gratitude to Professor Walter Ullmann, both for his kindness in including my book in his series, and for all the help he has given me in preparing my work for publication; and Miss Sheila Lawlor, for checking my proofs.

Many scholars who have had no formal connection with my studies have aided my research. In particular, I wish to thank Professor Bernhard Bischoff, for allowing me to use his transcripts of glosses from a Leningrad manuscript, and for providing me with palaeographical information about a number of other codices; and my friend, Mr Peter Godman, whose learning and good sense have made this book much less bad than it might have been. Other scholars who have discussed my work with me, or read parts of it in earlier drafts include: Professor D. Bullough; Dr C. Burnett; Dr J. Contreni; M. J. Devisse; Mr D. Ganz; Dr M. Gibson; Dr C. Ineichen-Eder; Mr P. Meyvaert; M. J. Vezin.

My work would have been impossible without the co-operation of a large number of libraries throughout Europe, who allowed me to examine their manuscripts or sent me microfilms of them. In

Acknowledgements

particular, I should like to thank the staff of the Warburg Library in London, a treasure-trove for anyone who works on medieval intellectual history; and the curator and staff of the Bibliothèque Nationale in Paris, for their efficiency and courtesy.

I would also like to thank the Syndics and Staff of the Cambridge University Press for the great patience and care they have shown in the production of this book.

My research has been supported by a scholarship from the French Government and a grant from the Department of Education and Science. But, above all, it has been Trinity College which has made my research financially possible; I count myself very lucky indeed, to be part of this College which supports scholarship with such generosity and constancy.

Trinity College   October 1979
Cambridge

INTRODUCTION

To most educated laymen, the term 'medieval philosophy' conjures up the names of the great scholastics of the thirteenth and fourteenth centuries: Aquinas, Duns Scotus and William of Ockham. Occasionally, this mental picture will be extended backwards in time to include the 'Platonism of the School of Chartres' and Anselm; but, almost invariably, the period before the eleventh century will be omitted. This book is a contribution to the study of that neglected age of philosophy. It is not a comprehensive history of early medieval thought, but an attempt to illustrate the character and continuity of the first main period of medieval philosophy, which stretched from the Circle of Alcuin in the late eighth century, to the School of Auxerre in the early tenth.

Such an enterprise raises two immediate questions. Why pick Alcuin as a starting-point and not, say, Cassiodore, Isidore or Bede? And what aspect of the thought of the early Middle Ages can sensibly be called 'philosophy', as opposed to 'logic' or 'theology'? My answers to these questions, which cannot be given entirely separately one from the other, have determined much in what I have chosen to discuss, and what pass by in silence, in the pages which follow.

Whatever doubts there may be about the originality of much of Boethius's work, it is beyond question that his writings contain substantial discussion, at first or second hand, of philosophical issues: the problem of Universals, free-will and determinism, and the nature of time are just a few examples. Moreover, in his *Opuscula Sacra*, Boethius did more than merely use logical techniques to clarify doctrinal distinctions. In his discussion, logical terms are loaded with metaphysical and theological implications. A correct understanding of the concept of essence and its ramifications is tantamount, Boethius appears to suggest, to a knowledge of the relationship between God and his creation. This characteristic of Boethius's thought

I

in especial makes him important both as a source and forerunner for the philosophy of the late eighth to early tenth centuries; and it is as such that I shall examine him in some detail.[1]

Between the death of Boethius and the time of Alcuin, there is no evidence of any similarly active philosophical speculation.[2] Cassiodore possessed a manuscript of dialectical works at Vivarium;[3] he included a short section on the divisions of philosophy and logic in his *Institutiones*;[4] and he compiled a work on the soul, which contained a certain amount of Neoplatonic teachings.[5] Yet there is no indication that he regarded logic as more than a technique for determining the correctness of ways of arguing;[6] nor that he made a connection between the Neoplatonic psychology he borrowed in his *De anima* and the dialectic he expounded in the *Institutiones*. In his *Etymologiae*, Isidore of Seville provided a fuller exposition of elementary Aristotelian logic than Cassiodore had done; and this encyclopaedia also includes information on the history of philosophy.[7] But of an active interest in logic or metaphysics there are few traces.[8]

Ireland has been represented, often with more enthusiasm than accuracy, as the refuge of culture in the dark period of the seventh and eighth centuries.[9] Grammatical and literary works by Irish

---

[1] See below, pp. 16–19 and 22–8.

[2] For general accounts of the intellectual life in this period, see P. Courcelle, *Les lettres grecques en Occident de Macrobe à Cassiodore* (Paris, 1948), pp. 342–88; M. L. W. Laistner, *Thought and letters in Western Europe A.D. 500 to 900* (rev. edn, London, 1957), pp. 91–185; P. Riché, *Éducation et culture dans l'Occident barbare: VIe – VIIIe siècles* (2nd edn, Paris, 1962.) (*Patristica Sorboniensia* 4), pp. 84ff.

[3] See his *Institutiones* (ed. R. A. B. Mynors (Oxford, 1937)) II, iii, 18, pp. 128: 14–129: 11; and cf. Courcelle, op. cit., pp. 342–56, esp. p. 353. This manuscript has not survived.

[4] Ed. cit., II, iii, 1–18, pp. 109–29.

[5] *De anima*, ed. J. W. Halporn (Turnholt, 1973) (*CC* 96). For a discussion of the sources of this work, see pp. 507–11 of this edition.

[6] Cf. *Institutiones*, ed. cit., II, 4, pp. 91: 19–92: 3: 'logica, quae dialectica nuncupatur . . . disputationibus subtilissimis ac brevibus vera sequestrat a falsis'.

[7] See ed. W. M. Lindsay (Oxford, 1911) II, xxii–xxxi & VIII, vi; and cf. J. Fontaine, *Isidore de Séville et la culture classique dans l'Espagne Wisigothique* (Paris, 1959), pp. 593–732.

[8] Fontaine (op. cit., p. 593) comments: 'Il y a . . . chez [Isidore] des pensées philosophiques, des idées et des expressions d'âge et d'origine divers, généralement détachés de leur contexte et réduits à l'anonymat par leur instrument de transmission immédiat. Il n'y a que très rarement une pensée philosophique proprement dite.'

[9] L. Bieler presents a somewhat old-fashioned picture of early Irish culture in *Irland: Wegbereiter des Mittelalters* (Lausanne/Freiburg i. Breisgau, 1961) (Stätten des Geistes 5). Useful modifications to his views are presented by E. Coccia, 'La cultura irlandese precarolingia, miracolo o mito', *Studi Medievali*, 3a serie, 8,1, 1967, pp. 257–420; M. W. Herren, ed., *The Hisperica Famina I: The A-text* (Toronto, 1974); M. Lapidge, 'The authorship of the adonic

scholars of this age survive, but nothing which indicates the study of dialectic. Modern scholarship suggests that the principal achievement of early medieval Ireland lay in the field of biblical exegesis.[10] This raises the question of whether these Irish scholars, like some of the Church Fathers, wove metaphysical discussion into their scriptural commentary. Those texts which have been published, and the accounts of modern specialists in the tradition, suggest the very opposite: fanciful allegorical exegesis is the norm, varied occasionally by more literal, 'historical' commentaries. There is an exception to this general characterization.[11] Faced by the task of recounting the various miracles recorded in the Bible, an Irishman of the mid-seventh century proceeded to a conclusion which is intellectually exciting.[12] None of these miracles, he contended, need be explained by divine intervention in the working of nature: they are comprehensible in natural terms alone. From such a distinction between the realms of nature and of God, the most interesting metaphysical consequences might have been elaborated. But the author confined himself closely to the task in hand; and the *De mirabilibus sacrae scripturae* remained virtually without influence until the twelfth century.[13]

In England, too, the achievements of the seventh and eighth centuries lay in fields other than philosophy. Aldhelm had a taste, developed by his reading of Isidore, for a display of encyclopaedic learning through the use of a precise technical vocabulary; but none of his works show even the slightest inclination towards logic or metaphysics. Bede's attitude to philosophy may be gathered from the way

verses "Ad Fidolium" attributed to Columbanus', *A Gustavo Vinay* = *Studi Medievali*, 3a serie, 18,2, 1977, pp. 249–314.

[10] See B. Bischoff, 'Wendepunkte in der Geschichte der lateinischen Exegese im Frühmittelalter', *Sacris Erudiri*, 6, 1954, pp. 189–281 (= *Mittelalterlichen Studien* I (Stuttgart, 1967), pp. 205–73).

[11] I also except from this characterization three related commentaries: the *Commemoratio Geneseos* in *Paris BN 10457*, the *Interrogatio de singulas questiones quem discipulus tolauit magistrum* in *Paris BN 10616* f. 94r ff. (both no. 3 in the catalogue in Bischoff, op. cit.), and the excerpts from the 'Irish reference Bible' in *Paris BN 614a* (Bischoff, no. 1B). These works *do* show an interest in the more metaphysical aspects of Augustine's exegesis; but, although they were certainly written before the turn of the ninth century, there is no strong evidence that they were written in Ireland, and they may well reflect the intellectual interests stimulated by Alcuin and his circle.

[12] *De mirabilibus sacrae scripturae*, MPL 35, 2149ff. (published under an attribution to Augustine). For the date and place of origin of this treatise, see P. Grosjean, 'Sur quelques exégètes irlandais du VIIe siècle', *Sacris Erudiri*, 7, 1955, pp. 67–98, esp. p. 84ff.

[13] See M. Esposito, 'On the pseudo-Augustinian treatise De mirabilibus sacrae scripturae . . .', *Proceedings of the Royal Irish Academy*, 35C, 1919, pp. 189–207.

in which he removed metaphysical and scientific digressions when he adapted patristic exegetical works.[14] There remains the question of what Alcuin owed, in the way of a philosophical training, to his insular background. Information on Alcuin's life in England is sparse; and on the details of his education there, sparser.[15] In his poem on York, Alcuin lists among the authors represented in the cathedral library Aristotle and Boethius.[16] If he is to be trusted, it is possible that texts of, say, Aristotle's *Categories* and *De interpretatione* (in translation or paraphrase) and Boethius's *De consolatione philosophiae* or his *Opuscula Sacra* were available. Were these works studied, or was the role of York limited to the preservation and transmission, if that, of these texts? In the absence of evidence, speculation is futile. The study of medieval philosophy can begin only from the place and time to which the first philosophical works and manuscripts can be assigned: the court of Charlemagne.

In my study, a set of connected philosophical problems will occupy a central, though not exclusive, position: essence, the Categories and the Universals. This choice is not an arbitrary one. The framework of early medieval studies and beliefs allowed no obvious place for the activity which, in a broadish sense of the word, may be described as 'philosophy': the analysis and elaboration by reasoning of abstract concepts explicative of sensibly or intellectually perceptible reality. Early medieval philosophy grew out of the fusion of two disciplines which were not themselves philosophy: logic and theology. The tools of logic were summoned to clarify and order Christian dogma; and, far more important, concepts and arguments logical in origin were charged with theological meaning. Early medieval thinkers had Boethius and the long tradition behind him to guide them in achieving this combination. But the fusion they made was their own; and, as they made it, they began, not consistently nor always self-consciously, to be no longer theologians or students of formal logic, but philosophers. It was, for the most part, in discussion of essence,

---

[14] See C. Jenkins, 'Bede as exegete and theologian' in *Bede: his life, times and writings*, ed. A. Hamilton Thompson (Oxford, 1935), pp. 152–200, esp. p. 171.

[15] See P. Hunter Blair, 'From Bede to Alcuin' in *Famulus Christi*, ed. G. Bonner (London, 1976), pp. 239–60; and P. Godman, edition of Alcuin's poem on York, to be published in *Oxford Medieval Texts*.

[16] *MGH PLAC* I, p. 204, ll. 1547 and 1549.

the Categories and the Universals that this fusion took place. The continuity between the different schools of the early Middle Ages which their interest in these problems reveals is therefore neither co-incidental nor imposed by the historian from without: it is the very reflection of the gradual rediscovery of philosophy, by men whose lifetimes followed an age that had been without philosophers.

The idea that a set of problems, logical in their origin, is central to early medieval philosophy is not a new one. In his pioneering *Histoire de la philosophie scolastique*,[17] Barthélémy Hauréau recognized the question of Universals as the main philosophical problem, not just of the ninth and tenth centuries, but of the whole Middle Ages. Subsequent historians have done little to challenge or develop Hauréau's view, in so far as it applies to the thought of the early Middle Ages.[18] I shall try to show that the question of Universals can only be properly understood as part of the larger complex of problems already mentioned, concerning Aristotle's ten Categories and, in particular, the first of these, essence.

The problem of Universals has exercised the minds of philosophers since the time of Plato. What is the relationship between a class and its individual members? Is the class a descriptive term, devised by observers who have noted the similarities between a number of members of the class? Or do the members possess their distinctive characteristics by virtue of their relationship to an independent, im-material Universal? The most influential account of this problem in the early Middle Ages was, as Hauréau recognized, a passage from Boethius's second commentary to Porphyry's *Isagoge*. Porphyry wrote this work as an introduction to Aristotle's *Categories*; and the *Categories* were available widely in early medieval times in a Latin paraphrase. But the connection between the problem of Universals and that of essence and the Categories is not just an accident of

---

[17] Volume I (2nd edn, Paris, 1872). See esp. pp. 42–60.
[18] E.g. F. Picavet, *Esquisse d'une histoire générale et comparée des philosophies médiévales* (Paris, 1905), pp. 125–50; M. Grabmann, *Die Geschichte der scholastischen Methode* I (Freiburg i. Breisgau, 1909), pp. 178–214; J. A. Endres, *Forschungen zur Geschichte der frühmittelalter-lichen Philosophie*, pp. 1–20; É. Gilson *La philosophie au Moyen Âge* (3rd edn, Paris, 1947), pp. 180–232; F. Copleston, *A History of Philosophy* II. *Medieval philosophy* (London, 1950), pp. 106–55; M. de Wulf, *History of Medieval Philosophy* I, translated from the 6th edn by E. C. Messenger (London, 1952), pp. 117–48.

history: it is intrinsic and intellectual. A theory of categories can become the instrument through which a philosopher uses his decision on the status of Universals to shape his entire view of the world. The most fundamental caregories of description, such as place, time, quantity and quality, assume the most divergent of functions, as they are treated, on the one hand, as useful, accepted ways of classifying perceptions; or regarded, on the other, as entities eternal and immutable, to be apprehended by the intellect as the result of intensive metaphysical speculation. Of none of Aristotle's Categories is this more true than of the first, essence. When essence is treated as a Universal, separable from, and productive of, those things that are, then every ontological statement becomes charged with a metaphysical weight that can easily be put to the service of theology.

This modification of Hauréau's view of the central problem of medieval philosophy is achieved by the use of Hauréau's own principles. For Hauréau, unlike many historians, was always scrupulous in demanding of the thought of the Middle Ages that clarity and logical coherence which are the prerequisites of all philosophy; and in using a terminology which, without misrepresenting the ideas of medieval scholars, is readily comprehensible to the modern reader. I have tried to do the same in my analyses of the arguments of Aristotle, Porphyry, Boethius and their early medieval followers. The result, I hope, is that it is possible to see exactly what these philosophers argued, and what were the intrinsic links between their various arguments and concepts.

The recognition of the connection between the problems of the Universals, essence and the Categories has an important historical consequence. It enables the observer to trace an important line of development which ran from the work of Alcuin's circle, by way of John Scottus (Eriugena), to the School of Auxerre. Hauréau's limited conception of the range of the problem of Universals prevented him from seeing the relevance of much material from the late eighth and ninth centuries to what he had identified as the central theme of medieval philosophy. Moreover, by viewing the problem of Universals in isolation, Hauréau and those who followed him were led to distort the views of many early medieval philosophers. Thinkers of this period were, by their account, either Realists, who believed that Universals had a real existence, independent of the objects they classified, or Nominalists, who thought that Universals were just names.[19] In fact, no philosopher of the early Middle Ages will fit neatly into one or the other of these parties. The issues that they considered were more complex than has been allowed; and so were their solutions.

It is not only in my interpretation of the central problem of early medieval philosophy that I differ from previous writers. The material which I discuss is far more extensive, and my attitude to it radically different from that of Hauréau and his followers. The period from the late eighth to the tenth centuries is, in philosophy, one of new beginnings, based on the rediscovery of old texts. The evidence of such beginnings will not, for the most part, be found in independent, original treatises, explicitly and completely devoted to philosophy. What the historian must discover are the traces of the philosophical teaching and discussion which took place in schools and among groups of scholars. He will find them in collections of passages, some of them quotations from authorities, others original; in glosses to logical and theological works; and in florilegia.

Modern scholars have tended to discuss whatever philosophical material from the early Middle Ages comes nearest to their conception of a complete, authentic work; and either to neglect the remainder utterly, or to distort it so as to fit this preconception of integrity and originality. Thus the terrain of early medieval thought, as it has been painted, is an odd one: a sombre, featureless plain, where the few landmarks can be seen from afar – the Alcuin Hills, the Forest of Auxerre, and, more prominent than them all, the great plateau of Eriugena, dominated by its splendid cathedral, the *Periphyseon*.

The only way to avoid so distorted an account of early medieval philosophy is to extend the range of evidence to be examined, and to approach this material with respect for its every revealing feature, its most meagre informative capacity. I have tried to follow this counsel in my study. A consequence is that many pages will be devoted to methodological discussion, examinations of textual minutiae and editions of texts not edited, or not properly edited, previously.

Such an approach gains its full value only if it is combined with a more sophisticated conception of originality than historians of philosophy have often entertained. Throughout the early Middle Ages,

---

[19] See, in addition to the works cited in n. 18 above, C. S. Barach, 'Zur Geschichte der Nominalismus vor Roscellin'; and J. Reiners, *Der aristotelische Realismus in der Frühscholastik.*

philosophy was studied on the basis of texts from the past: the writings of the Fathers (in particular, Augustine and Boethius); and a few late antique books of logic.[20] In the circle of Alcuin, the characteristic method for studying these works appears to have been excerption and compilation. But, from the time of John Scottus, a new method gradually predominates: the texts are glossed, thoroughly and sometimes at length. It is easy to dismiss florilegia and sets of glosses as unoriginal, informative only of *what* early medieval scholars read, not of *how* they read it. But this is misleading. In choosing which texts to excerpt and how to group them, a thinker could demonstrate his own interests and even his opinions. Indeed, often quotations and original passages stand side by side in a collection: to remove the original pieces from their context, and consider them alone, would be to miss the author's intentions. Glosses can provide evidence of a most important kind. They can show both how much of an ancient text a medieval thinker understood, and how many of its arguments he accepted. Very frequently, a glossator will try to modify a theory put forward in his text, or suggest an alternative hypothesis; and sometimes he will take the opportunity to expound the ideas most fashionable in his milieu, or to develop his own arguments. Early medieval philosophers thought *through* the ancient texts they studied, but their ideas were not bounded by their sources.

Since it is a tradition of teaching and discussion, of which only the traces survive, which represents the substance of early medieval philosophy, the historian cannot ignore details which may seem merely circumstantial. It is important to ask whether a given thinker worked in isolation, or in the company of colleagues and pupils; to enquire after the identity and character of these followers; and to assemble the evidence, however slight, for the nature of their intellectual life. Even such unpromising details as the size and external appearance of manuscripts can give valuable clues to the way in which an author was read, and what sort of people read him.

My study thus has cut across the traditional boundaries between the work of the philosopher, the historian, the philologist and the palaeographer. I have done so without compunction, for such a

---

[20] See É. Jeauneau, 'L'Héritage de la philosophie antique durant le haut Moyen Âge' – a study which, however, excludes logical works from its consideration.

'mixed' approach is, I suggest, a necessity, if the history of early medieval thought is ever to be written.

Briefly to illustrate the application of my general principles: in the first chapter I discuss the sources which early medieval thinkers used as starting-points for their discussions of essence, the Categories and the Universals. What I present is a summary history of a tradition of philosophized logic, and an examination of its availability to the thinkers of the late eighth and ninth centuries who revived and re-formed it. Chapter 2 is mainly devoted to a study of a set of material which has in the past been dismissed as entirely derivative. By an examination of the circumstances under which the material was pro-duced, and a detailed comparison of it with its sources, I suggest that Alcuin and the followers of his who were responsible for it were con-cerned, not passively to assimilate, but to understand and transform their intellectual heritage. In Chapter 4, I devote myself entirely to establishing what may be known about the followers of John Scottus, using the scraps of evidence presented by notes in manuscripts, brief allusions, and even the physical appearance of the manuscripts them-selves. In Chapter 5, I deal with the early medieval glosses on the problems of essence, the Categories and the Universals (in particular those to a paraphrase of Aristotle's *Categories*) which were, it seems, first written by the generation immediately following Eriugena's. It is not, I believe, sufficient for an intellectual historian merely to transcribe the glosses from a single manuscript and base his comments on these alone. Nor is it correct to treat sets of glosses as if they were literary texts, stable in form and the work of a single author. For this reason, I consider the problem of what can be said about the relations of glossed manuscripts of the same work one to another, without making assumptions beyond the evidence and without resigning one-self to utter confusion. None of the textual or methodological dis-cussions has been introduced for its own sake; and the conclusions of each lead back to my central theme. Chapter 3, where I devote myself to the two outstanding ninth-century discussions of essence and the Universals – those of Ratramnus of Corbie and, especially, John Scottus – is placed consciously at the heart of my study.

Indeed, although he does not appear in its title, John Scottus is the central figure in this work. John, I suggest, is at once a more important, and less outstanding, figure than has been imagined. Historians have in general been content to portray John in grand isolation, an Irishman, working at the court of a foreign king, who brought Greek Neoplatonism to its final development.[21] A man, they say, who owed nothing to the ideas of his contemporaries; whose principal sources were in a language and a tradition alien to the West; and whose works were misunderstood, then quickly forgotten, by the men of his age. A little has been done by modern scholars to modify this view. The wealth of documentation presented by Maieul Cappuyns in his study of Eriugena makes it apparent that John was a man living and working among other men at a certain time and place.[22] More recently, scholars such as Jeauneau[23] and Contreni[24] have published evidence of John's contacts with some of his contemporaries and of his influence upon them. By assembling this scattered material and adding to it a considerable amount never before investigated, I hope to have shown, historically, that, so far from being isolated, John was a thinker whose work was read eagerly by a sizeable band of followers, and whose ideas were copied, developed or distorted with enthusiasm by his contemporaries; and that, moreover, even John's more recondite Greek sources were used by other members of his circle. Parallel to this historical point is a more philosophical one. I argue that one of the central problems in the *Periphyseon*, John's masterpiece, is the complex of questions concerning essence, the Universals and the Categories. This interest John shared with the most gifted of his contemporaries and predecessors. He drew his approach to it mainly from the Western tradition of philosophy; and his account greatly influenced the handling of the problem by his successors. John's discussion of these problems is the most thorough and bold of the early Middle Ages; but neither is it free from the confusions characteristic of his contemporaries, nor are they entirely lacking in John's typical originality.

[21] E.g. Copleston, op. cit., p. 112, refers to the system of Eriugena 'which stands out like a lofty rock in the midst of a plain'. The account of John's philosophy provided by I. P. Sheldon-Williams in *The Cambridge History of Later Greek and Early Medieval Philosophy* (Cambridge, 1967), pp. 518–33, is a good example of the view of Eriugena as the last of the Greek Neoplatonists.

[22] *Jean Scot Érigène: sa vie, son oeuvre, sa pensée.*

[23] See especially: 'Dans le sillage de l'Érigène'; 'Influences érigéniennes dans une homélie d'Héric d'Auxerre'; and 'Quisquiliae e Mazarineo codice 561 depromptae'.

[24] See especially *The Cathedral School of Laon from 850 to 930: its manuscripts and masters.*

Introduction

I should like to end this introduction by expressing an intellectual gratitude to two scholars whom I have never known personally, but whose published work has had the profoundest influence – one that the acknowledgement of a footnote could not sufficiently express – on this study. One is Laurenzio Minio-Paluello. Without his catalogue of manuscripts of the early Latin translations of Aristotle,[25] it would have required years' research in libraries throughout the world to collect information which, with the aid of Minio-Paluello's work, was available at the cost of a certain limited time and labour. The other is the late Étienne Gilson. My direct debts to Gilson are few: only rarely did he touch on the philosophy of the ninth and tenth centuries, and this work was among his least original. My indirect debts to him are profound. Through Gilson's many writings on medieval philosophy there runs his concern with one theme in especial: essence.[26] My limited study of a limited period of medieval thought is centred largely around the same theme. My view of ontology is largely different from Gilson's; but any coherence which I succeed in giving it owes a great deal to my contact with the products of so fine a mind.

[25] *Aristoteles Latinus: Codices supplementa altera* (Bruges/Paris, 1961).
[26] Two works of Gilson's deserve a special mention in this respect: 'Notes sur l'être et le temps chez Saint Augustin'; and 'Éléments d'une métaphysique thomiste de l'être', *Archives de l'histoire doctrinale et littéraire du Moyen Âge*, 1973, pp. 7–36.

Chapter 1

ARISTOTLE'S *CATEGORIES* AND THE PROBLEMS OF ESSENCE AND THE UNIVERSALS: SOURCES FOR EARLY MEDIEVAL PHILOSOPHY

I have argued above that the problem of Universals in the early Middle Ages was part of a larger complex of problems, which can be finally traced back to Aristotle's *Categories*. The present chapter forms a necessary introduction to the detailed studies of early medieval thought and thinkers which follow. I shall begin by offering an abstract of the various patterns of interpretation to which the *Categories* lends itself. I shall then consider which earlier discussions of the *Categories*, and which versions of the *Categories* itself, were available in the early Middle Ages. Finally, I shall summarize the arguments of these sources and indicate their implications. In this way, it will be possible to gain the fullest and clearest impression of the complex of problems related to the *Categories*, as it presented itself in the early Middle Ages.

I

In the *Categories*,[1] Aristotle divides 'things said without any combination' into ten classes: *usia*, quantity, qualification, relation, place, time, being-in-a-position, having, doing and being-affected. By 'things said without any combination', Aristotle means, as he explains at the beginning of the work (1a16), terms such as 'man' and 'runs' as opposed to 'man runs'. The *Categories* is a discussion of these ten classes, although the treatment of the final six is cursory; a consideration of opposition, priority, simultaneity and change concludes the

---

1 In my translations of Aristotle's terminology, I have made considerable use of the excellent translation by J. L. Ackrill, *Aristotle's Categories and De Interpretatione* (Oxford, 1963), although I have not followed Ackrill consistently.

book. The designation of the nine latter categories is self-explanatory; that of the first, *usia*, requires definition. 'Substance' or 'essence' are often given as English translations for *usia*; but since each of these English terms has its own range of connotations, it will avoid confusion if, both here and in all subsequent discussions, the term *usia* is used to stand for the first of Aristotle's Categories. *Usia*, according to Aristotle, is the individual, this man or that horse (2a11); and this definition is supported by reference to a distinction made earlier in the book. A thing may be *said of a subject*, as for instance 'man' is said of an individual man; or it may be *in a subject*, as for example the individual white is in a particular body; or, again, it may be both *said of a subject* and *in a subject* – thus knowledge is both *said of a subject* (knowledge-of-grammar, for instance) and may be *in a subject*, such as the individual soul (1a20). *Usia*, Aristotle distinguishes, is that which is neither *said of a subject* nor *in a subject*. Besides *usia* proper, Aristotle classifies a secondary type of *usia*, by which are described the species and genera of primary *usiae*: so, as examples of secondary *usiae*, Aristotle gives Man (the species to which individual men belong) and Animal (the genus of the species Man)(2a14).

Modern scholars have sought to excuse Aristotle from charges of heterogeneity and incompleteness in his choice of the ten Categories by suggesting that his intention in the work was never to give a systematic classification of all things.[2] Aristotle's remarks, they say, are about things, not words, despite several passages which would suggest the contrary; but Aristotle thought of the Categories simply as questions most pertinently askable of a particular human being as subject. Certainly, in its working-out, it is difficult to imagine a work of comparable generality which is so sparing in its metaphysical presuppositions as the *Categories*. And where Aristotle touches on points of metaphysical interest, he is in general brusquely reductive in this book. On the question of Universals and their dependence on, or independence from, particular things, he simply says: 'All other

---

[2] For modern analysis of the *Categories* see the commentary to Ackrill's translation; E. Kapp, *Greek Foundations of Traditional Thought* (New York, 1942), pp. 36–42; G. E. M. Anscombe and P. Geach, *Three Philosophers* (Oxford, 1961), pp. 7–19; W. C. & M. Kneale, *The Development of Logic* (Oxford, 1962), pp. 25–32; and E. Vollrath, *Studien zur Kategorienlehre des Aristoteles* (Ratingen bei Düsseldorf, 1969) Excurs I, pp. 105–10. A lengthy study, lacking in insight, is provided by A. Trendelenburg in his *Geschichte der Kategorienlehre* (Berlin, 1846).

things are either said of the primary *usiae* as subjects or in them as subjects. So if the primary *usiae* did not exist it would be impossible for any other things to exist' (2b4). Why did the scholars of the early Middle Ages use the *Categories* as a basis for metaphysical speculation, usually of the most markedly un-Aristotelian kind? And how were Aristotle's ideas developed or distorted, to provide the basis for so dissimilar a structure of thought? The answer to the former of these questions depends at least in part on historical evidence, and is consequently best postponed until after a survey of the sources available to the early medieval scholars who studied the doctrine of the Categories. To the latter question, however, the sketch of a solution may be given here: it will serve as a point of reference in the detailed discussion of individual thinkers which follows.

There are two obvious ways in which the concept of *usia* can be charged with the ontological implications which the *Categories* carefully denies it. On the one hand, *usia* can become that which is permanent in any individual, that by which the individual remains this individual and not any other. By this 'interpretation', *usia* is not, as Aristotle had intended, the individual which can be pointed to, inseparable from *some* accidents *or others*, though mentally distinguishable from any *given* group of accidents; but rather, a uniquely differentiated substrate, to which accidents are considered to be fixed.[3] On the other hand, *usia* may be taken as a class-description. This is not in itself contrary to Aristotle's theory: presumably, *Usia* might, in the terms of the *Categories*, be *said of* any single *usia*, just as Man may be *said of* any single man. There is the temptation, however – a temptation that was to prove irresistible – to forget that the class of all *usiae* can only be a species, since its members can only be individuals, and to describe *Usia* as the *genus generalissimum*, the summit of a hierarchical class-system, which thence branches multifariously into genera, species and, finally, individuals.

Aristotle's assertion of the ontological primacy of individuals over species and genera was uncompromising in the *Categories*: if there were no primary *usiae*, there would be no secondary *usiae*. This might be softened, although in explicit contradiction to the text, into a statement of epistemological primacy: classes can only be known through the individuals which comprise them. Or, under Platonic

---

[3] Cf. Anscombe and Geach, op. cit., p. 16–17.

influence, it might be dropped altogether. A Realist theory of Universals has momentous implications when coupled with the re-interpretations of the concept of *usia* just indicated. If *Usia* is a *genus generalissimum*, and members are dependent on their classes, rather than vice versa, then *Usia* is the ontological prop of the universe. Without it there is nothing: it is the very linchpin of reality. If the class *Usia* is thus conceived, what more plausible as a definition of the individual *usia* than the first of the re-interpretations suggested above, *usia* as the unchanging substrate by which each individual is uniquely itself?

There is nothing in this 'argument' which will stand a close logical scrutiny. Even its terms dissolve before a close gaze: what is there in an individual which is unique or permanent, save a changing group of self-resemblances which the onlooker interprets by criteria which convenience has taught custom? How can reality depend on anything? Is it meaningful to envisage the possibility of the universe's not being? Notwithstanding, the pattern of the argument outlined above recurs, in part or whole, through centuries of late antique and early medieval philosophy. The modern interpreter cannot blind himself to the problems of signification raised by such discussions, but he must, so to speak, suspend his disbelief, if he is to trace and assess the development of early medieval thought. It is to the specific sources on the *Categories* and its problems available to the scholars of the ninth and tenth centuries that I shall now turn.

II

Scholars frequently refer to the 'availability' of a given classical text at a certain period in the Middle Ages: what do they mean by this expression? In some cases they are referring to its initial *introduction* into the West, as in the case of the writings of the pseudo-Dionysius, a copy of which was presented to Louis the Pious by the Byzantine Emperor, Michael the Stammerer, or in that of those Classical Greek writings which reached the west via translations from the Arabic. In other cases, they are referring to the first evidence for the *use* of a work, copies of which previously remained unread in some library (or libraries). It is this second concept of availability which is applicable to the antique and patristic texts on the *Categories* and its problems used by scholars of the ninth and tenth centuries. All of these works were *introduced* to the West by their authors at the time of publication: their *use* in the early Middle Ages does not reflect the luck of discovery, but rather interest in their subject-matter and method of treating it. Mere fashion might play a part, but one limited to conferring popularity on to a work which had already gained a limited but definite readership. To a considerable extent, therefore, the sources used by medieval scholars concerned with the problems of the *Categories* do not determine these scholars' point of view, but are themselves selected according to the individual medieval thinkers' preconceptions.

My final point is clearly illustrated by the case of the text of the *Categories* itself. In the early Middle Ages, there were three Latin versions of this;[4] a close translation of Aristotle's text by Boethius; a composite translation, formed from the lemmata of Boethius's Commentary on the *Categories* with the missing passages supplied by an unknown translator; and a paraphrase – in no sense a close or accurate translation – of Aristotle's text, attributed in the Middle Ages to Augustine (the *Categoriae Decem*). The earliest surviving manuscripts of Boethius's own translation are from the eleventh century; there is no evidence of its use in the Middle Ages before then, although some medieval library must have preserved a copy of it. Three ninth-century manuscripts of the composite translation survive[5] but it was not until the eleventh century that this translation began to be used and copied widely. In the ninth and tenth centuries, it was the *Categoriae Decem* from which scholars gained their knowledge of the *Categories*: nineteen manuscripts of the paraphrase from these two centuries survive, many of them with extensive glosses.[6] Ratramnus of Corbie, John Scottus, Heiric and Remigius of Auxerre, all knew the *Categories* through the *Categoriae Decem*;[7] a poetic version was made from the paraphrase;[8] and where, in one ninth-century manu-

---

4 See L. Minio-Paluello, 'The text of the *Categoriae*: the Latin tradition'; (corrected and supplemented by) *Aristoteles Latinus* I, 1–5 (Bruges, 1961), pp. x–xxiii & lxvii–lxxx and 'Note sull' Aristotele Latino Medievale: xv – Dalle *Categoriae Decem* pseudo-Agostiniane (Temistiane) al testo vulgato aristotelico Boeziano'. The first and third of these items are reprinted in Minio-Paluello's *Opuscula: the Latin Aristotle* at pp. 28–39 and 448–58 respectively.

5 *Karlsruhe Reichenau 172* (before 822); *Leningrad F.V. Class. lat. 7*; *Vercelli Arch. Capit. S. Eusebii 138*.

6 See below, pp. 116–38 and 173–206.   7 See below, pp. 67–87.

8 Preserved in *Paris BN 14065*, written in a hand of the eleventh century; published (with

script, a text of the composite translation of the *Categories* is glossed, the glosses derive from those to the *Categoriae Decem*.[9] The prestige of Augustine's name does not alone sufficiently explain the popularity of the paraphrase attributed to him: in the glosses, little capital is made of the great Father's supposed authorship. As I shall argue in my analysis of the *Categoriae Decem*, the popularity of this paraphrase appears to be due in the main to its very differences from Aristotle's text – differences which made the work far more sympathetic to the concerns and aims of most thinkers of the ninth and tenth centuries. Only in the eleventh and twelfth centuries did an increasing interest in the technicalities of logic, and a stronger respect for textual authenticity, lead, first to the replacement of the *Categoriae Decem* by the composite translation, and then to the supersession of both by Boethius's own version. But this story, which has already been sketched in a masterly fashion by Minio-Paluello,[10] lies outside the scope of the present study.

Porphyry's Introduction (*Isagoge*) to the *Categories* was translated into Latin by Marius Victorinus[11] and then by Boethius. Numerous copies of Boethius's translation in ninth- and tenth-century manuscripts testify to the interest in the work which early medieval thinkers displayed: its close connection with the *Categoriae Decem* in their scheme of study is suggested by the coincidence of the two works in a considerable number of dialectical manuscripts.[12] Boethius wrote two commentaries on the *Isagoge*: a simpler one, in dialogue form; and a more complex commentary in five books. By manuscript evidence alone, it would appear that neither version was much

abridgements) by V. Cousin in *Ouvrages Inédits d'Abélard*, pp. 657–69; cf. Minio-Paluello, *Aristoteles Latinus* I, 1–5, p. lxxix n. 2.

[9] In *Leningrad F.V. Class. lat.* 7; cf. Minio-Paluello, ibid.

[10] See 'Nuovi impulsi allo studio della logica: la seconda fase della riscoperta di Aristotele e di Boezio'.

[11] This survives only in fragments, edited by L. Minio-Paluello and B. G. Dodd in *Aristoteles Latinus* I, 6–7 (Bruges/Paris, 1966), pp. 63–8, cf. pp. xxxvi–xxxix; and P. Monceaux, 'L'Isagoge Latine de Marius Victorinus' in *Philologie et Linguistique. Mélanges offerts à Louis Havet* (Paris, 1909).

[12] There are six or seven manuscripts of Boethius's translation of the *Isagoge* which date from the ninth century (cf. Minio Paluello and Dodd, ed. cit., p. xvi). This translation is found among the following dialectical collections: *Roma Bibl. Padri Maristi A. II. 1* (before 814), *Vercelli Arch. Capit. S. Eusebii 138* (s. ix), and the manuscripts, discussed in detail below, pp. 173ff., to which I give the sigla *A, C, F, H, L*. For general information on the contents of dialectical collections, see Minio-Paluello, 'Nuovi impulsi' and A. van de Vyver, 'Les étapes du développement philosophique du haut Moyen Âge'.

studied before the tenth century, and then that it was only the second commentary which achieved a limited circulation: no complete copy of the commentary, and only one copy of the dialogue, survives from the ninth century; five manuscripts of the commentary, but none of the dialogue, survive from the tenth century.[13] Other evidence, however, suggests that this picture is somewhat misleading. John Scottus probably uses the commentary in his *Periphyseon*;[14] and a set of glosses to the *Isagoge*, written in the School of Auxerre not later than the early tenth century, make use of both the commentary and the dialogue.[15] Boethius's two commentaries to Porphyry did not, then, reach a wide early medieval readership; but they were not entirely neglected.

Early medieval scholars appear to have made very little use of the commentary to the *Categories* itself which Boethius composed. The text was available in the ninth century, but copies of it do not appear to have been multiplied.[16] One reason for this commentary's unpopularity may be that it was precisely the sections from the *Categoriae Decem* which were *not* paraphrased from the *Categories* that scholars of the ninth and tenth centuries found most worthy of copy or imitation; and another reason may lie in the commentary's concentration on strictly logical matters, which are treated with considerable fidelity to Aristotle.[17] By contrast, no part of Boethius's

---

13 *Paris BN 12598* (s. ix ex./x in.) contains the entire dialogue and the commentary in part; *Paris BN 12957* (s. ix ex./x in.) contains part of the commentary. The manuscripts of the commentary from the tenth century are: *Einsiedeln 315, 338*; *København Thott 167 fol*; *Paris BN 13955*; *Vaticanus Reg. 1332.* Cf. *Aristoteles Latinus*, I, 6–7, p. xxi.

14 See Van de Vyver, op. cit., p. 435.

15 See *Frühmittelalterlichen Glossen des angeblichen Jepa zur Isagoge des Porphyrius*, ed. Cl. Baeumker and B. von Walterhausen (Münster i.W., 1924) (= *Beiträge zur Geschichte der Philosophie des Mittelalters* 24, 1), sections 259–61 and Introduction, p. 14.

16 *Clm 6374* (Freisingen) dates from the ninth century; one manuscript from the tenth century and two from the late tenth or early eleventh century also survive. See *Aristoteles Latinus* I, 1–5, pp. xlii–xlvii and Addendum. A suggestion by Prantl in his *Geschichte der Logik im Abendlande* II, p. 28, n. 113, that John Scottus used this commentary, has been dismissed by Van de Vyver, op. cit., p. 435.

17 At the beginning of his commentary, Boethius refers to a second, more complex commentary on the *Categories*, in which he will deal with issues omitted in this work. P. Hadot claimed to have found a fragment of this otherwise lost commentary in *Bern 363*, a manuscript which has important links with John Scottus (see below pp. 106–9: 'Un fragment du commentaire perdu de Boèce sur les *Catégories* d'Aristote dans le Codex Bernensis 363', *Archives d'Histoire Doctrinale et Littéraire du Moyen Âge*, 26, 1959, pp. 11–27. But Minio-Paluello shows (art. SEVERINO BOEZIO in *Dizionario Biografico degli Italiani* XI, p. 13 of offprint) that there is no evidence to prove that the commentary from which this fragment derives is that of Boethius.

work had so much influence on early medieval thought about logic
as three of his *Opuscula Sacra*, the *De Trinitate*, the *De hebdomadibus*
and the *Contra Eutychen et Nestoren*. All of Boethius's *Opuscula Sacra*
enjoyed a very wide diffusion in the ninth and tenth centuries, and in
many cases were accompanied by glosses (composed at the end of the
ninth century).[18] Their popularity indicates the great interest which
Boethius's logical approach to doctrinal controversy inspired; their
special value for early medieval scholars tackling problems of ontology lay in the very fact that in these works, as opposed to his commentaries, Boethius did not feel a constraint to expound an Aristotelian (rather than a Platonic) position, nor to curtail metaphysical
discussions.

Two other Christian writers made a very important contribution
to the ninth- and tenth-century discussions on the *Categories*: Marius
Victorinus and Augustine. Although the diffusion of Marius Victorinus was very limited throughout the Middle Ages, his work was
certainly known in two of the most important centres of the ninth-
century thought. Alcuin demonstrates his acquaintance with both of
Victorinus's theological works, the *Adversus Candidum* and the
Adversus Arium;[19] and the *Adversus Candidum* was annotated by a
scribe or (as I shall argue) a pupil very closely associated with John
Scottus.[20] Many of Augustine's works contributed to teaching early
medieval scholars how to apply logic to theological questions, but
one, the *De Trinitate*, was of especial importance as a source for
discussion of the Categories. This work appears to have been
available at most major centres from the ninth century onwards.[21]

Finally, two minor sources for the material of the *Categories* should
be mentioned. The fourth book of Martianus Capella's *De nuptiis
Philologiae et Mercurii* is devoted to logic. Although the discussion of
the Categories here is brief and insubstantial compared with that
found in other sources, the great popularity of Martianus ensured that

---

[18] See E. K. Rand, *Johannes Scottus* (= *Quellen und Untersuchungen zur lateinischen Philologie des Mittelalters*, hrsg. L. Traube, 1) (München, 1906); M. Gibson; '*The Opuscula Sacra*' in *Boethius, his life, thought and influence* (Oxford, 1981), forthcoming; and below, pp. 119–20.

[19] See P. Hadot, 'Marius Victorinus et Alcuin'.

[20] See below, p. 94.

[21] Two manuscripts of the *De Trinitate* survive from the eighth century, twelve from the ninth and nine from the tenth. See A. Wilmart, 'La Tradition des grands ouvrages de Saint Augustin', in *Miscellanea Agostiniana, Testi e Studi* II (Roma, 1931), pp. 257–315, esp. pp. 269–78.

it was read thoroughly and furnished with a variety of sets of glosses. Quite often, Book Four is found, detached from the rest of the *De nuptiis*, as part of a manuscript of logical works.[22] Cassiodore's *Institutiones* contain a short discussion of the Categories which is far more faithful to Aristotle than the *Categoriae Decem*. Despite the wide readership of the *Institutiones*, this discussion appears to have been used only at the earliest period of medieval study of the Categories.[23]

III

Such were the sources for the doctrine of the Categories most used by scholars of the early Middle Ages: the more difficult question remains, as to what interpretations of this doctrine these sources would have suggested. The *Categoriae Decem* was, of all these works on the Categories, the most studied, and so it will be helpful to preface a consideration of more general issues raised by the sources with a look at its particular peculiarities.

The *Categoriae Decem* has either been entirely neglected by historians of logic, or else represented as a simple paraphrase of the *Categories*.[24] It would be more accurate, however, to describe it as a summary of Aristotle's book, interspersed with commentary. It is this commentary-material which, as their glosses show, particularly interested early medieval scholars. Passages of commentary which provided the subject for important glosses include discussions of the relationship between *usia* and the nine other Categories, an explanation of Aristotle's distinction between δύναμις and ἐνέργεια and a reference to the Peripatetic theory of virtues as a mean.[25] The passage added by the *Categoriae Decem* to the beginning of the discussion of quantity, on the way in which a geometrical body is built up from

---

[22] The Categories are discussed on pp. 164–84 of the edition by A. Dick, revised J. Préaux (Stuttgart, 1969). For details of the manuscripts of the *De nuptiis* and their glosses, see C. Leonardi, 'I codici di Marziano Capella', esp. 33, p. 457 (for mss. with Book IV apart from the rest of the work).

[23] The Categories are discussed in Book II, iii, sec. 9–10, pp. 113–114 of ed. cit.; for manuscripts, see Introduction, pp. x–xlix. For the use of the *Institutiones* at the beginning of the ninth century, see below, p. 51.

[24] For the view of the *Categoriae Decem* as a simple paraphrase, with just a few additions, see Prantl, *Geschichte der Logik im Abendlande* I, pp. 669–72.

[25] All references to the *Categoriae Decem* are to the edition by Minio-Paluello in *Aristoteles Latinus* I, 1–5, pp. 133–75; arabic numerals refer to the numbers of sections in this edition. The passages in question are, respectively: 52–4, 102, 160 second part.

length, breadth and height, gave rise to a number of speculations on the difference between *usia* and quantity and helped in the formulation of the early medieval theory of place as something incorporeal.[26] The expansion of the section on time and place, from Aristotle's dismissive mention to a fleeting paragraph in the *Categoriae Decem*,[27] begins a process which leads to John Scottus's extensive treatment of these categories and the various glosses on them which appear in a number of ninth- and tenth-century manuscripts. The *Categoriae Decem* also adds a passage on the ontological status of Aristotle's remarks and modifies Aristotle's definition of *usia*; on these questions, the early medieval scholar could also turn to a variety of other sources.

The explicit view of the *Categoriae Decem* as to the ontological status of Aristotle's remarks in the *Categories* is that they are about neither language nor external reality as such, but about things which are perceived. But, according to the paraphraser, a discussion of things that are perceived necessarily implies a discussion of the other two classes: what is perceived arises from what exists, and it could not be discussed without the aid of speech.[28] Certain other passages in the *Categoriae Decem*, however, do not wholly support this view. Although the paraphraser recognizes that Aristotle's interest is in what is signified, not what signifies, he adds considerably to the discussion of purely linguistic points.[29] The opening section of the *Categoriae Decem* is also a little confusing on this matter.[30] Aristotle, the paraphraser states, showed admirable scrupulousness in beginning his work with a discussion of the beginning (*origo vel principium*) of *oratio*, since all knowledge can only be treated by *oratio*. *Oratio*, he explains, does not mean any type of speech, but only that which signifies something: only, therefore, nouns and verbs. The paraphraser goes on to explain class-theory in purely verbal terms: the word 'Man' includes all men; man, beast and horse are all indicated by the word 'Animal'; and finally *usia* embraces all things 'with a vast and infinitely capacious name'.[31] The paraphraser most probably intended that his initial definition of *oratio* as 'speech which signifies' should suggest that what is here expressed in linguistic terminology should be

---

[26] 72–3.   [27] 145–6.   [28] 19–20.   [29] For example, 13–16 & 22–5.   [30] 1–5.
[31] 'Postremo, licet abunde prospexerat dispersa passim genera speciali nota concilians, tamen ingenti quodam et capaci ad infinitum nomine omne quidquid est comprehendens dixit οὐσίαν, extra quam nec inveniri aliquid nec cogitari potest.' 5, p. 134; 16–19.

understood as referring principally to those things which are signified by language; but he fails to make this interpretation explicit.

In his commentary on the *Categories*, Boethius puts forward an altogether simpler view of the ontological status of Aristotle's discussion. Aristotle's intention, he says, was to consider the names of things, not *qua* words subject to grammatical and syntactical rules, but 'in so far as they denote objects' (*in eo quod significantes sunt*).[32] Porphyry's *Isagoge* treats the *Categories* as a work about the nature of things; moreover, he extends the claims of its scope. The ten categories become universal classes which, between them, embrace all things.[33] This view of the scope of the doctrine of the Categories was taken over by Christian writers who discussed the relations between the ten Categories and God.

In the *Categoriae Decem* and the other works on the Categories available to the early Middle Ages there could be found both uncompromising statements of the truly Aristotelian definition of *usia* as the individual, and a variety of passages which contradicted this view. Thus the writer of the *Categoriae Decem* takes directly from Aristotle the expression that '*usia*, properly and principally so called, is that which is not in a subject nor is said of a subject, such as this man or this horse'.[34] This was one of the views advanced by Boethius when commenting the *Isagoge*,[35] and the only definition of *usia* to be given in his commentary on the *Categories*.[36] One example of a different, contradictory statement on *usia* from the *Categoriae Decem* has already been mentioned in connection with a different question. There *usia*, 'outside which nothing may be found or thought of', was said to embrace all things with a name of infinite capacity.[37] Similarly, when the paraphraser is talking about definition, which, he says, should begin from the genus and then narrow itself down until it includes only the particular *definiendum*, he remarks that *usia* cannot be defined in this way: *usia* has no genus since it sustains all things

---

[32] All references to Boethius's commentary on the Categories are to *MPL* 64, cols. 159–294. This passage is at 159C.

[33] All references to Porphyry's *Isagoge* are to the edition in *Aristoteles Latinus* I, 6–7, pp. 5–31. This passage: 11: 18–12: 2.

[34] 57, p. 146: 2–4.

[35] All references to Boethius's commentaries on the *Isagoge* are to ed. G. Schepss and S. Brandt (Wien/Leipzig, 1906) (*CSEL* 48). This passage: Dialogue p. 19:2–6.

[36] Cf. ed. cit. 182D.

[37] See above, n. 31.

(*ipsa autem usia genus non habet cum omnia ipsa sustineat*).[38] Here the paraphraser appears to fuse two views of *usia*, each equally un-Aristotelian: the idea that *usia* is a *genus generalissimum*, and so has no genus above it; and the notion of *usia* as a substrate, sustaining the accidents which make up the world of appearances. A definition of *usia* as a *genus generalissimum* is also put forward by Porphyry in his *Isagoge*[39] (where, most inconsistently, he states in another passage that there can be no one genus of all things).[40]

The idea of *usia* as a *genus generalissimum* will depend on the nature of a theory of Universals for its implications. Little in the way of such a theory is put forward in the *Categoriae Decem*, except for a single statement upholding the epistemological priority of the individual: no one could know what, for instance, a man was, unless someone placed a man before his eyes as a subject for 'Man'.[41] However, in the *Isagoge*, and, especially, in Boethius's commentaries on the *Isagoge* and the *Categories*, the problem of Universals is discussed in some detail. Porphyry himself avoids a direct discussion of the question, but his opinion emerges in a couple of incidental comments. He offers as a reason for constructing a theory of classes the fact that there can be no ordered knowledge (*disciplina*) about the infinity of individuals – a view which is explicitly recognized as Platonic.[42] And at one point Porphyry says openly that genera and species are prior by nature to individual substances.[43] Warren, whose notes on the *Isagoge* are normally perceptive and useful, suggests here that Porphyry is putting forward merely a distinction of conceptual priority, in which existence is not involved.[44] But this interpretation must be incorrect:

---

[38] 57, pp. 145:25–146:2: 'usian, quoniam secundum artem definiri non poterat – quae praecipit ut definitio, quo possit tendi latius, a genere sumat exordium, ipsa autem usia genus non habet cum omnia ipsa sustineat – per partes eam voluit definire, ut quid sit, non solum eius definitione, verum partium quoque cognitione noscatur' and cf. 37.

[39] p. 10:8–9; cf. p. 9:19–23.

[40] pp. 11:18–12:2.   [41] 6, p. 134:22–4.

[42] p. 12:12–13: 'infinita, inquit [Plato] relinquenda sunt, neque enim horum, posse fieri disciplinam. Cf. below, Chapter 3, pp. 82–3.

[43] p. 25:20–1: 'genera vero et species naturaliter priora sunt individuis substantiis'.

[44] *Porphyry the Phoenician: Isagoge*, translated with introduction and notes by E. W. Warren (Toronto, 1975), pp. 54–5, n. 50. In a brilliantly argued article ('Neoplatonic and Aristotelian logic'), A. C. Lloyd suggests that Porphyry treated logic as a discipline separate from, and subordinate to, his Neoplatonic metaphysics. Stripped of metaphysical implications, the logic of Porphyry's was almost nominalist, by Lloyd's account. My remarks in this chapter do not contradict the drift of Lloyd's theory, but they do suggest that in the *Isagoge* there were several instances where Porphyry allowed his metaphysical ideas to

if genus is merely a concept, then it is formulated by the mind from the observation of individuals; and so individuals must be conceptually prior to genera, since it will be from individuals that the concepts which constitute genera are derived: in short, to affirm the conceptual priority of genera is to deny that they are merely concepts.

In line with the consistently Aristotelian view which he takes in this work, in his commentary to the *Categories* Boethius clearly denies that Universals have any real existence. A Universal is simply that which is predicated of a subject, as Animal or Man is predicated of Socrates or Plato. If all individual men were to perish, then the Universal, Man, would perish too, says Boethius – a clear statement of the ontological priority of individuals.[45] One or two of the expressions he uses, however, illustrate some of the problems or doubts which Boethius attempts to leave out of consideration. Genera and species are understood, 'not from one single individual, but from all the single individuals [of a given class] conceived by the reason of the mind' (*non ex uno singulo intellecta sunt, sed ex omnibus singulis, mentis ratione concepta*). But that which was first of all called 'man' was not the concept derived from all single men, but a given individual man. The problem which is implied by the juxtaposition of these two ideas is this: if the Universal, Man, is to be gathered only from all individual men, how will any individual man be known to be a man? Boethius's pragmatic observation that 'man' was a name first given to an individual man suggests an *ad hoc* procedure of class-grouping, in which family resemblances replace hierarchically ordered genera and species as the terms of analysis. However, no philosopher of Antiquity or the Middle Ages contemplated doing away with the theory of ordered classes, and Boethius was not an exception: he leaves the problem raised by his two ideas implicit and unresolved. There are other awkward consequences to Boethius's theory. In an

colour his exposition of logic. Indeed, Lloyd himself (p. 156) is forced to admit that the passage under discussion here contradicts Porphyry's general 'nominalist' tendency.

[45] 171AB; 183B–D, esp. 183CD: 'Neque enim cuncta individuorum substantia in uno Socrate est, vel quolibet uno homine, sed in omnibus singulis. Genera namque et species non ex uno singulo intellecta sunt, sed ex omnibus singulis individuis, mentis ratione concepta. Semper etiam quae sensibus propinquiora sunt, ea etiam proxime nuncupanda vocabulis arbitramur. Qui enim primus "hominem" dixit, non illum qui ex singulis hominibus conficitur concepit, sed animo quemdam singularem atque individuum cui hominis nomen imponeret. Ergo, sublatis singulis hominibus, homo non remanet, et, sublatis singulis animalibus, animal interibit.'

attempt, apparently, to deny that the Universal exists in any individual member of the given class, Boethius writes: 'The whole substance of individuals (*cuncta individuorum substantia*) is not in one Socrates or in any single man at all, but in all single men.' If the whole substance of any individual is outside itself, then its own substance must be either partial or participatory. In trying to assert the ontological primacy of individuals, Boethius has succeeded in undermining their ontological independence altogether.

In his second commentary to Porphyry's *Isagoge* Boethius again denies the real existence of Universals, but here he is willing to allow that, in a sense, a genus must be entire in its subordinate species, and a species entire in its individual members. This assertion, and the consequent unity but multiplicity of any genus, are preliminaries to a denial that Universals exist at all. The mind considers men, who are all dissimilar and yet have each a certain point of similarity, and this similarity, 'considered in the mind and truly envisaged', constitutes the species. By a similar process of mental collection among the species the genera are produced. The similarity by which an individual belongs to its species is sensible in each individual, but when it is grasped by the understanding it becomes an incorporeal Universal.[46] One manner of raising an objection to this theory has a special importance for the early medieval discussion of Universals. If the characteristics by which an individual belongs to a species exist in that individual, then how is one member of a species to be distinguished from another? The answer is supplied by Boethius in his *De Trinitate*: 'it is the variety of accidents which constitutes numerical difference'.[47] If individuals owe their independence only to their accidents, then essentially they are not individual. This conclusion accords excellently with Boethius's initial concession, that the species exists entire in its individual members. Thus it is easy to up-end the theory of Boethius's

[46] Commentary, pp. 159:10–167:20. This passage has been much discussed by historians of medieval philosophy: in particular, M. M. Tweedale (*Abailard on Universals*, pp. 53–88) gives an excellent summary and critique of Boethius's theory of Universals. My account is rather different from his, not because I entertain any disagreement with his views, but because my interest is to show how, on a certain reading, Boethius could lead the way towards the hyper-Realism of a John Scottus and the various alternative theories of Eriugena's contemporaries and followers.

[47] All references to the *Opuscula Sacra* are to *Boethius: the Theological Tractates and the Consolation of Philosophy*, edited and translated by E. K. Rand, H. F. Stewart & S. J. Tester (Cambridge, Mass., 1973). This passage, p. 6:24–5: 'numero differentiam accidentium uarietas facit'.

Isagoge commentary into a 'hyper-Realism', whereby the existence of individuals is entirely dependent on that of the classes to which they belong.[48] The disclaimer which Boethius attaches to his exposition of the theory – he expounds it not because he thinks it true but because it is Aristotelian, and he is commenting a work based on Aristotle – must have made such an 'elaboration' of Boethius's idea all the more tempting to the early medieval scholar.

Boethius could well have extended his disclaimer. In his commentaries on the *Categories* and the *Isagoge* he may not show himself consistently or strictly an Aristotelian, but he provides few signs of the Platonic ontology and theory of Universals which surface in the *Opuscula Sacra*. Even here, certain comments, taken out of context, would suggest an Aristotelian approach. Thus in the *Contra Eutychen* he remarks, 'The understanding of universal things is taken from particulars.'[49] But this remark need only imply the epistemological priority of individuals; and a study of this and other passages in the *Opuscula Sacra* supports this limitation. Essences, says Boethius in the very same passage from the *Contra Eutychen*, can indeed *be* (*esse possunt*) in Universals, but only in particulars and individuals do they *have substance* (*substant*). Universals are hereby accorded a different sort of existence from particulars.

In his *De Trinitate*, Boethius puts forward two arguments which distinguish God's mode of being from that of other things. Concrete wholes, he says, are made of matter and form; but God is pure form.[50] The *esse* of anything, however, derives not from matter but from form:[51] that is, a piece of formless matter (pure potentiality) becomes such-and-such a thing by virtue of its form. Boethius argues also that all things except God are made of parts, and that their *esse* derives from their parts. Therefore, he says, only of God can it be said that he is what he is.[52] The connection between these two arguments is

---

[48] A similar conclusion emerges from the survey of H. J. Brosch *Der Seinsbegriff bei Boethius* (Innsbruck, 1931) (= *Philosophie und Grenzwissenschaften* IV, 1); see especially pp. 74–92.

[49] pp. 86:35–88:36: 'Intellectus enim universalium rerum ex particularibus sumptus est.'

[50] Ed. cit., p. 10:29–31; 'Divina substantia sine materia forma est atque ideo unum et est id quod est. Reliqua enim non sunt id quod sunt.'

[51] Ibid., p. 10:21: 'Omne namque esse ex forma est.'

[52] Ibid., p. 10:32–7: 'Unum quodque enim habet esse suum ex his ex quibus est, id est ex partibus suis, et est hoc atque hoc, id est partes suae coniunctae, sed non hoc vel hoc singulariter. Igitur non est id quod est.' I have discussed this passage from the *De Trinitate* in a paper entitled, 'Making sense of the *De Trinitate*; Boethius and some of his medieval

unclear. Certainly, all things except God cannot be held to be made from parts because they are composed of matter and form. *Esse*, Boethius has said, which comes from form, derives from the parts of which things are composed: these parts cannot therefore be *matter and form*.

The ontology of the *De hebdomadibus* is equally hierarchical. 'Being (*esse*) is different from that which is (*id quod est*). For being itself is not yet (*nondum est*), whereas that which is, once it has received the form of being (*essendi forma*), is and consists (*est et consistit*).'[53] Here *id quod est* seems to stand for *usia* in the Aristotelian sense, the individual, and *esse* for *Usia* in general; although *esse* 'is not yet', the individual requires the *forma essendi* in order to 'be and consist'. Schrimpf most convincingly interprets this passage, and related discussion in the *De hebdomadibus*, to mean that men can only know what is through the individuals; but that every particular thing derives its being from participation in universal *Usia*.[54] Indeed, an ontology of participation may be surmised from much of the *De hebdomadibus*; and such an ontology is central to another work of Boethius's widely studied in the early Middle Ages, the *De consolatione philosophiae*.

Moreover, when Boethius is not thinking ontologically, his tendency towards an extreme realism becomes manifest. In the passage from the second chapter of his *De Trinitate* discussed above, he states that a concrete individual owes its existence as such-and-such a thing to its form. But he then goes on to distinguish between the forms in matter, which are not really forms but images (*imagines*) of the true forms which exist outside matter.[55] This may just be the result of a tendency to hypostatize run wild – one could, after all, so easily posit real, immaterial Universals which determine their individuals, without imagining that the Universals would become literally embedded

commentators', given to the Eighth International Conference on Patristic Studies in Oxford, September 1979. Proceedings of this conference are to be published in 1981 under the editorship of Miss E. A. Livingstone.

[53] p. 40:28–30: 'Diversum est esse et id quod est; ipsum enim esse nondum est, at vero quod est, accepta essendi forma, est atque consistit.'

[54] G. Schrimpf, *Die Axiomenschrift des Boethius*, esp. pp. 27–8; and see pp. 8–29 in general for an account of the ontology of the *De Hebdomadibus*. See also P. Hadot, 'La Distinction de l'être et de l'étant dans le "De Hebdomadibus" de Boèce'. Hadot considers that *esse* translates the Greek τὸ εἶναι, and *quod est* translates τὸ ὄν.

[55] Ed. cit., p. 12:51–4: 'Ex his enim formis quae praeter materiam sunt, istae formae venerunt quae sunt in materia et corpus efficiunt. Nam ceteras quae in corporibus sunt abutimur formas vocantes, dum imagines sint.'

in the matter they inform. Or it may possibly be a result of Boethius's worrying that, since any given individual is the member of many classes, it cannot properly be said to resemble any single Universal; and so feeling that, if a relationship of exemplar to image holds between Universal and particular, this can only be through the intermediary of the images of individual Universals.

Further on in the *De Trinitate* Boethius develops his idea of the relationship of *usia* to God.[56] On the one hand, Boethius says that the word 'God' seems to indicate a substance, but that substance which is beyond substance. On the other hand, he remarks that whilst both Man and God are called 'substance', Man is not a substance, since he is not entirely himself: he owes what he is to things that are not Man. God, however, is entirely himself.[57] Boethius therefore offers two contradictory views on the question of God's relationship to *usia*. First, that God is, strictly speaking, beyond substance. Or, second, that it is of God alone that substance may be properly predicated, since he alone is entirely himself, owing nothing to things outside himself. Boethius then goes on to consider the other categories and their relationship to God and to Man. None of them is properly predicable of God, and only quantity and quality are properly predicable of Man, since the other categories attribute what is merely incidental to a man.[58]

The negative theology implicit in Boethius's treatment of the categories in relation to God is present in a clearer form in Augustine's *De Trinitate*.[59] Augustine begins by denying that any of the nine categories besides *usia* may be applied to God, although he goes on to allow that certain categories – position, condition (*habitus*), place and time – may be said of God metaphorically (*non proprie sed translate per similitudines*), and to discuss at some length the special way in which the category of relation (*ad aliquid*) must be treated if it is to be used in describing the relationship between the Father and the Son.

But the first of the categories, *usia*, is applicable to God. Indeed, for Augustine, it is God – the God who said, 'Ego sum qui sum' – who most properly instantiates this category. Created things have only a partial being, which resembles the true being of God, in which they

---

[56] pp. 16:14–18:36.   [57] p. 18:31–36.   [58] pp. 18:36–24:98.
[59] All references to Augustine's *De Trinitate* are to ed. W. J. Mountain and Fr. Glorie (Turnholt, 1968) (= *CC* 50). This passage v, 1–8, pp. 207:2–216:34.

participate. This partial being is mixed with non-being, so that the created universe is subject to continual change and ultimate destruction.[60]

Marius Victorinus had taken his negative theology further. A pagan rhetorician turned Christian in old age, he drew on a tradition formalized by Porphyry to deny that God could in any way be among the things that are.[61] God excels all the divisions of being and not-being; he is superior even to those things which truly are, since he is their cause. God is therefore μὴ ὄν, 'that which is not'.[62]

There was, then, a rich variety of thought on essence, Categories and the Universals to stimulate the minds of early medieval scholars. In the next chapter I shall turn to consider how the earliest philosophers of the Middle Ages – Alcuin and his followers – assimilated this aspect of antique learning and, falteringly, made their own fusion of logic and theology.

[60] Cf. É. Gilson, 'Notes sur l'être et le temps chez Saint Augustin'; and G. Huber *Das Sein und das Absolute* (Basel, 1955) (= *Studia Philosophica* suppl. 6), pp. 129–31.

[61] For the sources of Marius Victorinus's negative theology of being, see P. Hadot, *Porphyre et Victorinus* I (Paris, 1968), III–iii, pp. 171–8.

[62] All references to the theological works of Marius Victorinus are to ed. P. Henry and P. Hadot (Wien, 1971) (= *CSEL* 83–i). This passage: *Ad Candidum* 13, p. 30:1–12. Cf. Hadot. 'La Distinction' for the limitation of the meaning of μὴ ὄν.

Chapter 2

LOGIC AND THEOLOGY AT THE COURT OF CHARLEMAGNE

I

The circle of pupils which Alcuin gathered round him at the court of Charlemagne provided the setting for the first attempts in the medieval West to assimilate the techniques of logic and apply them to theology. In particular, the scholars of Alcuin's circle had to take measure of the problems concerning essence and the Categories which they inherited from the Schools of Antiquity and the Fathers. Historians have not been flattering in their estimates of the philosophical activity carried on at Charlemagne's court: the most charitable commend Alcuin for his part in introducing various logical texts into the curriculum, but they are unanimous in declaring that he was not at all a thinker in his own right.[1] And a writer as learned as Grabmann is willing to extend this judgement to the age as a whole.[2] Charlemagne's, he suggests, was a time of intellectual 'hyperconservatism', in which philosophy could be conducted only as a slavish imitation of past thinkers.

This low estimate of Alcuin's philosophy is misleading only in that it posits a crude distinction between the assimilation of old material and the creation of new ideas. Nowhere in the works certainly attributed to him does Alcuin put forward an argument that is original and striking. Yet in his choice and juxtaposition of second-

---

[1] See e.g. Hauréau, op. cit., pp. 123–7; Picavet, op. cit., pp. 126–7 (a charitable estimate); J. B. Gaskoin, *Alcuin: his life and work* (1904; reissue New York, 1966), pp. 194–6; Gilson, op. cit., pp. 191–2; Copleston, op. cit., pp. 106–11; de Wulf, op. cit., pp. 21–2; M. L. W. Laistner, *Thought and Letters in Western Europe A.D. 500 to 900*, (rev. edn London, 1957), pp. 321–3. The best treatment of the philosophy of this time remains Endres, op. cit., pp. 1–20. A study by M. Cristiani *Dall' 'unanimitas' all' 'universitas'. Da Alcuino a Giovanni Eriugena. Lineamenti ideologici e terminologia politica della cultura del secolo IX* (Istituto storico Italiano per il Medio Evo, Studi Storici, 100–2) (Roma, 1978) was not available to me before my book was complete.

[2] Op. cit., I, pp. 179–80.

hand material he reveals a mind clear and resolved in its purpose. His works against the Adoptionist heresy efficiently marshal the patristic testimonies for his case.[3] His didactic simplifications of the teachings of Augustine and other Fathers do not indicate an inability on his part to understand their thought in its full ramifications, but rather, the sane judgement of a teacher as to the abilities of a particular audience.[4] Alcuin's use of Boethius's *De consolatione philosophiae* in his *De vera philosophia* has often been discussed,[5] but scholars have been slow to recognize the skill with which he transforms Boethius's ideas to his purposes. In particular, the central theme of Books I–III of the *De consolatione* – that in seeking after lesser, transitory goods men are really searching, in a mistaken manner, for beatitude – is used to justify the pursuit of wisdom. Another good example of Alcuin's method of transforming borrowed material is provided by the *dicta Albini*, which is studied below in detail.[6] Logic was among Alcuin's strongest interests. He was responsible for putting the *Categoriae Decem* into general circulation,[7] and, in his *De dialectica* he provided a useful, though entirely derivative, compendium of logical doctrine.[8]

The only member of Alcuin's circle whose thought has attracted more than the most fleeting attention from historians is Fredegisus. I shall try to demonstrate that by far the most sophisticated and exciting intellectual products of Charlemagne's court are associated with another of Alcuin's pupils, the lesser-known Candidus. Fredegisus's philosophical work, produced entirely after the death of his master, will be examined later:[9] although it cannot bear the weight which some scholars have placed on it, it provides some interesting clues as to the history of philosophy between the break-up of Alcuin's circle and the rise of Charles the Bald's Palace School.

I shall focus my discussion of philosophy at the Palace School of Charlemagne on one particular set of material which originated

---

[3] Principally, the *Liber adversus Felicis Haeresin* (MPL 101, 87–230) and the *Liber adversus Elipandum* (ibid., 243–300). Cf. W. Heil, 'Der Adoptianismus, Alkuin und Spanien'.

[4] See especially, the *De Fide s. Trinitatis* (MPL 101, 11–58) and the letter to Eulalia, *De animae ratione* (ibid,. 639–50). Both these works draw heavily on Augustine's *De Trinitate*.

[5] The *De vera philosophia* is printed, as a preface to the *De Grammatica* in MPL 101, 849–54. Cf. F. Brunhölzl, 'Der Bildungsauftrage der Hofschule' esp. pp. 32–9; and P. Courcelle *La Consolation de philosophie dans la tradition littéraire*, pp. 33–47.

[6] See below, pp. 33–46.

[7] Cf. Prantl, op. cit., II, p. 14; *Aristoteles Latinus* I, 1–5, pp. lxxxvi–xci, and B. Bischoff, 'Die Hofbibliothek Karls des Grossen' in *Karl der Grosse: Lebenswerk*, pp. 42–62, esp. p. 48.

[8] Cf. Prantl, op. cit., II, pp. 15–17.   [9] See below, pp. 62–6.

there: a group of passages ('the Munich Passages') preserved most
fully in a manuscript now at Munich (*clm 6407* = v). Although these
passages have been printed before (though never in their entirety or
from the best manuscripts),[10] and they have been discussed by scholars,[11] their value as testimony to the philosophical interests of Alcuin
and his circle has never been fully exploited. This value emerges only
when the sources of the Passages are set forth, and the interests to
which the Passages testify are placed in the context of the assimilation
of logical material and techniques. It will then be seen that the level of
philosophical discussion at the court of Charlemagne was a good deal
more sophisticated than historians have allowed, and that the interests
and methods of scholars of the mid- and late ninth-century were anticipated to a surprising extent. To this end, I give below a complete
text of the Passages, edited from the best manuscripts and with an
apparatus of sources and parallels; and in the following pages I shall

[10] Twelve of the passages (the *dicta Albini*, IV and VI are omitted) were printed by Hauréau,
op. cit., I, pp. 134–7) from *Paris BN 13953*, unfortunately with many serious errors
of printing and transcription. Substantial extracts from III and IV, again from *BN 13953*,
appear in G. Grünwald, *Geschichte der Gottesbeweise zum Aufgang der Hochscholastiker*
(Münster, 1907) (= *Beiträge z. Gesch. der Philosophie des Mittelalters* VI, 3), pp. 18–24. The
dicta Candidi has been printed by Froben (*Alcuini . . . opera*, St Emmeram, 1777, II, p. 596
= *MPL* 101, 1359–60 from *clm 6407* and *Wien 458*; and, in letter-form, by Dümmler
(*MGH Epp.* v, pp. 615–16) from *Würzburg Theol. Fol. 56*. The *dicta Albini* has been
printed by Duchesne, alias 'Quercetanus' (*Alcuini . . . opera*, Paris, 1617, col. 54–6) from a
transcript by Sirmond of *Berlin Deutsche Stadtsbibliothek 181* (cf. *Handschrift-Verzeichnisse* of
the Berlin königliche Bibliothek, ed. V. Rose, II (Berlin, 1893), p. 414); and by Froben (ed.
cit., I–2, p. 339–40) = *MPL* 100, 565–8) from *clm 6407*, *Wien 458* and a St Emmeram
manuscript. O. Richter ('Wizo und Bruun, zwei Gelehrte im Zeitalter Karls des Grossen',
esp. pp. 34–5) edits the *dicta Candidi* from *clm 6407*, collated with the editions of Froben and
Hauréau. (I am grateful to Professor D. Bullough for lending me a copy of this exceedingly
rare article.) Zimmerman ('Candidus. Ein Beitrag zur Geschichte der Frühscholastik',
prints a number of the passages in whole or in part. His work appears to have been done
without any fresh references to the manuscripts; but his texts include a large number of
fresh errors. For pseudonymous publication of the *dicta Albini* and *dicta Candida*, see
Appendix 1 (below, pp. 144–51).

[11] Besides Hauréau, Zimmerman and Richter, loc. cit., see: Endres, op. cit., pp. 5–19; M.
Schmaus, 'Das Fortwirken der Augustinischen Trinitätspsychologie bis zur karolingishen
Zeit', in *Vitae et veritati: Festgabe für Karl Adam* (Düsseldorf, 1956), pp. 44–56; esp. 51–3;
Heil, op. cit., esp. pp. 150–1; G. Mathon, *L'Anthropologie chrétienne en Occident de saint
Augustin à Jean Scot Érigène*, II, pp. 210–24; F. Brunhölzl, *Geschichte der lateinischen Literatur
des Mittelalters* I (München, 1975), pp. 287–8; L. Wallach, *Diplomatic studies in Latin and
Greek Documents from the Carolingian Age* (Ithaca/London, 1977), pp. 254–5; and C.
Ineichen-Eder, 'Theologisches und philosophisches Lehrmaterial aus dem Alcuin-Kreise',
esp. pp. 193–4. Dr Eder has kindly informed me of her forthcoming publication of a paper on
the origin of the *dicta Albini* and the *dicta Candidi* in 'The authenticity of the Dicta Albini,
Dicta Candidi and some related texts' in the proceedings of the Toronto Conference on
Insular Latin (550–1066), held in April 1979.

discuss in detail the content of these passages and its significance. First, however, I shall consider the authenticity of the Passages, which has been questioned by some scholars, and present what may be said with some certainty about their origin and authorship.

II

Of the fifteen passages, all but two are anonymous: one is entitled *dicta Albini de imagine Dei*, and another *dicta Candidi presbiteri de imagine Dei*. Albinus was Alcuin's nickname in his scholarly circle, and it would be most natural to conclude that this *dicta* was[12] the work of Alcuin. For various reasons – none of them well founded, I shall argue – scholars have resisted this conclusion. As for Candidus, historians hesitated for a long time as to whether he was Witto, pupil of Alcuin, or Bruun, a monk of Fulda and pupil of Einhard. But, in 1940, Heinz Löwe showed that the earliest manuscript of the *dicta*, *V*, could be dated to c. 800, a time at which Bruun would have been no more than a child.[13] Löwe, however, advanced the theory that the *dicta Albini* and the *dicta Candidi* were not original compositions, but merely two extracts – the beginning and end, and the remaining middle section, respectively – of a work thought in Carolingian times to be by Ambrose, the *De dignitate conditionis humanae*.

Löwe's surmise is based on two very different pieces[14] of evidence. First, in Migne's *Patrologia* there appears a work called the *De dignitate conditionis humanae*, which is classed as an Ambrosian pseudepigraph. This treatise does, indeed, consist of the *dicta Candidi* sandwiched between the two halves of the *dicta Albini*. But a study of the tradition of the two *dicta* suggests that the *De dignitate*, so far from being their original, was compiled from the *dicta Albini* and the *dicta Candidi* by a twelfth-century scholar; and, moreover, that it was not attributed to Ambrose until the end of the Middle Ages.[15] This piece of evidence is therefore valueless.

Löwe's second piece of evidence concerns the context in which a

---

[12] I shall treat *dicta* as if it were singular, though, grammatically, it is plural. This is in order to avoid confusion between the *dicta Albini*, the *dicta Candidi*, and the Munich Passages as a whole.

[13] 'Zur Geschichte Wizos', *Deutsches Archiv für Geschichte des Mittelalters*, 6, 1943, pp. 363–73.

[14] Ibid., p. 369, n. 1.

[15] For the tradition of the *dicta Albini* and details of its pseudepigraphical appearances, see below, Appendix I, pp. 144–51.

substantial part of the *dicta Albini* is quoted in the *Libri Carolini*, the treatise on the place of images in Christian worship issued under Charlemagne's name.[16] The quotation there follows, without break or comment, a brief extract from a work genuinely by Ambrose, the *De fide*. The author of the *Libri Carolini* precedes this quote from Ambrose with the introductory phrase: 'Ait enim beatus Ambrosius . . .'. Löwe assumed that this introduction applied to both the quote from the *De fide* and the piece of the *dicta Albini* which followed; and that, therefore, the *dicta Albini* was thought in Carolingian times to be by Ambrose. But this second piece of evidence is no stronger than the first. On the one hand, Löwe gives no evidence at all to show why the introductory phrase should apply to anything more than the extract from the *De fide*. On the other hand, even supposing that this phrase *did* apply to the passage from the *dicta Albini* which follows, this would still not be sufficient to prove that this *dicta* was not an original work of Alcuin's. It is the common practice of the author of the *Libri Carolini*, where a quotation is followed by another extract from the same author, taken from a different work or a different part of the same work, to indicate this fact by a brief, interposed comment.[17] He would therefore be very unlikely to place, after a quote from the *De fide*, an extract from another work he thought to be by Ambrose (or, indeed, by any other authority) without some intermediate introductory phrase. It follows that, if the author of the *Libri Carolini* did think that the extract from the *dicta Albini* was by Ambrose, he must have read it in a manuscript of the *De fide* where it was interpolated immediately after the passage quoted before the *dicta* in the *Libri Carolini*. This possibility was in fact suggested by M. Mathon some years ago.[18] If the *dicta Albini* was interpolated into a manuscript of the *De fide* (or if it was confused with the *De fide* in a florilegium), this does not show that the *dicta* was not, nevertheless, the work of Alcuin.

---

[16] See ed. H. Bastgen, *MGH Legum*: III Concilia II-suppl. (Hannover/Leipzig, 1924), pp. 22:21–23:11 (collated in the edition of the *dicta Albini* below as C). A parallel also exists, as Löwe observed, between, Passage VI, *De loco Dei*, and the *Libri Carolini*, ed. cit., p. 162:30–1, 32–6. But in this case direct borrowing by the *Libri Carolini* is extremely unlikely, since there the author identifies the quote as being from Augustine, whereas in the Munich Passages it is given anonymously.

[17] See, for example, ed. cit., pp. 114–15, 162, 217–18. I should like to thank Mr Paul Meyvaert for drawing my attention to this aspect of the problem.

[18] Op. cit., II, p. 219.

Whilst the evidence which Löwe brings against Alcuin's author-ship of the *dicta Albini* may thus be dismissed with reasonable cer-tainty, considerable doubt remains about the form in which the author of the *Libri Carolini* used the *dicta*. This doubt is in part the result of the controversy which still exists over the authorship of the *Libri Carolini*. Bastgen, their editor, argued strongly that they were written by Alcuin.[19] This view still has at least one distinguished pro-ponent, Professor Luitpold Wallach.[20] If Alcuin were the author of the *Libri Carolini*, then the extract from the *dicta Albini* could be very simply explained, as a piece of *authorial* commentary and expansion on the quote from the *De fide*. But recently historians, foremost among them Miss Ann Freeman, have advanced an impressive array of arguments against Alcuin's authorship and for that of the Visigoth, Theodulf of Orleans.[21] The student of the Munich Passages cannot, therefore, shirk the task of explaining Theodulf's use of a work by Alcuin, assuming that Theodulf did compose the *Libri Carolini*.

There are three possible explanations. Either Theodulf found the *dicta* interpolated in Ambrose's *De fide* (as suggested above); or he found the work anonymously; or he found the work attributed to Alcuin but thought it unnecessary to mention the name of a contem-porary who was not, therefore, an authority. There are arguments for and against each of these possibilities. The strongest argument for the theory of an interpolated copy of the *De fide* is based on

---

[19] 'Das Capitulare Karls den Grossen über die Bilder', III, 10, 'Der Verfasser des Capitulare über die Bilder', *Neues Archiv*, 37, 1911–12, pp. 491–533.

[20] See Wallach's 'The unknown author of the Libri Carolini ...', in *Didascaliae: studies in honour of Anselm M. Albareda*, ed. S. Prete (New York, 1961), pp. 469–515; his 'The *Libri Carolini* and patristics Latin and Greek ...' in *The Classical Tradition: ... studies in honor of Harry Caplan*, ed. L. Wallach (Ithaca, 1966), pp. 451–98; and his *Diplomatic Studies*, pp. 161–294. One of Wallach's arguments for Alcuin's authorship is drawn from the variety of logical texts known to the author of the *Libri Carolini* (see esp. 'The *Libri Carolini* and patristics', pp. 456–65; *Diplomatic Studies*, pp. 64–70; and also Bastgen, op. cit., pp. 495–504). Although my study of the Munich Passages provides added evidence for the interest in logic showed by Alcuin and his followers, it does seem that the author of the *Libri Carolini* was fascinated by logical techniques, but not by the philosophical implications of logic which caught the attention of Alcuin's circle.

[21] See A. Freeman, 'Theodulf of Orleans and the *Libri Carolini*', *Speculum*, 32, 1957, pp. 663–705; 'Further studies in the *Libri Carolini* I & II', *Speculum* 40, 1965, pp. 203–89; III, 'The marginal notes in Vaticanus latinus 7207', *Speculum* 46, 1971, pp. 597–612. See also, for further arguments in favour of Theodulf's authorship: E. Dahlhaus-Berg, *Nova antiquitas et antiquitas nova* (Wien, 1975) (*Kölner historische Abhandlungen* 23), esp. pp. 169–80; and P. Meyvaert, 'The authorship of the "Libri Carolini": observations prompted by a recent book', *Revue Bénédictine*, 89, 1979, pp. 29–57.

the ending of the chapter in the *Libri Carolini*. There, a quotation from Augustine follows the passage from the *dicta Albini*. Finally, the author summarizes the gist of the whole chapter, attributing its arguments to *sancti viri*, a term which would probably indicate Fathers of the Church as opposed to contemporaries.[22] From this it might seem that the author of the *Libri Carolini* must have believed that the whole of the preceding chapter was taken from authorities such as Ambrose and Augustine. Yet it is also possible to interpret the concluding remark more loosely: the doctrine of the quote from the *dicta Albini* may be attributed to 'holy men' because it is an elaboration of ideas expressed in the two passages from Ambrose and Augustine which are juxtaposed with it. Against the theory of interpolation it may be added that there is no manuscript evidence that the *dicta Albini* was ever inserted into the *De fide*.

The other two explanations – that the *dicta Albini* was found anonymously; or that it was not thought necessary to mention that it was Alcuin's work which was being quoted – are both plausible. There are a number of manuscripts, including two from the beginning of the ninth century, in which the *dicta Albini* is anonymous.[23] And, indeed, anonymity was the rule for such school material: only the *dicta Albini* and the *dicta Candidi* amongst all the Munich Passages are assigned to authors in *V*. But, even if the author of the *Libri Carolini* knew that the *dicta* was the work of Alcuin, would he have mentioned the fact? Throughout his work, he cites only the names of the illustrious men of the past as his authorities. The borrowings from the *dicta Albini* by other Carolingian writers are also unacknowledged:[24] whether from ignorance of its author's identity, or from the tendency to treat any school-text anonymously, it is not easy to decide.

One of the few modern scholars who have been willing to recognize in the *dicta Albini* an original composition of the late eighth century is Mathon. But Mathon has argued that the greater part of

[22] Ed. cit., p. 24:33–6: 'Ecce quam subtiliter quamque salubriter sancti viri hominem ad imaginem et similitudinem Dei factum esse, imaginem videlicet in anima, in qua est intellectus, voluntas et memoria, similitudinem in moribus, id est in caritate, iustitia, bonitate et sanctitate, quae omnia incorporea sunt, intellegentes disseruere!'

[23] *Roma Bibl. Padri Maristi A. II. 1* and *Vaticanus Pal. lat. 1719*. See below, Appendix i, pp. 149–50.

[24] See below, Appendix i, p. 145.

the *dicta Albini* and the *dicta Candidi*, as well as five of the other passages (nos. II, III, IV, XII, and XIII) were written by Benedict of Aniane.[25] This hypothesis was based solely on the use of the material in Benedict's *Munimenta Fidei*.[26] Since the *Munimenta* were assembled between 800 and 814,[27] whereas the *dicta Albini* cannot have been composed after 791,[28] nor the other Passages after about 801, it would seem far more likely that Benedict should have borrowed from the Passages, rather than vice versa. And this supposition is made the more probable, when it is added that the *Munimenta* are by and large a compilation of extracts from the works of others, including Alcuin. An additional detail confirms that Benedict did not compose the material which he shares with the Passages. Passage VI is a literal quotation from Augustine's *De diuersis quaestionibus*. In the *Munimenta*, Passage VI is reproduced, shortly after Passage IV; but the title (which is Augustine's) is omitted, and the first sentence is altered.[29] So long as Benedict is considered to be copying from the Munich Passages, there is nothing at all strange about the procedure: he uses one of the passages, then decides to quote another, but omits the title and adapts the beginning to fit his context. But if the *Munimenta* is the original, the Munich Passages the copy, then the author of the Passages must be supposed to have referred back to Augustine's original, in order to restore the title and the first sentence of the passage. Such laborious scrupulousness strains credibility.

None of the various arguments which have been brought against Alcuin's authorship of the *dicta Albini* or Candidus's authorship of the *dicta Candidi* are, therefore, compelling. There is no good reason to doubt the attributions of the two *dicta* in *V*, a very early copy of a manuscript from the circle of Alcuin's pupils. Moreover, a variety of circumstantial and internal evidence makes Alcuin's authorship of the *dicta Albini* even less to be doubted. The *dicta Albini* is first used in

---

[25] Loc. cit.

[26] The *Munimenta Fidei* are edited by J. Leclercq in *Analecta Monastica* I^e serie (= *Studia Anselmiana* XX, Roma, 1948), pp. 27–66. The correspondences between the Munich Passages and the *Munimenta* are as follows: *dicta Albini* paras. 2 and 3 = pp. 36:9–37:40; *dicta Candidi* paras. 2 and 3 = pp. 35:34–36:58; II = p. 35:24–34; III = p. 29:51–72; IV = pp. 50:6–52:89; XII = p. 53; XII = p. 54.

[27] See Leclercq, op. cit., pp. 66–8.

[28] For date of the Munich Passages, see below, p. 43.

[29] 'Iam ergo quia Deum esse fateris, restat ut neque eum corporeum nec alicubi esse arbitreris, quia quod alicubi est continetur loco ... quam ipse alicubi' (ed. cit., p. 52:89–93; the italicized portion represents the divergence from Passage VI and from Augustine).

works influenced by Alcuin, and by authors who had close connections with him.[30] The main source of the *dicta*, Augustine's *De Trinitate*, indicates little about authorship, because of its great popularity; but a subsidiary source for the *dicta*, the *De statu animae* of Claudianus Mamertus, is revealing.[31] Whilst it is impossible to affirm categorically that the *De statu animae* was never read or used between the time of Cassiodore and that of Alcuin, there seems to be no evidence of such use. It is in other of the Munich Passages,[32] written by pupils of Alcuin, and in a manuscript possibly associated with the court circle,[33] that the first signs of the revival of interest in Claudianus Mamertus, apart from his use in the *dicta*, appear. Finally, there are a number of striking verbal parallels between the *dicta Albini* and works certainly by Alcuin, especially his *De animae ratione*.[34] Such parallels would, on their own, prove little; but, in combination with all the other evidence, they provide yet another argument for Alcuin's authorship of the *dicta Albini*.

The Munich Passages offer the names of two possible authors, Albinus – that is, Alcuin – and Candidus. The life and work of Alcuin has been the object of considerable research; but Candidus is an obscurer figure.[35] An Anglo-Saxon by birth, he was probably Alcuin's pupil in England, where he also came under the authority of Bishop Hygbald of Lindisfarne. The Latin nickname 'Candidus', by which Alcuin almost invariably refers to him, is presumably based on the meaning of his English name, Hwita. He came to the Continent probably in 793, but returned to Lindisfarne a year later.[36] Soon he was back on the Continent: by the time of the beginnings of the Adoptionist controversy, he was to be found acting as a messenger

---

[30] See below, Appendix I, p. 145.

[31] See below, Passage VII, n. 5 (& n. 14).

[32] See below, Passage II, n. 2; Passage XII, n. 1.

[33] *Paris BN 2164*; on this manuscript, see below, p. 57, n. 83.

[34] See below, Passage VII, nn. 2, 5, 7, 9, 10, 11, 13, 14.

[35] Brief accounts of his life and work are given in A. Hauck, *Kirchengeschichte Deutschlands* II (Leipzig, 1912) pp. 151–3; H. Löwe, op. cit., *passim*; G. Drioux, *CANDIDVS WIZO* in *Dictionnaire d'Histoire et de Géographie Ecclésiastique* II, col. 735–7.

[36] Cf. letter no. 24 (in Dümmler's edition *MGH Epistulae* IV, esp. p. 65:28–32). Dümmler's dating of this letter to 794 is preferable to Jaffé's date of 783–5 (*Monumenta Alcuiniana* = *Bibliotheca Rerum Germanicarum* VI (Berlin, 1873), p. 146) on the balance of evidence. In particular, Professor Bullough points out (letter of November 16th, 1978) that the unique manuscript of Letter 24, *British Library Cotton Tiberius A XV*, brings together a number of smaller collections, none of which appears to come from the period before 789.

between Alcuin and Charlemagne.[37] Candidus was often to fill this role of confidential messenger between his master and the great men of the realm. In especial, Candidus acted as a link between Alcuin and Arno, Bishop of Salzburg, with whom he spent about a year in 798.[38] He made at least two journeys to Rome: in 799, with Arno, and in 800–1. In 801–2 he was definitely a part of Charlemagne's court circle, although he still kept in close contact with Alcuin, who was in retirement as Abbot of Tours.[39] What happened in the rest of Candidus's life is a little unclear. Most probably he died shortly before or just after his teacher;[40] but it has also been argued that he went on to become Bishop of Trier, only to be dispossessed of his diocese some years before his death.[41]

Candidus was one of Alcuin's closest followers. Alcuin's regard and concern for him is evident both from the *Vita Alcuini*,[42] and the various references to him in his master's poems and letters.[43] One remark of Alcuin's is particularly revealing. He tells Arno that he has been especially careful with a letter of Arno's to him, containing compromising complaints about the behaviour of the Pope: only Candidus and he read it before he destroyed the document.[44] Evidence of Candidus's learning is provided by Alcuin's suggestion to Arno that he use Candidus as a teacher;[45] and by Charlemagne's use of Candidus to transmit his queries on time and eternity to Alcuin.[46] A high level of intellectual curiosity is evidenced by the only work besides the *dicta* which can be attributed to Candidus with a very high degree of certainty.[47] This is a letter discussing whether it is possible

---

[37] Cf. Alcuin's Letter no. 41 (ed. Dümmler, p. 84: 5–6). Jaffé dates this to 793, Dümmler more convincingly to 794–5.

[38] Cf. Letter no. 156 of Alcuin's (ed. Dümmler, p. 253–34).

[39] See Hauck, op. cit., p. 152, n. 1.

[40] The opinion of Richter (op. cit., p. 6), Hauck (op. cit., p. 153, n. 2.) and Löwe (op. cit., p. 373, n. 1.)

[41] By G. Morin: see below, pp. 57–9.

[42] See Jaffé, *Monumenta Alcuiniana* (cit.), p. 20.

[43] Note especially Poem 44 (ed. Dümmler, *MGH PLAC* I, pp. 255–7).

[44] No. 184 (ed. Dümmler, p. 309: 9–11).

[45] Reference as in n. 38.

[46] Cf. Alcuin letter no. 163, ibid., p. 263–7.

[47] Edited in *MGH Epp.* IV, pp. 557–61 (also in *MPL* 106, 103–7). The work is discussed by Richter, op. cit., pp. 26, 28–30; Zimmerman, op. cit., pp. 32–5; and by Cappuyns, 'Note sur le problème de la vision béatifique au IXe siècle', esp. pp. 99–100. Richter and Cappuyns both attribute this work to Candidus Bruun; given the content of the work, and the certainty that Wizo wrote the *dicta Candidi*, their attribution is almost certainly incorrect. Dr Christine Eder kindly informs me of her forthcoming publication of a paper arguing

to see God with bodily eyes. Candidus argues that God, being incorporeal, can only be seen by what is itself incorporeal. Man must become pure in spirit if he is to have any sort of vision of God; but even then he will only see God to the extent that God permits himself to be seen. If Candidus was also author of the other Munich Passages, except the *dicta Albini* (as I shall suggest is likely); and if he was also responsible for a number of other philosophical passages,[48] he must be considered pre-eminent among the philosophers of Charlemagne's court. Also probably by Candidus are a straightforward, synoptic account of the Passion,[49] and four sermons.[50]

There are two questions which must be answered before the authorship of the Munich Passages may profitably be discussed: to what extent the individual passages come together to form an integral work; and how far the passages are original works rather than excerpts from patristic writings. In my analysis of the sources and content of the Passages, I shall try to show how the individual passages are linked in concerns, method and material. The manuscript tradition also suggests that, with the exception of the *dicta Albini*, the passages were composed together.

Besides *V*, there are two early manuscripts which contain a considerable selection of the Passages: *München clm 18961* (s. ix²) (*B*),[51] and *Paris BN 13953* (s. x in.) (*P*).[52] If the Munich Passages were conceived apart from one another, and merely happened to be brought together in *V*, then the chances of finding many of the passages together in another manuscript would be slight, unless that manuscript were a copy of *V*. Moreover, one would expect to find the

---

the authorship by Candidus Wizo of this work and the *De passione Domini* (cf. n. 49 below): 'Candidus Bruun von Fulda: Maler, Lehrer und Schriftsteller' in *Rabanus Maurus Festschrift* (Fulda, 1980).

[48] See below, pp. 55–7.

[49] Printed in *MPL* 106, 58ff. For mss., see M. Manitius, *Geschichte der lateinischen Literatur des Mittelalters* I, (München, 1911), p. 668. Richter (op. cit., p. 26) puts forward an argument – not in itself very persuasive – for thinking that this work and the letter on the vision of God are by the same author. Cf. n. 47, above.

[50] See below, pp. 57–61.

[51] Cf. Ineichen-Eider, op. cit., p. 192, & pp. 194–7 (for a description of the contents of *B*); and B. Bischoff, *Die südostdeutschen Schreibschulen*, pp. 161–2. The folios containing the Passages and some other material form a separate book, which has been bound with later material.

[52] On this manuscript, see U. Blech, *Germanische Glossenstudien zu handschriften aus französischen Bibliotheken* (Heidelberg, 1977), pp. 150ff.

Passages mixed indiscriminately with other material. If, on the other hand, the Passages were conceived as a whole, it would still be likely that different manuscripts would present different selections of them, in accordance with the interests of the compilers of the various manuscripts.

In *V*, the Passages occur without interruption except for an excerpt from Augustine's *Soliloquia* (identified as such) which is directly related to Passage no. XI.[53] *B* contains all the Passages except for the *dicta Albini* and nos. X and XI. The order is different from that in *V*, but all the passages are together except for the *dicta Candidi*. The omission of X and XI might be explained by a loss of a folio, since one or more folios seem certainly to have been lost just before the block of twelve of the Passages.[54] *P* contains all of the Passages, except for the *dicta Albini* and no. VI. The order is different from both *V* and *B*; and all the Passages are together, except that an extract from Augustine's *De doctrina christiana* (identified as such), which is also found earlier on in *V*, separates III from IV. Although the readings of *V* are in general superior to those of *B* and *P*, these manuscripts share a number of readings obviously correct where *V* is corrupt; but they do not, for the most part, share each other's errors or eccentricities. It is very likely, therefore, that *V*, *B* and *P* all derive independently, and perhaps through intermediate manuscripts no longer extant, from the same archetype. A ninth-century manuscript, *Würzburg Theol fol. 56 (W)* contains an epistolary version of the *dicta Candidi*, followed by Passage I as a sort of footnote. According to the criteria specified in the last paragraph, all these facts indicate that the Munich Passages, with the exception of the *dicta Albini*, had a common origin. And if, as classroom material, their original form was other than that of a bound manuscript, this would explain the differences in their order between the three main manuscripts. Finally, a piece of internal evidence supports the integrity of the Passages. The opening sentence of Passage X reads, 'what *I* have named "being", "knowing" and "loving" *above* . . .': almost certainly a reference to the *dicta Candidi*.

The separate origin of the *dicta Albini* is suggested by its omission from both *B* and *P*; and by evidence of a separate tradition for this

---

[53] For a detailed description of the contents of *V*, see Löwe, op. cit., pp. 368–70.
[54] The extract from Boethius's *De Trinitate* breaks in the middle of a sentence at the foot of f. 38v; but the same hand continues with the title for Passage I on f. 39r.

dicta apart from the other Passages, dating from the earliest times. The *dicta Albini* alone is found in *Roma Bibl. Padri Maristi A.II.1* (written before 814) (*L*),[55] a manuscript which belonged to Alcuin's associate Leidrad; and in *Vaticanus Pal. lat. 1719* (s. viii–ix/s. ix in.).[56] The *dicta Albini* alone of the Passages is also used by Paulinus of Aquileia,[57] Hrabanus Maurus[58] and an anonymous letter-writer who was a missionary to the Slavs.[59] Moreover, the *dicta Albini* is quoted at length in the *Libri Carolini*; Passage VI is also found, elsewhere, in the *Libri Carolini*, but this Passage is merely a verbatim extract from Augustine.[60] However, although the origin of the *dicta Albini* may have been separate from that of the other Passages, Alcuin's *dicta* is most intimately connected to them, since the *dicta Candidi* extends the ideas of the *dicta Albini* and is based on the same source, Augustine's *De Trinitate*.

The Munich Passages appear, therefore, for the most part, to be integral; but are they original, or are they, as Löwe suggested, merely

---

55 On this manuscript, see L. Delisle, 'Notice sur un manuscrit de l'église de Lyon du temps de Charlemagne', *Notices et extraits des manuscrits de la Bibliothèque Nationale*, 35, II, 1896, pp. 831–42; B. Bischoff, op. cit., p. 85; *Codices Latini Antiquiores*, ed. E. A. Lowe IV, no. 417; *Aristoteles Latinus: Codices supplementa altera*, pp. 147–9; and see below, pp. 52–3.

56 See W. M. Lindsay, *Palaeographia Latina* III, 1924 (*University of St Andrews Publications* 19), p. 20; P. Lehmann, 'Mitteilungen aus Handschriften', *Sitzungsberichten der phil.-phil. Klasse der Bayerischen Akademie der Wissenschaften*, 1929, pp. 26–7; B. Bischoff, *Lorsch im Spiegel seiner Handschriften* (*Münchener Beiträge zur Mediävistik und Renaissance-Forschung – Beiheft*) (München, 1974), p. 31. Bischoff considers it possible that the part of the manuscript containing the *dicta* might even date from the end of the eighth century. This part of the manuscript he describes as West German but perhaps not written at Lorsch itself.

57 *Liber Exhortationis* (*De Salutaribus Documentis*), MPL 99, 197–282, cap. II and III, 199A–200A where three passages, one of them substantial, from the *dicta* are quoted almost literally; there are also a few summarial linking passages.

58 Commentary on *Ecclesiastes* (*MPL* 109, 763–1126, 874B–875B), where the central part of the *dicta* is quoted. This usage was first noted by Mathon (op. cit.).

59 Ed. Dümmler, *MGH Epp.* IV, pp. 484–90, pp. 488:44–489:21 (this text is collated in my edition of the *dicta Albini*, siglum *E*). Th. Sickel ('Alcuinstudien', *Sitzungsberichten der phil.-phil. Klasse der kaiserlichen Akademie der Wissenschaften* (Wien, 1875), 79, pp. 461–550, esp., pp. 535–41) considers that Wizo himself was the author of this letter; Hauck (op. cit., p. 152, n. 2) suspends judgement; Richter (op. cit., pp. 37–8) does not think that Candidus wrote it. My arguments against the attribution of this letter to Candidus are the following: (1) the author names himself, or refers to himself, as 'Blancidius'; this name is different though it might have the same meaning, as Wizo's otherwise invariable nickname, 'Candidus'; (2) if the letter is directed to Bishop Arno of Salzburg, then the tone of the letter is completely incompatible with authorship by Candidus, his subordinate; and so is the author's description of himself as 'senex' (p. 484:15), even if it was not to be taken literally; (3) the ornate style, involving the use of a very wide vocabulary and complex sentence-structure, is quite unlike any of Candidus's other writings.

60 See above, p. 37.

a set of patristic and other excerpts? Passage VI, as I have remarked, is a direct quotation from Augustine; and no. XII is copied from Claudianus Mamertus's *De statu animae* with only minor changes. Passage V presents a terse but accurate summary of an idea taken from Augustine's *Confessions*; and no. I is built around an extract from the same author's *De Trinitate*. The other passages are all lavish in their use of patristic sources, especially Augustine; but rarely do they copy directly, and they frequently combine ideas, develop them, or change their emphasis in an original way. Just as it would be wrong to consider glosses as forming a work quite separate from the text which they annotate, so these Passages must be studied along with the patristic material they summarize or develop. And, in the same way as a set of glosses, so the Munich Passages illustrate, not the passive assimilation of material, but the active selection and elaboration of it.

From the evidence just presented, the following sketch of the probable origin of the Munich Passages may be made. Before 791, the date of the uncorrected manuscript of the *Libri Carolini* (*Vaticanus lat 7207* – siglum *C*), Alcuin wrote his *dicta*. Candidus then wrote his *dicta* as an extension of his master's thought; and the other passages were composed at roughly the same time, in the same milieu, probably by Candidus himself. Sometime before the turn of the ninth century, the likely date for *clm 6407* (*V*), the Passages were brought together with the *dicta Albini*. A copy (*V*) of this manuscript was made at Verona and quickly found its way back to Germany.[61] The attributions in so early a manuscript as *V* make it almost certain that Alcuin wrote Passage VII (his *dicta*) and Candidus Passage VIII (his *dicta*). Candidus's authorship of the other passages is not certain; but the integrity of the collection (excepting the *dicta Albini*), Candidus's being named as author of one of the pieces, and the known facts of his life and work, all make his authorship highly probable.[62]

---

[61] For the dating and origin of *V*, see Löwe, op. cit., p. 368; B. Bischoff, op. cit., pp. 149–50; *Codices Latini Antiquiores* IX, no. 1282. Löwe suggests that Candidus himself took the exemplar of *V* to Verona on one of his trips to Rome.

[62] Zimmerman's arguments (op. cit., p. 36) to show that the various passages originated separately founder on his mistaken belief that *V* contains only four of the passages. Arguments by Zimmerman (ibid., p. 52) and Schmaus (op. cit., p. 51) in favour of multiple authorship of the Passages ignore both the full manuscript evidence and the integrity of thought and method found throughout the collection.

III

The Munich Passages may be divided, by their subject-matter, into four groups: (a) on the Trinity – II, VII, VIII, X; (b) demonstration of the existence of God – III, IV; (c) on the Ten Categories – I, XII, XIII, XIV, XV; (d) exercises in syllogistic method – V, VI, XI. Passage IX, *Propter quid homo factus est*, brings together, in terms of the greatest generality, ideas from the passages in groups a and b. There are, indeed, important connections between the groups; and the seemingly diverse sets of subject-matter are intricately linked to each other. But these connections will best emerge after a closer study of the individual passages.

(a) Group A: on the Trinity

The *dicta Albini* is a commentary on Genesis 1.26: 'Faciamus hominem ad imaginem et similitudinem nostram.' In part, the *dicta* is based on Augustine's *De Trinitate*, from which Alcuin took the parallel between the persons of the Trinity and the *intellectus, uoluntas*, and *memoria* which constitute the mind. However, Alcuin differs radically from Augustine in the way in which he draws a contrast between the two major terms, *imago* and *similitudo*, which the text from Genesis presents.

In an introductory paragraph, Alcuin follows a tradition dating back to Ambrose and discusses the implications of the use of the plural form *faciamus*. Then he turns to the subject of Man's image-relationship (*imago*) to God. This relationship is unchanging. It is a simple consequence of the structure of Man's soul, which bears the image of the Trinity in its composition from intellect, will and memory, and which bears the image of God by its omnipresence within the body. Alcuin goes on to consider Man's likeness (*similitudo*) to God. Godlikeness, he says, lies within Man's potential, but must be achieved by individual effort. God has created Man in such a way that any individual man is capable of possessing the same moral virtues as his creator, but may, through his misdeeds, lose any trace of such a resemblance to God.

For Augustine, image-relationships were a sub-class of likeness-relationships. A likeness may be called an image, when it is in some

44

way produced by that which it resembles (as a child by its parents or a picture by that which it portrays).[63] Likeness could not, therefore, be regarded as specifying a closer degree of resemblance than is indicated by image-relationship, since likeness is merely a general term for resemblance of any kind.[64] Consequently, it was not open to Augustine to interpret Man's likeness to God as something for the individual to attain by good behaviour, in contrast to his innate image of God: for Augustine, Man's creation in the image of his maker implies his Godlikeness. Where, then, did Alcuin find the distinction between the image of God in Man and Man's possible Godlikeness? In the Greek tradition, Man's likeness to God was interpreted in an active, potential sense, which Ambrose, too, adopted. M. Mathon[65] has suggested as a probable source for Alcuin's discussion of Godlikeness Gennadius of Marseille's *De ecclesiasticis dogmatibus*, which enjoyed a wide circulation in the early Middle Ages, sometimes with an attribution to St Augustine.[66] There is a single verbal parallel between Gennadius and the *dicta* which lends support to Mathon's view; but, otherwise, Ambrose has more to offer as a source for this interpretation.

One of Augustine's motives for breaking with the Greek tradition for exegesis of Genesis 1.26 may have been the logical neatness of the solution he adopts; but another was certainly a suspicion of the anthropological implications of the Greek interpretation. In their explanation of Man's Godlikeness, the Greeks had emphasized the power of Man to make himself like God by his own unaided efforts, given the excellence of his original state. Such moral optimism, which underplays the importance of Original Sin and the need for

---

[63] See *De diversis quaestionibus LXXXIII* no. 74 (*CC* 44A, pp. 213–14. For a perceptive analysis of this passage and its sources, see R. A. Markus, '"Imago" and "similitudo" in Augustine', *Revue des Études Augustiniennes*, 10, 1964, pp. 125–43. An excellent discussion of Greek and Augustinian doctrine on image and similitude is to be found in G. B. Ladner, *The Idea of Reform: Its Impact on Christian Thought and Action in the Age of the Fathers* (Cambridge, Mass., 1959), pp. 83–107, & pp. 185–203. My account of patristic doctrine on image and likeness is largely based on the work of Markus and Ladner.

[64] See *Quaestiones in Heptateuchon* v 4 (*CSEL* 28, pp. 371:30–372:7): 'Sed quod [Gen. 1.27] non addidit "et similitudinem", cum superius [Gen. 1.26] dictum esset "Faciamus hominem ad imaginem et similitudinem nostram", quibusdam visum est similitudinem aliquid amplius esse quam imaginem, quod homini reformando per Christi gratiam postea servaretur. Miror autem si non propterea postea imaginem solam voluit commemorare, quia, ubi imago, continuo et similitudo est.' Quoted by Ladner, op. cit., p. 180, n. 2.

[65] Op. cit. pp. 205–7.

[66] Cf. C. H. Turner, 'The *Liber Ecclesiasticarum Dogmatum* attributed to Gennadius', *Journal of Theological Studies*, 7, 1906, pp. 78–99, esp. pp. 78–9.

grace, would have been as unattractive to Augustine as it was enticing to a semi-Pelagian such as Gennadius. Nevertheless, human choice and effort, which are central to Greek thinking on Man's Godlikeness, do appear in Augustine's account of Man as the image of God. For Augustine, the trinities in the human mind are discovered by self-investigation. The analogy between the parts of the mind and the persons of the Trinity which Alcuin borrows is taken from a complex discussion in the *De Trinitate* of the process of seeking after and acquiring knowledge. At the core of this argument is an analysis of how the mind turns its attention away from God towards external things. The mind discovers the images of the Trinity which are innate within it as part of a recuperative process of introspection, which leads it back, through itself, to its maker. Thus, although the mind bears the image of God by its very nature, it discovers it only through its choice to seek God and by its effort in seeking him. When Alcuin borrowed Augustine's image of the Trinity, he omitted much of the complex psychological discussion surrounding it. It was therefore necessary for him to emphasize the part of human choice and effort in his account of Man's likeness to God, if he was not to turn his exegesis into a mere glorification of mankind.

The *dicta Candidi* (VIII) enlarges what Alcuin has to say about the soul as the image of the Trinity, chiefly by using another analogy from Augustine's *De Trinitate*, where the soul's being, knowing and loving are compared to the properties of Father, Son and Holy Spirit respectively. The most problematic but interesting part of the *dicta* is the beginning of its final paragraph. Before he draws a parallel between the actions of the soul and those of the Trinity, Candidus points to an important difference. Whereas God's goodness derives from himself, created things owe not only their existence, but also their qualities, to that which is outside themselves. God, however, always remains what he is. These ideas are almost certainly drawn from the passage in Boethius's *De Trinitate* discussing the relationship between God and the Categories. Then Candidus adds that, in a sense, the soul too is unchanging, in that it always exists, knows and wishes to know. The idea that the soul always knows may be linked with the definition, expressed earlier in the *dicta*, of knowing as the potentiality for knowledge rather than the sudden acquisition of it. Both these views about knowledge derive from Book Ten of Augustine's *De Trinitate*, where the knowledge for which the soul so often searches vainly in the external world is argued to be contained within the soul itself. But when Candidus says of the soul that it always exists, is he merely talking loosely and saying that the soul always exists from the moment it is created, or is he implying that all souls were created together at the beginning of time? In the period when Candidus wrote, a considerable breadth of views on the origin of the souls was held, as the controversy between Agobard of Lyons and Fredegisus in the 830s would show.[67] It is quite possible that Candidus believed that all souls had existed, and would go on to exist, eternally.

Passage II is a brief summary of ideas from VII and VIII, in which stress is laid on the use of psychological knowledge to explain the structure of the Trinity. The triad of being, knowing and loving is taken from the *dicta Candidi*; the concept of the soul's placelessly occupying the entire body from the *dicta Albini*. Passage X offers a more original application of the same material. Essentially, the author is concerned to show that, since the triads which compose the soul are abstract, incorporeal things, it is obvious that the soul itself is incorporeal and cannot be contained in space. The argument by which this conclusion is reached contains a number of stages not logically necessary, which illustrate the fascination with logical deduction for its own sake found throughout the Passages. There is one further, incidental point of interest. The treatment of space here does not identify space with bodies, but it does inextricably connect the two: 'that which is in space is the same as that which is bodily; and that which is bodily is the same as that which is in space'.

(b) Group B: on the existence of God

Of the two passages devoted to demonstrating the existence of God, IV, which takes the form of a dialogue, is by far the fuller. Arguments which are expounded fully in the dialogue are often so compressed in III as to be hardly intelligible. III is therefore presumably an abridgement of IV, although one parallel suggests independent reference to the main source of the dialogue, Augustine's *De libero arbitrio*.

The proof of God's existence set forth in the dialogue is one signifi-

[67] See below, pp. 64–6.

cantly different from that found in the *De libero arbitrio*.[68] Nevertheless, the medieval argument is best understood in relation to its
principal source. Augustine's argument has two distinct stages. He
begins by dividing all things into three classes: those that merely are,
such as inanimate objects; those that are and live, such as beasts; and
those that are, live and understand, such as men. These classes are
taken to possess ascending degrees of excellence. Augustine then turns
to consider the various means of perception: sense, interior sense and
reason. Whereas that which is sensed merely is, that which senses is
alive; therefore that which senses is better than that which it senses. It
cannot, however, be accepted, as a general principle, that everything
which senses is better than that which it senses, because this would
suggest that everything which understands is better than that which
it understands. But this consequence must be false, because the man
who understands wisdom is not better than the wisdom which he
understands. And so the interior sense – that faculty shared by Man
and the irrational animals, which controls and processes the workings
of the five bodily senses – cannot be held superior to the bodily senses
simply because it perceives them. Nor can it be put into the class of
things which understand, since it is possessed by the irrational
animals. It is to be considered superior to the bodily senses because it
controls and judges them. Reason can be placed above the interior
sense, both because it judges the interior sense, and because it does belong to the class of things which understand. Having placed reason at
the summit of the perceptive faculties, Augustine rejects the idea that,
if anything could be found superior to reason, it would necessarily be
God. God is not simply that which is above human reason, but that
to which nothing is superior. If, however, nothing can be found
above human reason except that which is eternal and immutable;
and if it is discovered without the use of any corporeal instrument:
then it will be justifiable to suppose that this superior thing is God.

The second stage of Augustine's argument might be said to take as
its point of departure the remark already ventured incidentally, that a
man who understands wisdom is *not* superior to the wisdom which
he understands. Each individual's perception of a given object is

---

[68] Ed. G. M. Green (Wien, 1956) = *CSEL* 74, pp. 40–72; for more precise references to
individual passages, see notes to Passage IV. The proof of God's existence in the Passages
is discussed by G. Grünwald, loc. cit.

distinct; and only in the case of touch is one person's perception affected by another's perception of the same thing. There is at least one thing perceptible by all rational creatures which remains intact whether or not it is perceived by them: the 'reason and truth of numbers', that is, the system which governs the relationships between numbers. Although wisdom is not as readily or universally perceptible as the reason and truth of numbers, it too remains constant, whether or not it is in fact perceived. Wisdom is stable, in contrast to the individual minds which seek it. The individual mind becomes wise through wisdom, and so wisdom is superior to the mind. Wisdom, therefore, satisfies the criteria for being considered God: it is superior to human reason; it is eternal and immutable; and it is found through reason alone, without the use of any corporeal instrument. Augustine can conveniently equate it with the scriptural designation of Christ as 'Wisdom', and then use the dogma of the equality of the Son and the Father to conclude his argument.

The writer of the Munich dialogue borrows heavily from the first stage of Augustine's argument, but almost entirely ignores the second. However, in some ways even the adaptation of the first stage of the argument is not direct. The medieval writer enunciates as a general rule that what senses is superior to what is sensed, whereas Augustine had scrupulously stated that this was not the case. A complex passage at the end of stage one (p. 156) is open to different interpretations. Following the sense suggested by a gloss found in *B* only, the argument might run: 'If there is anything better and more powerful in the nature of things, which understands, which is the reason by which everything understands, then it will far excel all that is in the nature of things.' Or, following the same gloss, that which is superior to all things might be 'that which understands what reason, by which all things understand, is'. Alternatively, preserving the text as it stands in *V*, it would be 'that which understands what reason (understands)' which excelled all other things. Only the first of these interpretations is at all in line with Augustine's thought. The other two adopt the principle, rejected by Augustine, of the superiority of the perceiver to that which is perceived.

The second stage of the Munich Passage dialogue is somewhat simplistic. The interlocutors agree that the being which is so much superior to all other things is God; and they then set out to discover whether there is in fact such an entity. The fact that the soul's powers are limited – it cannot, for instance, choose to remain in its body as long as it wishes – is taken to indicate that there must be a higher being, constraining the soul's powers and itself omnipotent: this being will be God. The final moments of the argument make what the author seems to consider a logical deduction, but which amounts to scarcely more than a verbal flourish. Throughout, superiority has been discussed in terms of goodness and power. Now, the interrogator asks whether the being who is better than what is best and more powerful than the most powerful exists. He must exist, comes the reply, otherwise he could not be so powerful. But the existence of each being in the ascending scale of superiority has been supposed throughout the argument: the author is not concerned here (as Anselm was, for example, in his ontological argument) to demonstrate the real existence of an entity known to exist as a concept.

Augustine's proof of God's existence relies on indicating the immutable, superhuman nature of Universals; and his division of nature into things which are, sense and understand is made as a preliminary to an exposition of the nature of Universals. The concept of Universals does not enter into the Munich dialogue. Its author tries to build his proof of God's existence by extending the principle of superiority, by which sense is to be preferred to mere existence, and reason to sense, so as to discover a fourth level, superior to ordinary reason, which will be uniquely instantiated by God. Only by one interpretation of the text, in which the superior being is the reason from which other things gain the power of reason, does the emphasis come at all to resemble Augustine's. But even in this case, the conclusion of the argument will still be made in terms of levels of being, rather than by an analysis of the nature of Universals.

(c) Group C: on the Ten Categories

The Munich Passages, and a collection of logical works in *Roma Bibl. Padri Maristi A. II. 1 (L)*,[69] are the two most important pieces of evidence which survive concerning the assimilation of the doctrine of the Categories at the time of Charlemagne. The first of the Munich

---

[69] For a discussion of this manuscript, see above, p. 42; below, pp. 52–3 and note 55 to the present chapter.

Passages is built around the piece in the *De Trinitate*, where Augustine states that God transcends all the Categories, except for the first, which is substance or essence. In the last sentence, the medieval author adds his own thought: 'Essence or substance may be called "every created thing", because what is created derives from it, and yet it remains constant in its own nature.' Everything that is must, in some way, participate in essence; but essence is unaltered by being participated. This theory of participation is close to Augustine's ontology, but it is cruder, since it does not distinguish clearly between God's perfect manner of being, and the less than perfect semi-being of created things.

It is interesting that the first Passage is given the title 'On Augustine's Ten Categories', since, although Augustine lists ten categories in the passage quoted from the *De Trinitate*, he does not identify them as the Ten Categories; nor does he use the term *categoria* – so frequent in the *Categoriae Decem* – here.[70] The author of the Passages was probably thinking of the *Categoriae Decem* even as he extracted the piece from the *De Trinitate*. The other passages devoted to the Categories reflect a greater concern with the technicalities of the doctrine. Passages XIV and XV on space and time appear to be derived from ideas in the *Categoriae Decem*. The concept of space put forward here is considerably more sophisticated than that employed in Passage X: space is an incorporeal capacity which circumscribes and separates bodies. The presence of these two passages shows that, even at this very early stage in the medieval study of the Categories, space and time had begun to assume a special importance. Two of the other passages concern the first of the Categories. Whereas the concept of *usia* given in Passage I was that which emerged after centuries of Platonic and Christian distortion of Aristotle's original idea, Passage XIII gives an accurate summary of the genuine Aristotelian concept of *usia*. Substance is the individual, such as Plato or Cicero, which is neither *in a subject*, nor *said of a subject*. The language here is far nearer to the authentic Boethian translation of the *Categories* than to the *Categoriae Decem*. There is no evidence that the Boethian translation was used before the eleventh century; but, at this point, its wording is preserved in Cassiodore's *Institutiones*: perhaps they were the compiler's source here. Passage XII is a near literal quotation from

---

[70] Augustine does use the term elsewhere, e.g. *Confessiones* IV, 16, 28.

Claudianus Mamertus's *De statu animae*,[71] a work probably used elsewhere in the Passages. It provides a concise definition of the terms *subject*, *in a subject*, and *said of a subject*, derived from Aristotle's *Categories*.

Roma Bibliotheca Padri Maristi A. II. 1 can be dated to before Leidrad's death (which probably occurred not long after his retirement in 814), because it contains notes of variant readings in Leidrad's hand.[72] The manuscript helps to place the logical passages just discussed in their context, because it provides an excellent illustration of the links between the theological concerns expressed in some of the Munich Passages and an interest in formal logic. It contains the *dicta Albini* and also constitutes the earliest collection of logical texts to have survived from the Middle Ages: Porphyry's *Isagoge*, the *Categoriae Decem*, extracts from Alcuin's *Dialectica*, Apuleius's *Periermenias* and Boethius's first commentary to Aristotle's *De interpretatione*. The last part of the manuscript contains a selection of creeds closely related to those in *V*, and a number of short exegetical pieces, including items by Augustine and Jerome, on the Psalms. By contrast to so many manuscripts of the late ninth and tenth centuries, this dialectical corpus contains no glosses at all, apart from a few 'Nota' signs. But, employing the characteristic early ninth-century method of comment by way of excerption, the compiler has added an extract from Boethius's *De arithmetica*.[73] Here Boethius defines wisdom as the understanding of the truth of things which are. Boethius continues: 'We say that those things are, which are not made bigger by any increase nor smaller by any diminution . . . but preserve themselves always in their own strength, striving with the aid of their nature.' As examples of things which are, Boethius lists qualities, quantities, forms, magnitudes and smallnesses (*parvitates*), equalities, habitudes, acts, dispositions, places and times – a different and rather less rigorous

---

[71] A parallel noted by Zimmerman, op. cit., p. 45; for a discussion of the use of Claudianus Mamertus in the Passages, see ibid., p. 59.

[72] See above, p. 42, n. 55.

[73] 'Est enim sapientia rerum, quae sunt suique inmutabilem substantiam sortiuntur, conprehensio veritatis. Esse autem illa dicimus, quae nec intentione crescunt nec retractione minuuntur nec variationibus permutantur, sed in propria semper vi suae se naturae subsidiis nixa custodiunt. Haec autem sunt qualitates, quantitates, formae, magnitudines, parvitates, aequalitates, habitudines, actus, dispositiones, loca, tempora.' Ed. G. Friedlein (Leipzig, 1867), pp. 7:26–8:7. The text as it appears in *L*, with a number of errors, is printed from fol. 28v by Delisle, op. cit., p. 832.

list of categories than Aristotle's. Although this set of categories was little used by medieval scholars, the definition of being given here by Boethius was often to be recalled by philosophers from John Scottus onwards.

(d) Group D: exercises in syllogistic method

The final group of passages is less tight than the other three. Passages V, VI and XI resemble each other, not in subject-matter, but by the high degree to which they each exemplify the taste for logical, and especially syllogistic, reasoning which is found throughout the Passages. Passage VI is a verbatim extract from Augustine's *De diversis quaestionibus*, in which a syllogism is used to show that God is not in any place. Passage XI shows a further stage of development in the process of learning how to reason syllogistically by following Augustine's example. It is closely related to the extract from Augustine's *Soliloquia*, which is quoted immediately following it. There it is argued that truth would remain, even if the world were to perish, for in that case it would be true that the world had perished. Passage XI presents a syllogistic development of a number of similar arguments of Augustine's. Although each of the argumentative steps is valid in itself, they lead, in conjunction, neither in the direction of Augustine's original discussion, nor in that suggested by the title, 'Can there be anything true unless Truth exists?' The conclusion to the passage is not, as might have been expected, that without truth, nothing can be true; but rather, that truth is not a body. This passage is a case where enthusiasm for the technique of the syllogism so outweighs discretion in its application, that a circuitous and irrelevant train of argument is produced.

Passage V is again based on Augustine. In his *Confessions*, Augustine had tackled the difficult theological question of whether God is prior to time by time or by excellence, by analysing and clarifying the terms in which the problem is stated. The medieval author makes clearer the reasoning which underlies Augustine's more elegant statement. If God preceded time by time, then he would have to begin to precede time at some given time; and in that case he would not precede time, since he would be placed in time.

(e) Links between the Passages

Passage ix serves mainly to link together the subject-matter of two different groups, A and B. 'For what purpose was Man made?', asks the title: 'to know God and to know himself', comes the reply. The process of finding God by starting with an investigation of the human mind is exemplified in both Group A, the passages on the Trinity, and Group B, the passages concerned to demonstrate the existence of God. In the present passage the importance of beginning from the human, if one is to explore the divine, is stressed: unless Man knows and loves the image of God himself, he cannot know and love the God who made him in his image.

Some individual passages from the four different groups are connected. No. xiv is a non-theological counterpart to vi, the quotation from Augustine on God's lack of place; similarly, no. xv explores time in the purely physical sphere, whilst v considers time in its relation to the divinity. The distinction between subjects and what is *in a subject*, in the sphere both of the corporeal and of the incorporeal, which is made specifically in Passage xii, also underlies the argument of Passage x.

More important, however, than any links between individual passages, are certain overall connections, which indicate the large extent to which the concerns behind the Passages are unified. Groups A and B are both, as I have said, concerned to understand God by first understanding the human mind; and between Groups C and D – the former discussing the theory of logic, the latter putting logical techniques into practice – the connection is obvious. But between Group C and Groups A and B there is also to be found an important connection, which has roots in the patristic period. The two most sophisticated Latin discussions of the Trinity to emerge from this time, Marius Victorinus's *Adversus Candidum* and *Adversus Arium* and Augustine's *De Trinitate*, both make extensive use of the doctrine of the Categories. The subtleties of Peripatetic logic were required, if the mystery of triune equality was to be made in the least intelligible, and then to be defended from heretical misinterpretation. But concepts which Aristotle had developed by studying the necessary relationships between parts of the physical universe took on a different, and often far more metaphysical, significance when they were used in an attempt to discuss the divine. The Munich Passages continue the connection, established by the Fathers, between the discussion of the Trinity and the elaboration, often markedly un-Aristotelian, of the doctrine of the Categories. In the proof of God's existence, the medieval author does not follow Augustine in his introduction of the concept of Universals, but he does introduce the notion of essence, as the lowest level of existence, and as that which God, being powerful, must also possess. The crudeness of this use of the concept of essence, just like the over-enthusiasm in the use of syllogistic reasoning, marks how early a stage the Munich Passages represent in the assimilation of logical doctrine.

IV

There are two further sets of material, connected with Candidus, which broaden the picture of the logical and philosophical interests of Alcuin's most sophisticated followers. The first is a copy (*München clm 18961 – B*), made in Brittany in the second half of the ninth century, of a schoolbook used in the circle of Candidus; the second is a fascinating discussion of the number three, which a variety of internal and external evidence suggests as Candidus's composition.

The later ninth-century section of *B* (ff.25–46) has already been mentioned, since it contains most of the Munich Passages, including the *dicta Candidi*.[74] These passages constitute part of a larger collection of extracts and original philosophical or theological pieces. This alone would provide grounds for associating the whole collection with Candidus and his followers; but, in fact, the manuscript provides far stronger evidence for such a connection. The first title to appear after the missing folio(s) between f.30 and f.31 is 'ITEM EIVSDEM'; the next item has exactly the same title, whilst the following piece is called 'ITEM EIVSDEM DE IMAGINE DEI'. Since this last-mentioned piece is none other than the *dicta Candidi*, there is every reason to assume that Candidus was the author of the two passages preceding it. What appears to have happened is that one of the pieces in the lost folio(s) was attributed to Candidus by name, and that the *eiusdem* of the following titles referred back to him.[75]

---

[74] See above, p. 40, n. 51.
[75] Ineichen-Eder (op. cit., p. 195, n. 20) seems to suggest the same argument: 'Da mit *Item eiusdem* die Texte von Nr. 10, 11 und 12 (= Dicta Candidi de imagine Dei) überschrieben

55

The content of the collection as a whole, and the two ITEM EIVSDEM passages in particular, strengthens this supposition. The first ITEM EIVSDEM piece (edited below, *A*) is an analysis of the Trinity into 'he who gives', 'he through whom he gives' and 'that which is given', highly reminiscent of the description of the Trinity as 'from whom', 'he who is from him' and 'by which', in the *dicta Candidi*. The second of these pieces (edited in part below, *B*) parallels the beginning of no. x of the Munich Passages by listing love, memory and thought as the things which proceed from the mind and are therefore incorporeal. However, the most striking affinity borne by this passage is to another which, I shall argue below, is also by Candidus; and the two are best considered together.[76]

Dr Ineichen-Eder has given a full and detailed description of the various excerpts which make up the bulk of *B*.[77] The collection begins with a set of extracts from Boethius's *Opuscula Sacra*,[78] including the *De Trinitate* which Candidus had probably used in composing his *dicta*. The second of these Boethius extracts, 'How God is omnipresent', deals with exactly the same topic as no. vi of the Munich Passages; and the third extract, on the difference between the human and the divine relationship to time, neatly adds to the discussion in nos. v and xv of the Passages. Augustine is the source for three of the extracts. As in the Munich Passages, his *De diuersis quaestionibus LXXXIII* is the source for a brief piece,[79] here an assertion of the idea, central to the doctrine of the Categories, that everything belongs to a species. The two other Augustinian items are both taken from the *De ciuitate Dei* and both illustrate the interest which antique philosophy held for the compiler of the collection.[80] One is Cicero's definition (as quoted by Augustine) of God as an unfettered, immortal mind, perceiving all things and moving them eternally. The other is

---

sind, so ist anzunehmen, dass alle drei, sowie das Fragment Nr. 9 von demselben Autor ("Candidus") stammen, der vielleicht in dem jetzt fehlenden Teil genannt war.'

[76] See below, p. 61.

[77] Op. cit., pp. 194–7. From an examination of *B* made before Dr Ineichen-Eder's work was published, I am able to add only one detail to her description of the quotations: no. 13, *AGVSTINVS DIXIT*, is not, as she says, a reminiscence of Augustine's *De Trinitate* XIV, xvi, 22, but a direct quotation from his *De ciuitate Dei*, XXII, 20 (*CC* 48, p. 840:7–11), where he is quoting Cicero *Tusculanae Disputationes* I, 66.

[78] Numbers in brackets refer to the items of Ineichen-Eder's catalogue: (1–6).

[79] (8).

[80] (13 and 18).

a definition of the nature of Man which Augustine quotes from 'Apuleius the Platonist'.

The remaining items in the collection, with the exception of a brief commentary on a verse from Job,[81] all testify even more strongly to this enthusiasm for the thought of the pagan past. There are two extracts from Seneca's *Quaestiones Naturales*,[82] a very rare work in the ninth century, each concerned with metaphysical questions of the greatest generality. Most exciting of all, however, is the passage entitled 'The Reasoning of a certain Platonist on how to discover the Artificer of the World' (edited below, *C*). Dr Ineichen-Eder has noticed that this piece contains a quotation from Calcidius's commentary on Plato's *Timaeus*, but does not comment on the importance of her discovery. Professor Bischoff has recently suggested that a manuscript containing the *Timaeus* in Calcidius's translation along with his commentary, previously dated to the eleventh century, was in fact produced in north-east France during the reign of Charlemagne.[83] Together with this quotation from Calcidius, the manuscript provides good evidence that the *Timaeus* was being studied by the beginning of the ninth century, probably in the circle of Alcuin's pupils. The passage which follows the one which quotes Calcidius, is, in effect, a commentary on it (edited below, *D*). It glosses the terms *harmonia*, *analogia*, *ordo* and *prouidentia*, around which the previous passage was constructed, and explains how they are linked together by their association with reason and understanding (*intellectus*).

The connection between a passage on the number three in *British Library Harley 3034* and Candidus was first suggested by Dom Morin in an article published at the end of the last century.[84] Not only does this article propose a number of additions to the corpus of Candidus's

---

[81] (7): 'Philosophus (*corrB* uel Philiphus) in Iob'. This little piece, dealing with the image and likeness of God in Man, is not taken, as the corrector appears to have imagined, from Philippus's commentary on *Job*. Neither I nor Ineichen-Eder have succeeded in finding its source.

[82] (16 and 17).

[83] *Paris BN 2164*; cf. B. Bischoff, 'Panorama der Handschriftenüberlieferung aus der Zeit des Karls des Grossen', *Karl der Grosse: Lebenswerk*, II, pp. 233–54, esp., p. 239. On this manuscript, see also above, p. 38. I should like to thank Dr Michael Lapidge for examining this manuscript on my behalf. On early manuscripts of the *Timaeus* and Calcidius's commentary, and library-catalogue references to them, see E. Mensching, 'Zur Calcidius-Ueberlieferung', *Vigiliae Christianae* 19, 1965, pp. 42–56.

[84] 'Un saint de Maestricht rendu à l'histoire', *Revue Bénédictine*, 8, 1891, pp. 176–83.

works; it also suggests the story of this scholar's later days. Morin began by identifying Candidus with the Waso/Wiso/Wizo, who is known to have been Bishop of Trier from 804 to about 809: not only is the name identical with Candidus's, but 'Wiso's' predecessor as Bishop of Trier, Ricbod, and his successor, Amalarius, were both, like Candidus, pupils of Alcuin's. Then Morin observed that at Maestricht, a town not far from Trier, a Saint Candidus was venerated from at least as early as the eleventh century. Saint Candidus, Morin conjectured, was none other than Wizo. Amalarius is known to have found himself uneasy in the high office which his connection with Alcuin had won him and to have been removed from his bishopric some time before his death. Could not the same fate have befallen Candidus, who would then have retired to Maestricht, where his holy life would confer him sanctity in the popular imagination of a later generation? So, at least, runs Morin's hypothesis; and it is as a final piece of evidence that *Harley 3034* (described in full below, p. 168) is introduced. This manuscript contains a group of sermons (3–5), the passage on the number three (6), and an account of the Passion, elsewhere attributed to Candidus (8): these pieces all follow on from one another without break. Morin conjectures that they are all the work of Candidus; and he uses the fact that the second of the sermons (5) was preached at Maestricht to support his theory of Candidus's retirement there.

Scholars have not generally accepted Morin's thesis. They have pointed out that the cult of Saint Candidus antedates Wizo and that the saint who was venerated at Maestricht in the eleventh century was most probably this older Candidus.[85] However, in using these as grounds to reject his hypothesis, scholars have ignored the fact that Morin's theory comprises three separable arguments: first, that Candidus, Alcuin's pupil, was the Bishop 'Wiso' of Trier; second, that items (3–6) and (8) of *Harley 3034* are the work of Candidus; and third, that Candidus retired to Maestricht, were he was venerated as a saint in the eleventh century. The first and second of these arguments, for which Morin presents good evidence, are not affected by objections to the third, which cannot be considered even probable. It is the second hypothesis which is of particular interest in the present context; and it appears to be particularly well founded. *Harley 3034* is a

[85] See e.g. Löwe, op. cit., p. 373, n. 1.

manuscript probably written in the region of Trier at the beginning of the ninth century. Lindsay considers, improbably in my opinion, that the manuscript could have been written at the end of the eighth century.[86] If this were the case, then it would make Morin's reconstruction of Candidus's later life impossible, but the attribution of material from the manuscript to Candidus would not, for this reason, be less probable. The nature of the contents of the passage on the number three (edited in full below, pp. 168–70) strongly supports this attribution.

Items (3–5) are clearly sermons in form: straightforward, unsophisticated expositions of Christian doctrine. These sermons are also to be found in another manuscript, of the early ninth century, *München clm 14510*,[87] where they are accompanied by another, rather more complex, sermon, on the Trinity, which is also very possibly the work of Candidus. The passage on the number three is very different in presentation from all these sermons. Clearly, it was not composed for public delivery: a dense study of philosophical and theological points, it can have been intended only for advanced students. The argument is often compressed and the Latin frequently strained: the passage requires detailed paraphrase and commentary.

All things, the author begins by saying, are constituted of being, being able, and willing. Being able and willing concern being – that is, being is logically prior to them, and they describe being. Being able is brought forth (from being); willing proceeds from being and being able – a person wishes because he has being and ability. This ability to do something is permanent: it is to be distinguished, that is, from the individual putting-into-practice of the ability to do a particular thing. Wishing, however, is always found in what is mutable: however many times something is wished, an act of wishing takes place. It is easy to see how this is the case in animate things. As for inanimate things, their being presents no problems of comprehension; their being able consists of their potentiality to become something, even if they do not in fact become it (for example, a tree *can* become a walking stick). Wishing in inanimate things is found in their lending themselves easily to the work of someone who is

---

[86] *Notae Latinae*, p. 55.

[87] This manuscript is mentioned, but not described at all, by Morin in his *Études, textes, découvertes* I (Maredsous, 1913), p. 61.

operating on them. If a tree lets me turn it into a walking stick easily, then this may be interpreted as its willing this; if I encounter difficulty in this task, this is the result of the tree's willing that it is not to be turned into a walking stick. Willing, then, in inanimate things is used by other, animate beings; and this is because all things without reason are made for the benefit of Man; but Man and the angels for God's benefit.

The argument so far does not seem to derive from any particular source. Indeed, the ingenious but faintly ludicrous notion that inanimate things have volition suggests a homespun train of reasoning. The statement that 'de esse sunt posse et uelle' may be reminiscent of the idea of something's being *de subiecto* – as put forward in the *Categoriae Decem* and the Munich Passages. Perhaps the underlying conception of the first paragraph is a free variation on Augustine's attempts in the *De Trinitate* – summarized in the *dicta Albini* and the *dicta Candidi* – to find trinities analogous to the Holy Trinity. The carefully made distinction between the second term, which is born from the first, and the third, which proceeds from the other two, suggests that the author is thinking of the Holy Trinity; but the parallel is left implicit. And the medieval writer is more ambitious than Augustine: he is not content merely to seek the image of the Trinity in the human mind, but finds it in all things.

Most of the second paragraph is based directly on a passage from Augustine's *De musica*; but this source is condensed and paraphrased, rather than quoted literally. Three consists of a beginning, a middle and an end. The way in which one must be a beginning, two a middle and three an end is set forth; and then the author goes on, following Augustine, to remark that, in a sense, two is also a beginning, since it has neither middle nor end. But this does not mean that there are two beginnings, as if there were one and then another one. Two is created by one's giving birth to another one, exactly the same as itself. The author now continues Augustine's argument in a direction implicit in the foregoing, but not pursued by its originator. Three is three ones; and it is also a beginning, since it is the 'first perfection', derived from one and two: the first one gives birth, two is the first to be born, and three is the first perfection of that which gives birth and that which is born. One cannot exist alone, since it would not be giving birth unless something were born. But nor can there be just two things, because the existence of two implies the existence of one and two. There must therefore be three things; but, to make three, one and two must be joined together. This joining, like love, makes three things of two. Unless they are one, they are not three. The author can conclude, tying up the argument of his second and third paragraphs with that of the first: 'See, therefore, that all perfection is a trinity, and indeed this alone; and that everything consists of a beginning, a middle and an end. And the beginning cannot exist without the middle and the end; nor the middle without the beginning and the end, nor the end without the beginning and the middle. It is necessary only that "one" be pronounced to say all things; and all things are told by the mention of the one that is perfect.'

The section on the number one in a passage from *B* (edited below, B) puts forward a very similar doctrine. There is no unity in which a trinity cannot be found, because we start to enumerate from unity, we number through it and finish our numbering in it. One is the vestige of God imprinted in the human mind, since God's unity is also a trinity. The author then lists two sets of trinities which are found in corporeal things: height, length and breadth; and number, measure and weight. These complement the different list – being, being able and willing – explored in the first paragraph of the passage in *Harley 3034*.

The chief difference between the passage in *B* and that in the Harleian manuscript is the explicitness of the former. The Harleian passage is remarkable for what it leaves unsaid. From Augustine's analysis of the perfection of the number three, its author has developed an account of trinitarian relations which dovetails with that presented in the first paragraph. Numerological analysis stresses the unity of the trinity; and the third term is described as 'love' – so frequently a name for the Holy Spirit. But the analogy between the numerical trinity and the Holy Trinity is left implicit. Perhaps, as it stands, the passage in the Harleian manuscript is rough or incomplete; more probably, its lack of explicitness is intentional.

There is, then, good evidence to attribute to Candidus, Alcuin's friend and pupil, a body of philosophical work which makes him the outstanding philosopher of his generation; and which, indeed, must encourage historians to modify their whole conception of the range and energy of thought at the court of Charlemagne. None of

Candidus's ideas is a sophisticated or durable solution to the problems he poses himself; and theological ideas are inextricably entangled in his attempts at philosophy. Nevertheless, his was an adventurous and original mind: in his decided ability to use the work of authorities as the basis for his own thoughts, he shows the sort of innovative traditionalism which was to characterize both his immediate and his more distant followers. How does Candidus's achievement compare with that of his far more famous near-contemporary, Fredegisus?

V

Fredegisus has received the lion's share of the meagre attention which historians have paid to the philosophy of the period of Charlemagne.[88] This has had three unfortunate consequences: seen in isolation, Fredegisus's thought has been incorrectly interpreted; some scholars have given an exaggerated idea of the complexity of the problems with which he deals; and, on the other hand, those who have arrived at a juster, lower estimate of Fredegisus's attainments have improperly extended this judgement to all of Alcuin's circle. In his intimacy with Alcuin, his master, who used him at times as a confidential messenger, Fredegisus resembles Candidus.[89] But Fredegisus's surviving philosophical work does not date from the period of Alcuin's mastership at the Palace School. The letter *De nihilo et tenebris* was written in 800, at the earliest dating.[90] Further, and in many ways more interesting, record of Fredegisus's philosophical activity relates to a controversy

---

[88] Detailed studies include: M. Ahner, *Fredegis von Tours* (Leipzig, 1878) and Endres, op. cit., pp. 5–15. L. Geymonat, 'I problemi del nulla e delle tenebre in Fredegisio di Tours', *Rivista di Filosofia*, 1952, pp. 280–8, and C. Mazzantini, 'Ancora intorno al "nulla" di Fredegisio da Tours', *Atti dell'Accademia delle Scienze di Torino, Classe di scienze morali* etc., 87, 1952–3, pp. 170–96, do not attempt to give faithful account of Fredegisus's own thought. I have seen only a summary of F. Corvino, 'Il "De nihilo et tenebris" di Fredegiso di Tours', *Rivista critica di Storia della Filosofia*, 1956, pp. 273–86; but Corvino's idea that Fredegisus's interpretation of *nihil* was intended to support a literal interpretation of the Bible, as opposed to allegorical exegesis, is at variance with what can be learnt of Fredegisus's views on exegesis from Agobard's letter (see below, p. 65). C. Gennaro, *Fridugiso di Tours e il 'De Substantia Nihili et Tenebrarum'* (Padova, 1963), makes no original contribution to a discussion of the content of Fredegisus's work.

[89] See Ahner, op. cit., pp. 3–14.

[90] See Gennaro, op. cit., pp. 57–66. Ahner (op. cit., pp. 13–14) suggests a later date – 804–14. This letter is edited by Dümmler in *MGH Epistolae* IV; pp. 552–5: my references are to this edition. The work is also edited in *MPL* 104, 751ff.; Ahner, op. cit., pp. 16–23; Corvino, op. cit.; and Gennaro, op. cit., pp. 123–38.

with Agobard of Lyons, which apparently took place in the late 820s. Fredegisus, therefore, provides a testimony to the thought of the years between Alcuin's retirement and the intellectual revival which took place under Charles the Bald.

Fredegisus' letter on the nature of nothingness and darkness was a contribution to a discussion of negative concepts which had been broached by Alcuin and which continued to perplex men at the Palace even after they had digested Fredegisus's opinions. The letter explains the reference of negative concepts by recourse to a simplistic theory of language. God is held to be the creator, not just of objects, but of their names. Moreover, God 'created nothing whatsoever for which a word was lacking, nor did he institute any word unless that object for which it was set up existed'.[91] A parallel argument claims that every *nomen finitum* signifies something: since *nihil* is a *nomen finitum*, what it signifies must really exist.[92] A variety of strictly redundant pieces of logic support or elaborate these astonishing presumptions; and a host of biblical references to *nihil* and *tenebrae* are used to confirm the real existence of these concepts.

The letter shows that Fredegisus, like the writer of the Munich Passages, was fascinated with the techniques of logic for their own sake; but it gives a distinctly unfavourable impression of the mental powers of its author. The brief discussion of reason and authority in no way anticipates John Scottus's sophisticated treatment of these ideas; nor does it use with any imagination the passages in Augustine which were the starting-point for both Fredegisus and Eriugena.[93] A reference to the concept of Universals rather ignores than treats the problem: the name of 'Man' or 'Stone', says Fredegisus, designates or embraces the generality (*universitas / generalitas*) of men or stones.[94] Some commentators have tried to represent Fredegisus' theory of nothingness as a contribution to the exegesis of the Hexaemeron; but

---

[91] Ed. cit., p. 554:30–2: 'Conditor etenim rebus, quas condidit, nomina inpressit, ut suo quaeque nomine res dicta agnita foret. Neque rem quamlibet absque vocabulo formavit, nec vocabulum aliquod statuit, nisi cui statueretur existeret.'

[92] Ibid., p. 553:8–18.

[93] Ed. cit., p. 553:4–7 and 19–22; cf. Ahner, op. cit., pp. 24–33. For John Scottus on reason and authority, see *Periphyseon* I, pp. 194:30–198:12; and cf. C. Allegro, *Giovanni Scoto Eriugena 1: Fede e Ragione* (Roma, 1974).

[94] Ed. cit., p. 553:9–11: 'Quippe hominis nomen praeter differentiam aliquam positum universalitatem hominum designat. Lapis et lignum suam similiter generalitatem conplectuntur.' Cf. Prantl, op. cit., I, p. 18.

a few, vague sentences in the letter form a very poor basis for such a view.[95]

Far more interesting, but far more elusive, is the part which Fredegisus played in a controversy with Agobard of Lyon. The only record of this controversy is provided by a letter of Agobard's, which has been dated to about 830.[96] From this letter it is possible to reconstruct the following sequence of events. In a work which has not survived, Fredegisus used the phrase, 'when the soul reached the body'.[97] Agobard was shocked by the implication that Fredegisus knew for certain of the soul's pre-existence, and he wrote a letter to him pointing out his error.[98] Fredegisus's reply was detailed and ill-tempered.[99] It was concerned not just to defend (and perhaps to elaborate) his original argument, but also to attack certain of the ideas which Agobard had mentioned, and to question his opponent's competence as an interpreter of Scripture. Fredegisus also raised a number of new questions. It is Agobard's reply to this letter which survives, although it is perhaps missing its final section.[100]

Historians of the dispute have been interested mainly by Fredegisus's ideas about the soul.[101] As to their details, Agobard is frustratingly vague. Fredegisus appears certainly to have thought that souls existed before the bodies they were to animate, otherwise he would not have tried to defend his use of the phrase, 'when the soul reached the body'.[102] Furthermore, he considered that souls were created from an unknown matter (*incognita materies*) in a vacuum (*in vacuo*).[103] Modern scholars have tried to identify both the unknown matter and the vacuum with the nothingness of Fredegisus's *De nihilo et tenebris*, in neither case with good reason.[104] There does, however, seem to be a

[95] See ed. cit., p. 533:24–6 and p. 554:1–2; and cf. Ahner, op. cit., pp. 41–50.

[96] Edited by Dümmler in *MGH Epistolae* v, pp. 210–21 (also in *MPL* 104, 159–74). c. 830 is Dümmler's dating.   [97] See ed. cit., p. 217:17ff.

[98] This reply is the *cartula* mentioned at ibid., p. 210:38.

[99] See ibid., p. 210:26–40.

[100] As found in the unique manuscript, *Paris BN 2853*, a collection of Agobard's letters, the letter ends without any sort of formal conclusion or summary. Had one been written, but lost in transmission? *BN 2853* is not a contemporary manuscript of Agobard, but dates from the tenth century according to the Bibliothèque Nationale's *Catalogue générale des manuscrits latins* 11 (Paris, 1952), pp. 164–5 (although Lindsay (*Notae Latinae*, p. 472) suggests c. 840).

[101] See Ahner, op. cit., pp. 48–53; Endres, op. cit., pp. 10–12.

[102] See Endres, op. cit., p. 12.   [103] Ed. cit., p. 217:27–8.

[104] These identifications are made by Ahner (op. cit., p. 50) and Endres (op. cit., p. 11) respectively.

real parallel between Fredegisus's notion of the pre-existence of souls and the view implied by a passage in the *dicta Candidi*.[105] The theory attacked by Agobard may well have been one popular among Alcuin's followers; for himself, Alcuin had refused to speculate about the origin of the soul.[106]

Other aspects of the controversy are also interesting. Fredegisus had said in his reply to Agobard that Scripture broke the rules of grammar only where there was some specific reason for doing so.[107] By contrast, Agobard asserts, and defends, the general 'rusticity' of biblical style: for him there is an absolute distinction between eloquence of language, to which Scripture does not aspire, and the richness of hidden, figurative meaning which distinguishes the Bible. On a couple of questions about Christ, Fredegisus is accused of using misleading arguments or perverting the meaning of the authorities he quotes.[108] Another problem shows most clearly the difference in intellectual temperament between the two men. Fredegisus asks whether God is one thing, truth another:[109] presumably this question was intended to raise the sort of problems about the predication of qualities to God which Boethius had discussed in his *De Trinitate*,[110] and perhaps those about God's relation to his Son (who could be called 'Truth') which Augustine had tackled in his work on the Trinity. But to Agobard such a question is merely ridiculous. Of course, he answers, 'truth' is used many times in the Bible to mean, not God, but that virtue which is the opposite of falsehood; this does not mean that God is not truth, but rather that he also is truth. And in this way, in his righteous indignation, Agobard misses all the problems which Fredegisus had most probably meant to raise.

The general tone of Agobard's letter is in keeping with this particular instance. Fredegisus has tried to defend false positions 'with his syllogisms'; he has sided with the (pagan) philosophers in his theory

---

[105] See above, p. 47.
[106] *De animae ratione* 13 (*MPL* 101, 645B): 'Origo vero animarum unde sit, solius Dei cognitioni relinquendum est. Quam multa exinde philosophi vana finxerunt, et plurimas Christiani doctores opiniones inde posuerunt, et nihil pene certum reliquerunt'; cf. Endres, op. cit., p. 11.
[107] Ed. cit., p. 214:28–9 (quoting Fredegisus): 'Nihil enim omnino contra regulam grammaticae dixerunt [*sc.* apostoli et evangelistae et divinae scripturae interpretes] quod non ita aut ratio aliqua aut causa mysterii dici exigeret.'
[108] Ibid., p. 211:4ff. and p. 218:19ff.   [109] Ibid., pp. 217:44–218:18.
[110] Cf. Boethius, *De Trinitate* IV (ed. cit. pp. 18:31–20:44).

of the origin of the soul.[111] In short, crude as Fredegisus's arguments appear by comparison with those of both his immediate predecessors and successors, they were far too sophisticated for Agobard to allow that they might be true or even honest. It is the sad reflection of a time when, according to Walahfrid Strabo, 'studies were falling into decline, and the light of wisdom, no longer so highly prized, was growing fainter'.[112] It would be the work of a brilliant generation, living under the rule of Charlemagne's grandson, to take up again the problems which had fascinated Alcuin and his followers, and tackle them with a depth and breadth of interest which would have astonished even the most adventurous of Candidus's generation.

[111] Ed. cit., p. 218:19 and p. 217:40–43; cf. Endres, op. cit., p. 10.

[112] Prologue to Einhard's *Life of Charlemagne* (in Einhard, *Vie de Charlemagne*, ed. and trs. L. Halphen (4th edn, Paris, 1967), p. 106): 'Nunc vero, relabentibus in contraria studiis, lumen sapientiae, quod minus diligitur, rarescit in plurimis.'

Chapter 3

PROBLEMS OF THE CATEGORIES, ESSENCE AND THE UNIVERSALS IN THE WORK OF JOHN SCOTTUS AND RATRAMNUS OF CORBIE

No early medieval treatment of the Categories and the problems connected with them is as wide-ranging or as original as that which John Scottus provided in his masterpiece, the *Periphyseon*. No other treatment had so much influence on the scholars of the late ninth and tenth centuries who tackled these problems. A study of the doctrine of the Categories as it appears in the *Periphyseon* will therefore provide a centrepiece to my whole survey. First, however, I will look at a piece of material which perhaps gives some clues to the direct antecedents to John's theory of Universals.

I

The only record which survives of a controversy on the World Soul between Ratramnus of Corbie and an unnamed monk of Saint-Germer de Fly is Ratramnus's *Liber de anima ad Odonem Bellovacensem*.[1] This book, written in the early 860s,[2] is a reply to the answer which the monk of Saint-Germer had written to Ratramnus's original objections to his ideas. However, the monk of Saint-Germer professed to be expounding, not his own views, but those of his master, a certain Macarius, who, despite several attempts, cannot convincingly be identified with any figure from other sources. This chronology

---

[1] The *Liber de anima ad Odonem Bellovacensem* is edited by D. C. Lambot (*Analecta Mediaevalia Namurcensia* 2: Namur, Lille, 1952). All references are to this edition. P. Delhaye's *Une Controverse sur l'âme universelle au IXe siècle* (*Analecta Mediaevalia Namurcensia* 1: Namur, Lille, 1950) is written as a companion to this edition, and discusses in detail the origin of the controversy, Ratramnus's sources and his doctrines.

[2] Lambot (ed. cit., pp. 8–11) suggests the late 860s as the date for this work, but J.-P. Bouhot (*Ratramne de Corbie: Histoire littéraire et controverses doctrinales* (Paris, 1976), p. 59) argues convincingly for a dating before the end of 863.

would suggest that Macarius began to expound his views to his pupils some time in the 850s, if not before. Moreover, Macarius is described as 'Scottus', an Irishman, and this makes some connection, or common background, with John Scottus particularly probable, since the links between the various Irishmen on the Continent were strong.[3]

A controversy on the World Soul is not, at first sight, a likely place in which to find a dispute on the nature of Universals. That this question found its way to the centre of Ratramnus's and the monk of Saint-Germer's arguments is another striking proof of the extent to which questions of logic were raised by early medieval theological discussions. The controversy was raised by a passage from St Augustine's *De quantitate animae*.[4] Here Augustine puts forward three possibilities: that all souls are one; that individual souls are entirely separate; or, as a compromise between the two extreme positions, that souls are both one and many. He finds neither of the first two alternatives satisfactory, and considers that the third would invite ridicule. In short, he leaves the dilemma unresolved.

Some caution is necessary in stating Macarius's position, since it is known only through the passages of his pupil's writings quoted by Ratramnus for the specific purpose of being refuted. It seems, however, that Macarius took Augustine's passage for the serious metaphysical discussion which its author doubtless meant it to be, but tendentiously argued that, by his phrasing, Augustine wished to convey his assent to the third of the alternatives, that the soul is both one and many. However, in attacking the writings of Macarius's pupil, Ratramnus immediately turned the dispute into a logical one; and it is the logical questions raised which are of particular interest here.

According to Ratramnus, when Augustine talks of a single, universal soul, he is merely referring to the species to which individual souls belong.[5] And, he continues, species have no real existence: they are simply concepts formed by the mind from the individuals which it perceives. Ratramnus bases himself on Boethius's *Contra Eutychen*[6]

---

[3] See below, pp. 105ff.   [4] *De quantitate animae* xxxii, 69 (*MPL* 32, 1073).

[5] E.g., p. 28:6–9: 'Porro anima cum est species, quod tunc existit quando rationalis accipitur, nunc de multis nunc de singularibus intelligitur. De multis cum dicitur omnis anima: de singularibus cum dicitur una.'

[6] He quotes Boethius's phrase 'Intellectus enim universalium rerum ex particularibus sumptus est' (see above, p. 26, n. 49) at pp. 71:15–16, 74:8–10.

and his first commentary to Porphyry's *Isagoge*.[7] But he goes far beyond the mere statement of the epistemological priority of individuals which he quotes from the former; and at times he even goes beyond the conceptualism of the latter, when he states sweepingly that species and genera do not properly exist outside the mind.[8]

It appears from a few incidental criticisms made by Ratramnus, that the theory of Universals advanced by the monk of Saint-Germer was radically opposed to Ratramnus's conceptualism. Among the statements of his opponent which Ratramnus mentions as being particularly erroneous, there is one which describes any singular, indivisible man as an abyss,[9] and another which suggests that, by the mere placing of Cicero as a subject for Man, all men are collected together.[10] Each of these rather vaguely phrased statements points to a problem which Ratramnus had ignored: that any individual, in so far as it is a member of a given class, must really possess all the defining characteristics of that class. The monk of Saint-Germer's two statements seem to propose for a solution to the difficulties raised by this consideration what I shall call 'hyper-Realism': each individual really contains every other individual member of the same class, and there is thus no difference between genera, species and individuals. Another of the monk of Saint-Germer's remarks which Ratramnus pillories compares the manner in which individuals emerge from their species to the birth of creatures, or to a river's flowing from its source, or a tree's growth from its roots.[11] It is impossible to tell whether these logical doctrines were those taught by Macarius, or whether the monk of Saint-Germer himself devised or discovered them as replies to Ratramnus's criticisms. Both in the

---

[7] p. 78:3–10: 'Dicit [Boethius] itaque quod species et genera, cum in singularibus habent considerationem, id est, de particularibus enunciantur, sint, id est, existant: cum vero sint universalia, non tunc dicantur esse, sed cogitari tantummodo: quoniam omne quod est universale, in cogitatione, id est, rationali consideratione consistit, non in aliqua subsistentia quae possit sensibus corporis apparere.' And cf. Boethius, commentary on *Isagoge* I, ed. cit., pp. 74:20–75:7, for a direct quote.

[8] p. 96:8–11: 'At vero genera seu species, quae sunt usiae secundae, in cogitationibus per mentis intellectum formantur: in rebus autem existentibus non consistunt . . .' *Consistunt* may be a term derived from the *De Hebdomadibus*; see above, p. 27, n. 53.

[9] p. 102:14–15: 'Nonne quilibet indivisibilis homo, quod est singularis, abyssus non est?'

[10] Cf. p. 102:19–22: 'Qua de re, si aliquis profert Ciceronem homini esse subiectum, non in hac voce sic haerebit ut cogitatio profundi cordis cunctos longe lateque sparsos non colligat homines'; cf. Delhaye, op. cit., pp. 35–7.

[11] See p. 108:37ff., esp. 'singularia, quae sunt individua sive propria, de specie producantur more nascentium creaturarum, veluti de fonte producitur rivus, vel arbor de radice . . .'

hyper-Realism and in the assimilation of logical processes to those of nature, the view of Universals so violently condemned by Ratramnus is that which John Scottus elaborated and wove into his system.

II

John Scottus was writing his masterpiece, the *Periphyseon*, at very much the time when Ratramnus was working on his *De anima*.[12] There is a sharp contrast between the two treatises. Ratramnus deals with a specific, limited problem. He transforms this problem, originally theological in nature, into a philosophical one; and he proposes a solution which is derived largely from Boethius. The *Periphyseon*'s subject-matter is, by contrast, of the greatest possible generality. In his dialogue, John proposes to discuss the ultimate divisions of universal nature: in doing so, he attempts to explain the relationship between God and his creation, the Fall of Man, his redemption by Christ, and the ultimate return of all things to God. The theological system which John proposes, with its emphasis on the idea of procession from God and return to him, owes a very great deal to the Greek Christian Neoplatonists, Gregory of Nyssa, the pseudo-Dionysius and Maximus the Confessor.[13] But, like all his contemporaries, Eriugena was a respectful and thorough reader of the greatest of the Latin Fathers, Augustine. The frequent contrasts and conflicts between Augustine's ideas and those of the Greeks provides a good deal of the *Periphyseon*'s matter for argument and is responsible for much that is characteristic in John's work.

Eriugena set about his ambitious task by using two different types of discussion, both familiar to his age, as a framework. The first book of the *Periphyseon* is based around a topic logical in its origin – the ten Categories and their relation to God; the remaining four books centre loosely around the interpretation of the opening verses of Genesis. It

[12] For the date of the *Periphyseon*, see Cappuyns, *Jean Scot*, pp. 188–90.

[13] On the sources of the *Periphyseon*, see J. Dräseke, *Johannes Scottus Eriugena*; I. P. Sheldon-Williams, 'Eriugena's Greek Sources'; and *Freiburg Conference, passim*. There are a number of studies of the theological system of the *Periphyseon*. Details of these will be found in M. Brennan, 'A bibliography of publications in the field of Eriugenian studies', esp. sec. vb, pp. 424–34. An outstanding general study is T. Gregory, *Giovanni Scoto Eriugena: Tre Studi* (Firenze, 1963) (*Quaderni di letteratura e d'arte raccolti da Giuseppe De Robertis*, xx). (The first and second sections of this three-part study were originally published in *Giornale critico della filosofia italiana*, 37, 1958, pp. 319–32; and 39, 1960, pp. 237–52, respectively.)

is, therefore, in Book I that most of the discussion of essence, the Categories and the Universals will be found. In considering these points, and thereby bringing together logical and theological ideas, John is most fully a philosopher. The remaining four books of the *Periphyseon* are devoted to an interpretative activity: an analysis of Holy Scripture and an attempt to reconcile some of the different authoritative views as to its meaning. In the course of this exegesis, John builds a theological system which is in many ways his own; but his task is not that of abstract explanation. Yet his discussion of essence, Categories and the Universals offers Eriugena the opportunity to consider some of the most fundamental concepts devised by philosophers in their attempts to give a rational explanation of reality. In handling these concepts he must, therefore, use to a considerable extent the methods of philosophy. But it is important to remember that philosophical discussion in the *Periphyseon* is always subordinated to the requirements of a system that, in its overall structure and meaning, is theological. This is one of the reasons why – as I shall suggest – there is much in John's thought on philosophical problems which is confused or contradictory.

The various discussions of essence, the Categories and the problem of Universals[14] in the *Periphyseon* may be drawn together to provide a glimpse, individual in its emphases but true in its overall bearing, of John's system as a whole. Unified in this way, John's comments on logic take on a definite but specious magnificence – specious because so many of the problems confronted have been circumvented by terminological ambiguity or mere self-contradiction. I shall try to steer a middle course between an artificial sympathy with John's system, and an entirely destructive critical investigation of his arguments. Neither of these two extremes would help to illustrate how the *Periphyseon* brought the early medieval discussion of the Categories to its intellectual peak, and yet left to John Scottus's successors plenty of room for changes which were not simply the result of their comparative ignorance.

---

[14] Partial treatments of this subject include: G. Anders, *Darstellung und Kritik der Ansicht von Johannes Scotus Eriugena, dass die Kategorien nicht auf Gott anwendbar sein* (Sorau, 1877); K. Eswein, 'Die Wesenheit bei Johannes Scottus Eriugena', *Philosophisches Jahrbuch*, 43, 1930, pp. 189–206; and M. Cristiani, 'Lo spazio e il tempo nell'opera dell'Eriugena' (summarized in 'Le problème de l'espace et le temps dans le . . . *Periphyseon*', *Dublin Conference*, pp. 41–8).

(a) God and the Ten Categories

John Scottus first introduces the Categories into the *Periphyseon* in order to affirm God's transcendence over all of them. If any one of these Categories, which are applicable to the things created by God, could be predicated of God himself, then God would no longer be that which can neither be spoken of nor understood.[15] This use of the Categories is clearly in the tradition of St Augustine, whose *De Trinitate* is explicitly acknowledged as a source.[16] The inapplicability of the Categories to God is made into a particularly firm assertion of divine transcendence by another view which John takes from Augustine and also from other late antique interpreters of the *Categories*: the ten categories are seen as embracing all things that can be discovered in created nature or imagined by the mind.[17]

There are two ways, however, in which John's account of God's relationship to the Categories differs from Augustine's. The first is the linking of this account to a theory of apophatic and cataphatic theology; the second lies in the thoroughness with which God's transcendence of the Categories is stated, and in its extension to the first of the Categories, *usia*.

Before he introduces the Categories into his discussion, John has explained the distinction between apophatic and cataphatic theology.[18] Strictly speaking, no quality may rightly be predicated of God: the only way of speaking about the divinity is to negate any attribute that may be applied to him and to affirm his superiority to it. This process of systematic negation constitutes apophatic theology. The attribution of certain qualities to God is, however, permitted, so long as it is recognized as merely metaphorical; and this is called cataphatic theology. John took this distinction from the pseudo-Dionysius, but,

[15] I, p. 86:9–13: 'Clare conspicio nulla ratione kategorias de natura ineffabili proprie possi praedicari. Nam, si aliqua kategoriarum de Deo proprie praedicaretur, necessario genus esse Deus sequeretur. Deus autem nec genus nec species nec accidens est: nulla igitur kategoria proprie Deum significare potest.'

[16] I, p. 84:32–4: 'Sed, ut ait sanctus pater Augustinus in libris de Trinitate, dum ad theologiam, hoc est ad diuinae essentiae inuestigationem, peruenitur, kategoriarum uirtus omnino extinguitur.'

[17] I, p. 84:17–21: 'Aristoteles, acutissimus apud Graecos, ut aiunt, naturalium rerum discretionis repertor, omnium rerum quae post Deum sunt et ab eo creatae innumerabiles uarietates in decem uniuersalibus generibus conclusit, quae decem kategorias, id est praedicamenta, uocauit.'

[18] I, pp. 72:32–84:13.

characteristically, systematized it and used it as the basis for a theory of logic. The inapplicability of the ten Categories to God is an epitome of apophatic theology.

The thoroughness of John's treatment of God's superiority to the Categories is partly illustrated by the very length of his survey, which lasts for most of the first book and painstakingly asserts for each Category that only cataphatically may it be predicated of the divinity. But far more important philosophically is one particular consequence of John's thoroughness, his insistence that *usia* cannot be predicated of God.[19] This view directly contradicts Augustine's, who identified *usia* with God. It owes something to the pseudo-Dionysius's statement, repeated by John, that the being of all things is God, who more-than-is;[20] and something, perhaps, to Marius Victorinus's description of God as what is not. But, most of all, the assertion of God's superiority to the first of the Categories is a result of John's characteristic tendency to follow through all the logical consequences of an idea. If God's ineffability is compromised by the possibility that any description of him in human terms may be appropriate, then *usia*, which is predicable of created things, cannot be predicated of God. John's extreme position here causes grave difficulties in the development of his ontology, since, unlike the pseudo-Dionysius, he is not willing to retreat into the learned ignorance of the mystic, and, unlike Victorinus, he has negated the essence itself of God, and not some derivative like 'that which is'. The attempt to surmount these difficulties shapes much of the rest of John's discussion of the Categories.

(b) The Five Modes of Being

At the very beginning of the *Periphyseon*, John puts forward two different divisions of Universal Nature. One of these is the fourfold division into that which is not created and creates, that which is created and creates, that which is created and does not create, and that which is not created and does not create; it is by this division that the structure of the whole *Periphyseon* is articulated. The other, mentioned

---

[19] I, p. 86:29–31: 'Non est igitur OYCIA quia plus est quam OYCIA, et tamen dicitur OYCIA quia omnium OYCIWN... creatrix est.'

[20] I, p. 38:25–7: 'ipse nanque omnium essentia est qui solus uere est, ut ait Dyonisius Ariopagita. "Esse enim", inquit, "omnium est super esse diuinitas".' Cf. Jeauneau ed., *Homily on Prologue to John*, Appendix II, esp. pp. 323–4.

first and described as being more fundamental, is into those things that are, and those that are not.[21] The very nature of this division is illuminating of John's ontology: those things which are not are considered to be a fundamental class, not a nullity; being must be a predicate of only limited application.

John proposes five ways in which things may be said to be or not to be.[22] These divisions derive from different sources and are incompatible with each other: each of them provides a point of departure for one of the *Periphyseon*'s strands of argument. Thus the fourth mode of being reflects a Platonic distrust for the perceptions of the senses: according to the philosophers (*secundum philosophos*) only those things perceived by the intellect may be said truly to be (*uere esse*). This concept of *truly being* is reminiscent of the ontologies of Augustine and Boethius. Again, the third mode of being is related to Augustine's theory of seminal reasons, derived from the Stoics, which John was to use extensively in Books II and following. That which is manifest in matter and form, time and place is said to be, whereas that which is as yet contained in the recesses of nature (*naturae sinus*) is said not to be. The fifth mode of being has a limited, moral application: human nature, corrupted by Original Sin, lost its image-relationship to God and ceased to be, until restored in the person of Christ. The second mode of being is based on a logical subtlety rather than a metaphysical perception: to affirm something of one order of nature is to deny it of the order above that one; and vice versa. For instance, what one affirms of a man – that he is rational, mortal and capable of laughing – one must deny of an angel, which is rational, but neither mortal nor capable of laughing.

It is the first of the modes of being which is of most importance in the development of John's ontology. Those things which can be grasped by the sense or the intellect may be said to be; those which 'escape sense and even all intellect' may be said not to be. This class of not-beings includes God, and the reasons (*rationes*) and essences (*essentiae*) of all things created by him.[23] The pseudo-Dionysius's

---

[21] I, p. 36:4–6: 'rerum omnium . . . primam summamque diuisionem esse in ea quae sunt et in ea quae non sunt . . .'

[22] I, pp. 38:19–44:24.

[23] I, p. 38:19–25: 'Quorum [modorum interpretationis] primus uidetur esse ipse, per quem ratio suadet omnia, quae corporeo sensui uel intelligentiae perceptioni succumbunt, uere ac rationabiliter dici esse, ea uero, quae per excellentiam suae naturae non solum omnem

statement that God's more-than-being is the being of all things is quoted in support of God's transcendence of being itself. To this John adds a remark which he takes from Gregory Nazianzen, by way of Maximus, to the effect that, just like God, so the substance or essence (*substantia seu essentia*) of any creature is beyond the comprehension of the intellect and therefore is not.[24] This position is even more paradoxical, and raises greater difficulties, than the assertion of God's not being: how can essence, the abstract particular or universal of being, itself not be? The strand in John's ontology which treats *usiae* as a special kind of unintelligible individuals, eliminating the idea that it is through participation in *usia* that things are, may be seen as a response to this problem. But before looking in detail at John's treatment of *usia*, I shall describe his theory of Universals.

(c) The Theory of Universals

John expresses his theory of Universals in the terminology of the *Categoriae Decem*. There is no difference, he says, between what is *said of a subject* and the subject itself. For example, Cicero, the individual subject, and Man, which is *said of* Cicero and of every other man, are one and the same. The species 'in its numerous members is whole and one in the individual, and these members are one individual in the species'.[25] This 'hyper-Realism'[26] is made more work-

<hr/>

sensum sed etiam omnem intellectum rationemque fugiunt, iure uideri non esse: quae non nisi in solo deo ... et in omnium rerum quae ab eo conditae sunt rationibus atque essentiis recte intelliguntur.' Sheldon-Williams's suggestion (n. 15 on p. 223) that *essentiae* here means the same as *rationes*, 'the primordial causes', is almost certainly mistaken: John goes on almost immediately to talk about the way in which essence, even the essence of a visible creature, is incomprehensible (passage quoted p. 75, n. 24 below).

[24] I, pp. 38:27–40:2: 'Gregorius etiam theologus multis rationibus nullam substantiam seu essentiam siue uisibilis siue inuisibilis creaturae intellectu uel ratione comprehendi posse confirmat, quid sit. Nam sicut ipse Deus in se ipso ultra omnem creaturam nullo intellectu comprehenditur, ita etiam in secretissimis creaturae ab eo factae et in eo existentis consideratus incomprehensibilis est.' For a summary of earlier discussions of the unknowability of *usia*, see Cristiani, op. cit., pp. 40–54. For a use of this passage by a follower of Eriugena (which confirms the unusual reading *secretissimis*), see below, p. 125.

[25] I, p. 102:11–21: 'Nam, iuxta dialecticorum opinionem, omne quod est, aut subiectum aut de subiecto est ... Vera tamen ratio consulta respondet subiectum et de subiecto unum esse et in nullo distare ... Si ergo species tota et una est indiuiduaque in numeris et numeri unum indiuiduum sunt in specie, quae quantum ad naturam distantiae est inter subiectum et de subiecto non uideo.' Sheldon-Williams's reference (n. 109 on p. 233) to Boethius's commentaries on the *Isagoge* for the categories of subject, in a subject, etc., seems somewhat beside the point, since the *Categoriae Decem* are the obvious source for this terminology.

[26] Two scholars, C. Prantl (op. cit., II, pp. 22–37) and P. Mandonnet ('Jean Scot Erigène et

able by John's theory of 'analytic' collection and 'diairetic' descent, which preserves a measure of distinction between particulars and Universals, despite their logical identity.

Porphyry had already referred to the process of descent from the highest genera through the intermediate genera and species to the lowest species; and the converse process of ascent back to the highest genera.[27] John took over these two processes, the first of which he called *diairetikē*, extending their range, so that they reached down to individuals.[28] These two processes became the organizing principles of John's entire system and gained a metaphysical dimension by their use. Diairetic descent is seen as analogous to the process of creation: from the divine unity is created the multiplicity of the primordial causes; these in their turn create the infinite variety of sensible nature. Analytic ascent is treated in parallel to the Return of all things to their maker – a neoplatonic theme which John took in the main from Gregory of Nyssa. The analytic and diairetic processes which separate the particulars from their Universals are in theory entirely logical: they simply deduce consequences from implied premises. As such, they do not compromise the identity of the particular with the universal. But, as they are used in the *Periphyseon*'s system, there lies between the two extremes which these processes span the whole

Jean le Sourd'), have argued that, in spite of his obviously realistic tendencies, John also manifested a nominalist streak in his treatment of Universals. This opinion, however, is founded on no more than a few expressions which employ the linguistic terminology used so *frequently* in the *Categoriae Decem*. Hauréau (op. cit., I, pp. 161–73), by contrast, subordinates every other feature of John's system to his 'unrestrained realism'.

27 Ed. cit., p. 12:7–15. Another important source for John on the processes of logical division and collection was Maximus; cf. *Ambigua*, *MPG* 91, 1177 B. The ultimate source for this procedure is Plato's *Philebus*; see esp. 16c–17e.

28 See esp. II, pp. 6:26–8:35; *De praedestinatione* (*CC c.m.* 50) pp. 5:18–6:27. The clearest statement of this theme occurs in John's preface to his translation of Maximus the Confessor's *Ambigua* (ibid., 1195BC): Maximus, says John, explains 'quomodo causa omnium, quae Deus est, una sit simplex et multiplex: qualis sit processio, id est, multiplicatio divinae bonitatis per omnia quae sunt, a summo usque deorsum, per generalem omnium essentiam primo, deinceps per genera generalissima, deinde per species specialiores usque ad species specialissimas per differentias proprietatesque descendens. Et iterum, ejusdem videlicet bonitatis qualis sit reversio, id est, congregatio per eosdem gradus ab infinita eorum, quae sunt, variaque multiplicatione usque ad simplicissimam omnium unitatem, qua in Deo est et Deus est; ita ut et Deus omnia sit, et omnia Deus sit.' On the inclusion of individuals in John's hierarchy, see II, p. 8:8–11, 22–6, and I, p. 106:6–9: 'Num OYCIA in generibus generalissimis et in generibus generalioribus in ipsis quoque generibus eorumque speciebus atque iterum specialissimis speciebus, quae atoma, id est indiuidua, dicuntur, uniuersaliter proprieque continetur?'

drama of creation, Fall, redemption and Return. In this way, extra-logical factors permit John's hyper-Realism to be useful in talking about the world of sensible reality; and the logic of particulars and Universals, viewed in its own strict terms, reflects John's meta-physics stripped of any consideration for historical contingency.[29]

Besides its value in the working-out of his system, and besides the possible influence of contemporaries such as Macarius, John's hyper-Realism may owe its development to three factors. First, there is the discussion of Universals by Boethius in his second commentary to the *Isagoge*. Boethius had admitted that, in some sense, the entire class was contained in each of its members. For him, this was a preliminary to asserting that classes had no real existence; but a subsequent thinker might feel himself free to adopt only the first part of his argument, especially as Boethius himself disowned his solution to the problem.[30] Second, there is the ease with which hyper-Realism solves a problem posed by John's theory of knowledge. John held that the mind could contemplate certain Universals, such as the 'reason of numbers', which yet remained distinct from it. In a case where the mind fully assimilated such a Universal, it is difficult to see how the particular accident, *that* knowledge in *that* mind, could be distinguished from the Universal, knowledge of that sort in general. John's hyper-Realism provides an explanation for this identity, whilst the theory of diairetic descent and analytic collection yet enables some distinc-tion to be preserved between the particular and the Universal. Finally, hyper-Realism supported certain fundamental features of John's anthropology. The substantial unity of all men provided an explana-tion for the subjection of humanity entire to Original Sin, since Adam, as a man, contained all men. Similarly, Christ's redemptive mission became less an article of faith than a consequence of logic, since by his incarnation Jesus became all men, and all men were thus saved in him.[31]

---

[29] Trouillard ('La notion d'analyse chez Érigène', *Laon Conference*, pp. 349–56, esp. p. 349) notes that already in Proclus's logic the relation of genus to species was assimilated to that of cause and effect.

[30] See above, p. 26.

[31] See esp. v, 921A–923C. John concludes (923C): 'Proinde si Dei Verbum humanitatem accepit, non partem ejus, quae nulla est, sed universaliter totam accepit. Et, si totam accepit, totam profecto in seipso restituit, quoniam in ipso resturata sunt omnia . . .'

(d) Usia

Usia is itself unknowable, John had stated at the beginning of his account of the Categories. Appropriately, therefore, John's concept of *usia* is best understood through the relationships concerning it: that between the particular *usia* and universal *Usia*; that between *usia* and the other Categories; and that between *usia* and the material world.

Two distinct relationships between individual *usia* and universal *Usia* are posited in the *Periphyseon*. The first is simply that implied by John's hyper-Realism. *Usia* is contained in the most general genera and in all their subdivisions down to the individuals (*atoma*); 'it subsists in these, its natural parts, as a whole'.[32] The characteristics of *usia*, both general and particular, are stated to be incomprehensibility and immutability. *Usia* can be known only by the categories which surround it, place, quantity, situation and time; the *usia* of each individual is a stable centre, which can be neither moved, increased nor diminished.[33]

In the context of a discussion of the triad, οὐσία, δύναμις and ἐνέργεια, which he borrowed from the pseudo-Dionysius and Maximus, John puts forward a different view of the relationship between individual *usia* and general *Usia*. From the *essentia* which is 'created one and universal in all things and is common to all things, and which, because it belongs to all those things which participate in it, is proper to no single one of them, there emanates by natural progression a certain specific substance which belongs to nothing except to that of which it is'.[34] The *usia* (and the δύναμις and ἐνέργεια)

---

[32] I, p. 106:10–14: 'Nil aliud esse uideo in quo naturaliter inesse OYCIA possit, nisi in generibus et speciebus a summo usque deorsum descendentibus, hoc est a generalissimis usque ad specialissima, id est indiuidua, seu reciprocatim sursumuersus ab indiuiduis ad generalissima. In his enim ueluti naturalibus partibus uniuersalis subsistit.'

[33] I, pp. 102:31–104:6: 'Si autem acutius uestigia sancti Gregorii expositorisque sui Maximi sapientissimi sequens inspexeris, inuenies OYCIAM omnino in omnibus quae sunt per se ipsam incomprehensibilem non solum sensui sed etiam intellectui esse, atque ideo ex his, ueluti ex circumstantiis suis, intelligitur existere: loco, dico, quantitate, situ, additur etiam his tempus. Intra haec siquidem, ueluti intra quosdam fines circunpositos, essentia cognoscitur circuncludi, ita ut neque accidentia ei quassi in ea subsistentia uideantur esse, quia extrinsecus sunt, neque sine ea existere posse, quia centrum eorum est, circa quod uoluuntur tempora, loca uero et quantitates et situs collocantur.'

[34] I, p. 182:7–12: 'Non enim ueritati obstrepat, ut aestimo, si dicamus ex ipsa essentia quae una et uniuersalis in omnibus creata est omnibusque communis atque ideo, quia omnium se

78

which is 'most particularly considered in individuals' is subject to
change, increase and diminution; this is because all things do not
participate to a similar extent in the universal triad of οὐσία, δύναμις
and ἐνέργεια.[35] The same distinction seems to be made in Book II,
where the *universalis essentia*, which is not subject to accidents, is
distinguished from *substantia*, the first of the Categories, which is
finite and subject to accidents.[36]

Essentia, according to this second version of the relationship, is not
universal *Usia*, but rather *usia* of all kinds, conceived, as it is in the
first version of the relationship, as one in many and many in one. This
is made clear when John adds that the universal triad of οὐσία,
δύναμις and ἐνέργεια, like light to the eyes, is not more or less in
anything that participates in it, but is whole both in itself and in its
participants.[37] According to this second version of the relationship,
therefore, each individual has two different types of *usia*: universal
Usia, entirely realized in that particular, just as it is in every particular;
and an *usia* peculiar to that individual, which participates to a greater
or lesser extent in universal *Usia*. This second version of the relationship thus attempts to subsume the first version. But it is doubtful
whether the two are really compatible. The hyper-Realism used by
the first version directly contradicts the theory of participation which
the second version employs, since the theory of participation maintains that individuals, so far from being the entire class to which they
belong, and thus their own Universals, share only to a limited degree
the possession of the characteristics of a Universal which is completely outside them.

participantium est, nullius propria dicitur esse singulorum se participantium, quandam
propriam substantiam, quae nullius alicuius participantium est nisi ipsius solummodo cuius
est, naturale progressione manare . . .'

[35] I, p. 182:22–6: 'Haec uero quae specialissime in singulis considerantur augeri possunt et
minui multipliciterque uariari. Non enim omnes similiter participes sunt uniuersalis
essentiae et uirtutis et operationis: alii enim plus, alii minus, nullus tamen participatione
ipsius penitus priuatur.'

[36] II, p. 160:31–6: 'Ea namque substantia quae primum in categoriis obtinet locum finita est et
accidentibus subiecta, ea uero uniuersalis essentia nullum in se accidens recipit. In suis quippe
subdiuisionibus usque ad indiuidua peruenientibus accidentium capax est; ipsa uero in se
simplex est nullique accidentium subiecta.' Confusingly, John here seems to imply that the
finite substance is simply the individual essence; but he does not attribute to it the unknowability and stability he elsewhere grants to individual *usia*. Eswein (op. cit., p. 198) places
undue emphasis on this passage.

[37] I, p. 182:26–9: 'Ipsa quoque in omnibus participantibus se una atque eadem permanet
nullique ad participandum se plus aut minus adest, sicut lux oculis. Tota enim in singulis est
et in se ipsa.'

Two different views of *usia* are also present in John's treatment of the relationship between *usia* and bodies. A third view, the opposite of the first, is found in a passage which was added in the course of revision.

By his first view, John maintains that *usia* has no direct relationship with anything corporeal or sensibly perceptible. Behind the world of appearances is envisaged an invisible world of *usiae*, species and genera, harmonizing with the world of sensible bodies, but not affecting it or affected by it. The best expression of this position is John's theory of essential and qualitative forms. The essential form of something is its species; and this is considered to be entirely distinct from its qualitative form, which consists of its dimensions and composition from parts.[38] Bodies consist of matter and qualitative form. Matter, at this point, is seen as something entirely different from essence: infinite, formless but capable of form, it has been created 'so that those things which by themselves could not reach the senses might in some way appear sensibly in it (i.e. matter)'.[39]

Elsewhere, however, John rejects the dualism implied by this view, and is even willing to venture a highly tendentious interpretation of a passage from Boethius's *De arithmetica* to support this end.[40] Bodies are formed by the concourse of things themselves incorporeal: *usia*, quality and quantity. *Usia* remains perpetually invisible, and quality and quantity, too, are contained invisibly by it. But when these three come together to form a sensible body, quantity brings forth a perceptible *quantum* and quality a perceptible *quale*.[41] A different expression of the same view is also made. Bodies are produced from

---

[38] I, p. 154:1–7: 'Formarum aliae in OYCIA, aliae in qualitate intelliguntur, sed quae in OYCIA sunt substantiales species generis sunt ... Genus nanque ... totum in singulis suis formis est, quemadmodum et singulae formae unum in suo genere sunt; et haec omnia, id est genera et formae, ex uno fonte OYCIAE manant inque eam naturali ambitu redeunt.'

[39] See I, pp. 166:9–168:5, esp. I, 166:18–25: 'Deus siquidem infinitus informisque quoniam a nullo formatur, dum sit forma omnium; materia similiter informis infinita, aliunde enim formari indiget finirique, dum per se non forma sed formabilis sit. Et haec similitudo causae omnium, ex qua et in qua et per quam et ad quam omnia sunt, et ipsius causae informis – dico autem materiae – quae ad hoc creata est ut ea, quae per se sensibus attingi non possent, quodam modo in ea sensibiliter apparerent, e contrario intelligitur.'

[40] I, p. 174:20–33, which overturns a far more plausible interpretation of the passage (ed. cit., pp. 7:26–8:13) advanced by the Alumnus at pp. 162:21–164:11.

[41] See esp. I, p. 156:23–8: 'Haec etenim tria in omnibus naturalibus inspiciuntur corporibus, OYCIA, quantitas, qualitas; sed OYCIA solo semper intellectu cernitur, in nullo enim uisibiliter apparet; quantitas uero et qualitas ita inuisibiliter in OYCIA, ut in quantum et quale uisibiliter erumpant dum corpus sensibile inter se coniunctae componunt.'

the four elements (themselves accidents of *usia*, qualities to each sensible instance of which a *quantum* must be added before they can become corporeal);[42] and it is to the elements that bodies return on their dissolution.[43] But the essence of each body remains immutable in the midst of this coming-together, changing and dissolution. So, indeed, do the accidents of *usia* (the elements). It is only the participation by the accidents in *usia* which undergoes change.[44] *Usia* is in this way at the basis of every bodily thing but separate from its embodiment. The *usiae* remain the particulars of a non-sensible, immutable world.

In a passage which was added during revision, there occurs a remarkable development in the discussion. Here, the requirement that every natural body must have *usia*, as well as quantity and quality, takes on a special importance. What is it that distinguishes a natural body from a geometrical one? John's answer is that a natural body has an *usia*, a geometrical body has not.[45] The peculiarity of such a statement within John's system becomes apparent when one considers that an obvious point of difference between a geometrical and a natural body would be that the former lacked matter. *Usia* and matter are supposedly at two extremes of John's conceptual system; but here the functions of these two concepts converge.

---

[42] I, p. 156:33–158:13: 'Non enim aliud te suadere aestimo quam ut cognoscamus quattuor mundi huius elimentorum in se inuicem concursu contemperantiaque materiam corporum fieri, cui adiecta qualicunque ex qualitate forma perfectum corpus efficitur . . . Si . . . elimenta quantitate qualitateque fiunt, et corpora ex elimentis, ex quantitate et qualitate corpora sunt.'

[43] I, p. 112:28–34: 'Constat etenim hunc mundum uisibilem quattuor generalibus quibusdam partibus compositum esse, et est quoddam corpus suis partibus compactum ex quibus, uidelicet partibus catholicis, omnium animalium, arborum, herbarum propria specialissimaque corpora mirabili ineffabilique mixtura coeuntia componuntur, inque eas iterum resolutionis tempore redeunt.'

[44] I, pp. 112:34–114:11: 'Vt enim totus iste mundus sensibus apparens assiduo motu circa suum cardinem uoluitur – circa terram, dico, quam ueluti quoddam centrum caetera tria elementa, aqua uidelicet, aer, ignis, incessabili rotatu uoluuntur; ita inuisibili motu sine ulla intermissione uniuersalia corpora, quattuor elementa dico, in se inuicem coeuntia singularum rerum propria corpora conficiunt, quae resoluta iterum ex proprietatibus in uniuersalitates recurrunt, manente semper immutabiliter quasi quodam centro singularum rerum propria naturalique essentia, quae nec moueri nec augeri nec minui potest. Accidentia enim in motu sunt, non essentia; nec etiam ipsa accidentia in motu sunt seu in incrementis detrimentisue, sed participatio eorum ab essentia tales patitur mutabilitates.'

[45] I, p. 152:21–5: 'geometrica solo animo consideramus, in nullaque OYCIA subsistunt atque ideo "phantastica" iure uocantur, naturalia uero corpora propterea naturalia sunt, quoniam in naturalibus suis OYCIIC, id est essentiis, subsistunt et sine quibus esse non possunt ideoque uera sunt – alioqui non in rebus naturalibus sed sola rationi cogitarentur . . .'.

The more John's *usiae* belong to an independent world of exact generic relationships, causally unconnected with the world of bodies, the less does the theory of *usia* constitute a theory of being. *Usiae* are just one sort of thing, bodies another: *usiae* are the individuals of which classes consist. By contrast, in so far as John posits a connection between *usiae* and bodies, he is supplying the basis for a theory of being: it is by its relationship to *usia* that something is or is not. Although John does not make an explicit connection, it seems true that John's hyper-Realistic explanation of the relation between universal *Usia* and individual *usiae* will best function where the world of *usiae* is most distinct, and that where the theory of *usiae* tends towards a theory of being, a theory of participation, such as John sometimes adopts, will best explain the connection between particular *usiae* and universal *Usia*.

The theory of *usia* is subject to a further ramification, when John discusses it in Book III as one of the primordial causes.[46] It is questionable how far John's general discussion of the primordial causes at this point is integrated with his overall system. Most often, the primordial causes are used to perform the function of Augustine's *rationes seminales*, immanent principles in created nature which explain ordered growth without the direct intervention of the deity. Here, however, the primordial causes are far more like Platonic Ideas, except that they are clearly considered to be the causes of their individual instantiations, and, in one particular way, are not their classes. The instantiations of each of the primordial causes may be arranged into a series of classes of ever-increasing generality; but the primordial causes themselves are not ordered, they are above order and number and are created immutably one in the divine Word.[47] How many primordial causes there are is not made clear: John lists in order Goodness, Essence, Life, Reason, Intelligence, Wisdom, Virtue (*virtus*), Beatitude, Truth, Eternity, Magnitude, Love, Peace, Unity and Perfection[48] – a strange medley which seems to have been inspired by the various descriptions of God listed by the pseudo-Dionysius. These, he adds, are merely the first in order, given by way

---

[46] III, 621A–632B.
[47] See III, 626A–D and 628D–630A, esp. 626B: 'ipsae per seipsas omnium quae sunt primordiales rationes uniformiter et incommutabiliter in Verbo Dei, in quo factae sunt, unum et id ipsum ultra omnes ordines omnemque numerum aeternaliter subsistunt'.
[48] III, 622B–623C.

of example; but is every Universal a primordial cause? And, if so, how can the strict generic hierarchy of the classes of their instantiations be maintained? In spite of the incoherence of this position, it is at least certain that here the theory of Universals being used is a type of Platonic Realism, not the hyper-Realism of *Periphyseon* Book I.

John places Essence second to Goodness.[49] This decision is justified in various ways. Scriptural support is adduced and it is argued that, if God, through his goodness, caused all things to be, then Goodness must precede Essence. Most interestingly, John follows the pseudo-Dionysius in arguing that, whereas Essence would disappear if Goodness were to vanish, Goodness would remain were Essence no longer to be, since those things which are not, because of their excellence, are nevertheless good.[50] Whilst this idea fits in well with John's 'apophatic ontology', in which essence is denied to God and his most sublime creations, it is highly confused. God is said not to be simply because no description of him in human language can be remotely accurate. *Ex hypothesi*, the statement, 'God is not', is not a statement about God, but about the limits of the human understanding. It cannot rightly be used to assert not-being as a real attribute of the deity. Moreover, the impossibility of description applies to goodness as much as to essence. Only cataphatically may God be called 'good'; but cataphatically he may also be said to be.

(e) Space and Time

Apart from his discussion of *usia*, the weight of John's account of the Categories falls on two of the others: space and time. Other interesting developments, such as the division of the ten categories into two super-categories, rest and motion,[51] are not elaborated to play any important part in John's system.

---

[49] III, 627C–628C; cf. *De hebdomadibus*, ed. cit., esp. p. 46: 119–27, and G. d'Onofrio, 'A proposito del "magnificus Boetius": un'indagine sulla presenza degli "Opuscula Sacra" e della "Consolatio" nell'opera eriugeniana', *Freiburg Conference*, publication forthcoming. The most direct source for John's argument here is the pseudo-Dionysius: see esp. *De diuinis nominibus* IV, 1–4 (*MPG* 2, 693B–700C).

[50] III, 628B: 'Non solum, quae sunt, bona sunt; verum etiam, quae non sunt, bona dicuntur. Eoque amplius meliora dicuntur quae non sunt, quam quae sunt: nam in quantum per excellentiam superant essentiam, in tantum superessentiali bono, Deo videlicet, appropinquant; in quantum autem essentiam participant, in tantum a superessentiali bono elongantur.' Cf. pseudo-Dionysius, *De divinis nominibus* V, 1 (ed. cit., 816B).

[51] See I, pp. 98:17–102:8 and II, p. 160:29–31. Prantl (op. cit., II, p. 36) suggests a neoplatonic origin for this theory; almost certainly it owes something to Maximus: cf. H. von Balthasar,

John takes the beginnings of the theory of space and time which he expounds in Book I of the *Periphyseon* from Maximus. Space and time cannot exist without each other. They are beyond the universe, since the universe cannot be its own place, and because everything besides God has a beginning and therefore must be subject to time.[52] Space and time, conceived in this way, are related to *usia* in two, incompatible, ways. Either *usiae*, from the most individual to the *genus generalissimum*, preserve their independence and unknowability: they can never be known for *what* they are, but it is known *that* they are from the accidents surrounding them, including space and time.[53] Or the spatio-temporality of *usiae* is considered to be a measure of their lack of absolute being: only of God, who is outside space and time, may it be said that he *is* absolutely and properly. Here John talks in terms of participation and his source appears to be Boethius's *Opuscula Sacra*.[54]

In addition to this very generalized concept of space, John develops the idea of the place of a thing as the limits within which it is enclosed – a notion which the *Categoriae Decem* might have suggested.[55] But John extends the idea to incorporeal things: their place is their definition.[56] This idea is allied to John's concept of definition to give space

Liturgie Cosmique: Maxime le Confesseur, trs. L. Lhaumet and H.-A. Prentout (Paris, 1947), pp. 89–104.

[52] I, pp. 124:30–126:18: 'Omne quodcunque est, praeter Deum ... intelligitur in loco; cum quo ... semper et omnino cointelligitur tempus ... Locus est ipsa extra uniuersitatem ambitus, uel ipsa extra uniuersitatem positio ... Sub tempore etiam uniuersa comprobabuntur, quoniam non simpliciter sed aliquo modo esse habent uniuersa quaeque post Deum esse habent, ac per hoc non carent principio.'

[53] I, p. 138:3–17, esp. ll. 3–8: 'OYCIAN per se ipsam diffinire et dicere quid sit nemo potest. Ex his autem quae inseparabiliter ei adhaerent et sine quibus esse non potest, ex loco dico et tempore ... solummodo diffiniri potest *quia* est.'

[54] I, p. 126:18–25: 'Omne enim quodcunque rationem recipit alicuius modi essentiae etsi est, non erat. Itaque aliquo modo esse, hoc est localiter esse, et aliquo modo inchoasse esse, hoc est temporaliter esse; ideoque omne quod est praeter Deum, quoniam aliquo modo subsistit et per generationem subsistere inchoauit, necessario loco ac tempore concluditur. Vnde Deum esse dicentes, non aliquo modo esse dicimus, ac per hoc et "est" et "erat" simpliciter et infinite et absolute in ipso dicimus.' Cf. Boethius, *De Trinitate*, ed. cit., p. 18:26–36, and *De hebdomadibus*, p. 40:28–30; these passages are discussed in Chapter I above, pp. 27–8.

[55] See e.g., I, pp. 130:35–132:2: 'Quis enim locum seu finem seu diffinitionem seu qualemcunque circumscriptionis speciem, qua uniuscuiusque substantia ambitu, inter ea quae sensibus corporeis succumbunt recte sapientium posuerit, cum uideat terminos liniae seu trianguli seu alicuius planae solidaeue figurae incorporeos esse?'; cf. *Categoriae Decem*, secs. 72–7; pp. 149:9–150:12.

[56] I, pp. 132:33–134:28, esp. p. 134:26–8: 'Videsne itaque non aliud esse locum nisi actionem intelligentis atque comprehendentis, uirtute intelligentiae, ea quae comprehendere potest, siue sensibilia sint, siue intellectu comprehensa?'

a use in the system of the *Periphyseon* which totally belies its stated nature. True definition, says John, is essential definition;[57] and definition is a function of the mind and so exists within the mind. Definition, therefore, relates neither to the world of appearances harmonized to that of *usiae*, nor to the limitations of less-than-divine essences; rather, it determines the very *usiae* themselves. It is on this basis that John erects his theory of creative cognition. The act of knowing is the act of defining, and the act of defining makes an *usia* into what it is.[58]

In Book v of the *Periphyseon*, the three notions of space and time found in Book I – Maximus's concept of these two categories as anterior to the world and necessary for its existence; the idea of an object's space as its boundary; and the identification of space with definition – are juggled in such a way as to leave the reader impressed by John's dexterity, but no less conscious for that of the muddle he has perpetrated. Augustine had put forward a theory of space and time completely contradictory to Maximus's: space and time did not precede the world but were created with it. In the course of his discussion, John moves towards the Augustinian point of view.[59] This is probably because he wishes to assert that at the end of the world space and time will disappear. But, he adds, he does not mean place as the definition of things – that will always remain in the mind; what will perish is the space 'by which the quantity of bodies is extended'. As for space and time, the two parts of the world which the Greeks (and here the reference is to Maximus) call 'those without which the other parts cannot exist', how will they remain when that of which they are parts perishes? When there is nothing to be placed or circumscribed, space will vanish; when there is no motion, time will cease.[60] Here John seems to assimilate Maximus's concept of

---

[57] I, p. 130:13–22. An essential definition is not concerned with the parts of an *usia* or anything outside it but only 'quod perfectionem naturae quam diffinit complet et perficit.'

[58] The theory of cognitive creation is intimately linked to that of theophany. It is beyond the scope of my discussion to go into either of these theories in any detail: for treatments of these subjects, see T. Gregory, 'Note sulla dottrina delle "teofanie" in Giovanni Scoto Eriugena'; J. Trouillard, 'Érigène et la théophanie créatrice'.

[59] v, 888A–889C.

[60] v, 889C–890A: 'Totus itaque mundus aut totus interibit, aut totus semper erit. Peribit autem. Totus igitur peribit, neque ulla pars sui post suum interitum remanebit sine interitu. Sunt autem partes ejus locus et tempus: in ipso igitur et cum ipso peribunt locus et tempus. Locum nunc dico non rerum definitionem, quae semper manet in animo, sed spatium, quo corporum quantitas extenditur. Nam quod Graeci duas illas mundi partes, locum dico et

space and time to the humbler one, of these categories as the immaterial dimensions of material things, which he had taken from the
Categoriae Decem. In a later passage, John says that, at the end of the
world, space and time return to their 'eternal reasons', which are
identified with the scriptural *tempora aeterna*.[61] But it does not appear
consistent with their use elsewhere in the *Periphyseon* that any of the
Categories should have primordial causes distinct from themselves, as
opposed to themselves being primordial causes.[62]

(f) Conclusions

In the preceding analysis, four directions of thought have emerged as
guiding principles in John's treatment of the Categories. First, a radi-
cal negative theology, which bars all of the Categories, including *usia*,
from any applicability to God. Related to this is a theory of being
which might be described as apophatic, because the state of non-
being is held to excel that of being. Second, a hyper-Realism, which
conflates individuals with Universals. *Usia* ceases to be a predicate
under such a theory and each *usia* becomes, as in Aristotle's original
theory, an individual; but, so far from being the everyday, sensibly
perceptible individual, it is an entity present in each sensible thing but
unknowable in itself, the lowest term in a world ordered according to
a strict logical hierarchy. Third, an ontology of participation – a line
of thought plainly in contradiction to the first and second directions.
Fourth, a theory of space as definition, which allows John to elaborate
his concept of creative cognition. Each of these different elements has

tempus, ὢν ἄνευ, hoc est, sine quibus ceterae partes esse non possunt, appellant, tamdiu illud
vocabulum non temere dixerim in eis praevalere, quamdiu totum illud, cujus partes sunt,
permanserit. Eo vero transeunte, simul et illius vocabuli virtus evacuabitur. Cum enim non
fuerit, quod locari et circumscribi indigeat, quomodo erit locus? ... Quando ... nullus
motus erit, quem mensura temporis non dividet et comprehendet, quomodo tempus erit?'

[61] v, 970D: 'Nam et ipsa loca et tempora cum omnibus, quae in eis adhuc in hac vita ordinantur
et moventur et circumscribuntur, in suas aeternas rationes redire necesse est, quas rationes
"tempora aeterna" divina vocat historia.'

[62] For this reason, I think that John's reference to the primordial causes of space and time is a
measure of his desperation in trying to reconcile the irreconcilably different concepts of
space and time furnished by Maximus and Augustine. Cristiani (op. cit., p. 132) thinks, on
the contrary, that by this move John preserves the overall unity of his theory: the *rationes
aeternae* of space and time are, in her view, 'the immutable categories, the ontological laws,
thanks to which, in the inverse order of the *processio*, the unity of the causes is defined and
made specific, right down to its final consequences'.

its importance in John's metaphysical scheme; but they do not themselves link to form a coherent logical picture.[63]

[63] At a conference in August 1979, I gave a paper ('John Scottus and the *Categoriae Decem*',
Freiburg Conference, forthcoming) which explored some of the material discussed in the
second part of this chapter from a rather different point of view. In the paper, I tried to
probe the philosophical validity of John's reasonings, and the implicit philosophical assumptions he made, in order to throw light on the nature of the enterprise he undertook in
composing the *Periphyseon*.

Chapter 4

THE CIRCLE OF JOHN SCOTTUS ERIUGENA

In the last three chapters, I have traced the development of a group of ideas and methods from the time of Charlemagne to that of Charles the Bald. In the final chapter, I will examine one of the principal routes by which these ideas were disseminated and developed during the course of the tenth and the eleventh centuries. At the centre of this story will have been John Scottus. His *Periphyseon* brings to a climax the discussion of the Categories begun in the School of Alcuin; and the scholars of the late ninth and tenth centuries were to turn to this work when they considered the problems of essence and the Universals. In this chapter, therefore, I wish to fill in some of the intellectual background to John's work. The 'circle of John Scottus' appears to have occupied as central a position in the philosophical development of the ninth century as its master himself. Who belonged to this circle and in what did its work consist?

There is good evidence that John's ideas attracted considerable, enthusiastic attention from his contemporaries; but this evidence is scattered and fragmentary. Whenever the possibility that a particular figure was deeply influenced by John's work is raised, it requires only a moderate amount of scepticism to dismiss it. I shall therefore begin by examining a set of material incontrovertibly associated with John: the notes and glosses written in two insular hands, each of which scholars have claimed as John's own. I will argue that neither of these hands belonged to John himself, but rather to two of his closest followers. I will then move on to another block of sure evidence for Eriugena's influence: the manuscript diffusion of the *Periphyseon* in the late ninth and early tenth centuries, and the external indications of how these manuscripts were read. Only then will I turn to consider the individual figures – Sedulius Scottus, Martin of Laon, Wulfad, Heiric of Auxerre – who have the best claims to have belonged to John's circle.

I

When Ludwig Traube examined the earliest surviving manuscript of the *Periphyseon*,[1] *Reims 875 (R)*, he was excited to discover in it extensive marginal additions in Irish script. He found corrections and marginalia in what he took to be the same hand in two further manuscripts: *Bamberg Ph 2/1 (B)*, which contains the second revision of *Periphyseon* Books I–III; and *Laon 81*, the unique manuscript of Eriugena's *Commentary on the Gospel of St John*. From the authorial nature of these additions, Traube concluded that the Irish hand – 'i' as he called it – must be that of John Scottus himself; and he sought confirmation for his hypothesis in the very nature of the handwriting: individual and spirited, how could it be the work of an unknown copyist and not the writing of the great Irish philosopher?

Traube's pupil, E. K. Rand, was content to subscribe without reserve to these views when he edited the paper expressing them from his master's literary remains. But when, some years later, he studied the material for himself, he was forced to reach very different conclusions.[2] Not one but two Irish hands – 'i¹' and 'i²' – were responsible for the marginalia in *R*; and they shared their work with a number of Caroline scribes. Rand then brought forward two strong arguments for supposing that neither i¹ nor i² was the hand of Eriugena. First, the work of these two Irish hands is divided, not on the basis of the contents or the length of their additions, but by groups of quires, in a purely businesslike way.[3] And, second, both i¹ and i² co-operate at times with Caroline hands in writing a single gloss. Could it be that John knew how to write both Irish and Caroline script? Rand dismissed this possibility, in the case of i¹ at least, by showing that the Irish hand co-operated with more than one Caroline scribe: no author, he suggested, would play with his copyists in this way. i¹ and i² were both scribes, Rand concluded; but they worked under John's

---

[1] 'Palaeographische Forschungen v: Autographa des Iohannes Scottus', *Abhandlungen der k. Bayerischen Akademie d. Wissenschaften*, phil.-phil. u. hist. Klasse, 26, 1.

[2] 'The supposed autographa of John the Scot'.

[3] See op. cit., p. 140: i¹ writes in quires I–X and XV–XLI (ff. 1–80 and 113–318); i² writes in quires XI–XIV and XLII–XLVI (ff. 81–112 and 319–58). The only exception to this are some lemmata, written by i² even in parts of the manuscript otherwise assigned to i¹: see T. A. M. Bishop 'Autographa of John the Scot', esp. p. 92.

immediate direction, and the material they copied was composed by John.[4]

In spite of the power of Rand's arguments, they have been ignored or brushed aside by most subsequent scholars.[5] In his edition of *Periphyseon* Books I and II,[6] Sheldon-Williams simply ignored Rand's discovery that the marginalia of *R* are written by two separate Irish hands. He criticized Rand for assuming that 'Eriugena invariably wrote in the same hand', whereas Rand had put forward a good argument against the possibility that John wrote in (one variety of) Irish and in (one variety of) Caroline script; and it must be beyond even the wildest of a palaeographer's fancies to suppose that Eriugena experimented with various types of one or both kinds of writing. Finally, Sheldon-Williams confused the point at issue, which is not whether John was the author of the marginalia in *R* (which Rand never doubted), but whether they are written in his hand.

By contrast, Edouard Jeauneau gave a full and fair account of the controversy on John's autograph in the Introduction to his edition of Eriugena's *Commentary on St John*.[7] Nevertheless, Jeauneau was inclined to set aside Rand's arguments and claim i^1 as Eriugena's hand. But Jeauneau had sought the advice of Bernhard Bischoff, and it was Bischoff's different conclusion which he favoured in the end. Bischoff has done more than any other scholar to further the discussion of John's autograph, by adding a number of items to the list of i^1's and i^2's appearances. Yet his contribution via Jeauneau's Introduction did little but confuse the issues. Bischoff proposed that i^1 was not John's hand (no reason is given for this opinion – was he convinced by Rand's arguments on this score?); and that i^2, being found in a range of manuscripts besides *R* and *B*, could hardly be the hand of a scribe, because it would be difficult to explain how John had kept the same scribe during the period required for the production of a range of manuscripts; and that i^2, therefore, was the hand of Eriugena. This reasoning appears to involve two near-contradictory assumptions.

---

[4] A third argument against identification of i^1 with Eriugena put forward by Rand is based on the mistaken assumption that i^1 was responsible for an addition containing serious errors: in fact it is written by the text-scribe: see op. cit., p. 139, and cf. P. Lucentini, 'La nuova edizione del "De divisione naturae (Periphyseon)" di Giovanni Scoto Eriugena', n. 39.

[5] An honourable exception is Lucentini (see op. cit. pp. 10–11).

[6] I, pp. 7–8.

[7] Jean Scot, *Commentaire sur l'Évangile de Jean* (SC 180), (Paris, 1972), pp. 63–80.

For Bischoff begins by taking it for granted that, even if i^2 is not John's hand, all his annotations in whatever manuscript must have been entered under Eriugena's direction: a point of view which implies that a scribe would never leave the employ of a single master. But then he proceeds to argue for i^2's identity with John, from the notion that a scribe would never stay long in the employment of a single master.

The most recent contribution to the controversy on John's auto-graph has been made by T. A. M. Bishop.[8] i^2, Bishop argues, is not John's hand: some of i^2's glosses contain errors unlikely to have been made by Eriugena; and his work on B may be regarded as editorial. He then goes on to argue that i^1 *is* Eriugena's writing – a conclusion for which Bishop has not better evidence than the old assumption that, if one of the i's is not John, then the other one must be. By way of support, Bishop falls back on the argument which Traube had used of the undifferentiated i, recognizing in this 'rapid, nervous, dispersed, sometimes rather disorderly hand' the 'more specious characteristics of an Irish-cosmopolitan intellectual'.

Neither Bishop nor any other scholar has succeeded in disposing of Rand's argument about the co-operation of Irish and Caroline scribes;[9] but this argument makes it inconceivable that i^1 should have been Eriugena. Bishop's paper, moreover, has the effect of hardening into virtual impossibility the meagre chances which remained, in spite of Rand's evidence, that i^2 could be John Scottus. Just as strange as the way scholars have ignored Rand's arguments is the manner in which they have assumed that one of the Irish hands in R must be John's. It is unlikely that, if Eriugena had another Irish scribe and a number of Caroline copyists at his disposal, he would still have taken a part in the demanding labour of copying long additions into narrowish margins. But oddest of all these oddities is that scholars as fine as Traube and Bishop should have seemed to argue as if the physical characteristics of a hand, its nervousness or spirit, could

---

[8] Op. cit. (n. 3 above). In the discussion which followed Bishop's paper, Bischoff retracted his earlier view that i^2 was the hand of John and gave his support to Bishop's conclusions: cf. *Laon Conference* p. 94. Another paper at this conference (J. Vezin, 'À propos des manu-scrits de Jean Scot: quelques rémarques sur les manuscrits autographes du haut Moyen Âge' (ibid., pp. 95–9)) added a useful note of caution but did not bring any new material or important arguments to the controversy.

[9] Bishop succeeds in finding just one instance where the collaboration between i^1 and a Caroline scribe was 'more apparent than real': see op. cit., p. 91, n. 1.

betray it as that of an intellectual, not just a scribe. Such a procedure is dubious even when applied to modern handwriting: for medieval script it is entirely inappropriate. Indeed, the indications point – if they point at all – in a direction exactly opposite to this line of argument. No qualities of speed, spirit or nervousness are evident in the authenticated autographs of two scholars associated with John, Martin of Laon and Heiric of Auxerre.[10] Theirs is the slow, deliberate, somewhat clumsy writing of those who are not professional scribes; by contrast, i^1's marginalia combine legibility with an obvious speed in execution.

Traube likened the experience of seeing the hand of Eriugena (as he thought) in R to that of watching the hand of Erasmus writing a paraphrase of Mark in Holbein's picture.[11] Were it not for the antiquarian thrill of feeling that one has the physical product of a great mind of the past before one, would scholars have been so tempted to ignore every argument which suggested that neither i^1 nor i^2 was the hand of John Scottus? It is a thrill which must be sacrificed; but in its place may be offered a greater, if less sensational, satisfaction. For i^1 and i^2, their independent identity vindicated, provide the most valuable of evidence for the activity of John's followers.

The hand i^1 appears in five, and i^2 in some eight manuscripts.[12] Only in R do they come together in the same manuscript. Here their work is clearly that of scribes, working under the author's direction and copying either from dictation or another manuscript. Although i^1 and i^2 contribute a majority of the longer marginal additions, the role of the Caroline scribes should not be underestimated, especially in Book IV. R shows only that i^1 and i^2 were both expert scribes, but not whether they were also scholars in their own right.

A few of the other appearances of both of these Irish hands are doubtless scribal. i^1 was used by Eriugena to enter corrections and additions in the manuscript of his *Commentary on St John*.[13] In two manuscripts i^2 shares the task of glossing with a Caroline scribe. One (*Leiden BPL 88*) contains glosses in i^2 to Book IX of Martianus

---

[10] See below, p. 109–11 and p. 122, n. 19.

[11] Preface to Rand, *Johannes Scottus*, p. ix (quoted by Jeauneau, ed. of John Scottus, *Commentary on . . . John*, p. 71, n. 14).

[12] See Jeauneau, ed. cit., p. 76; and Bischoff in *Laon Conference*, pp. 56–7 and p. 94.

[13] These are clearly distinguished from the main text by Jeauneau in ed. cit.

Capella's *De nuptiis* which are in all likelihood the work of John
Scottus. Claudio Leonardi has recently demonstrated that i^2's glosses
go back to an earlier stage in the tradition than those of his Caroline
counterpart, perhaps even having been written at the author's dictation.[14] This manuscript, then, is another indication of i^2's close contact with Eriugena. Less certainly Eriugenian are the glosses which i^2
contributed to *Paris BN 13908*, a copy of Boethius's *De musica*.[15]
Here there is little distinction between the type or quantity of glosses
contributed by i^2 and the Caroline scribe, except that the Irishman is
responsible for writing down the interlinear translation of a passage
in Greek [16] and may, implies Bishop, have composed a brief gloss in
Old Irish himself.[17] Eriugena may have been the originator of these
glosses: music was one of his special interests.[18] The comments are
for the most part technical; but there is at least one reference to
Servius and one to Martianus Capella,[19] and Jeauneau has detected
some characteristics of John's thought and style in these glosses.[20]

In the case of both i^1 and i^2 there is one appearance which is so
brief that it is impossible to suppose that a scribe would have been
called in to make such an entry. In *Paris BN 13345*, folios 88–116
form a separate book, which contains Hilduin's *Passio Sancti Dionysii*.
There are a number of glosses in a Caroline hand (s. ix ex./ x in?), and
just one brief note in i^1. Hilduin remarks that today Dionysius is
called 'ptergion [*sic*] tu uranu', 'wing of heaven'. i^1 corrects the first
word of the Greek to 'pterygion', places accents above the final letters
of *tu* and *uranu*, and notes the whole phrase, in Greek letters, at the
foot of the page.[21] *Paris Mazarine 561* is a copy of Eriugena's translation of Maximus the Confessor's *Ambigua*, again with extensive
glosses in Caroline script: i^2 contributes just one, brief gloss, defining

[14] 'Glosse Eriugeniane a Marziano Capella in un Codice Leidense', *Laon Conference*, pp. 171–
82. For the question of these glosses' authorship, see below, pp. 117–19.
[15] On these glosses, see 'Jean Scot Erigène, premier lecteur du "De Institutione Musica" de
Boèce', *Freiburg Conference*, forthcoming, esp. pp. 182ff.
[16] However, the Caroline scribe also uses and explains Greek words in his glosses: e.g. (f. 59r)
'id (est) contemplatio regularum ex mente quae grece ΘΗΩΡΗΝΑ [*sic*] dicitur'.
[17] Cf. op. cit., p. 91 – a gloss which Bishop characterizes as 'intelligible but not intelligent'.
[18] For John's interest in music, see J. Handschin, 'Die Musikanschauung des Johannes Scotus
(Eriugena)', *Deutsche Vierteljahrsschrift für Literaturwissenschaft und Geistesgeschichte* 5, 1927,
pp. 316–41; B. Munxelhaus, 'Aspekte der Musica Disciplina bei Eriugena', *Laon Conference*,
pp. 253–62; and Duchez, op. cit.
[19] On f. 57r and f. 60r respectively.
[20] As reported by Bishop, op. cit., p. 91.
[21] On f. 96v; see *MPL* 106, 31D for the passage in Hilduin.

the word *intelligentia*.[22] These two notes, unimportant in their content, were almost certainly made by i[1] and i[2] independently, not from dictation; and so they raise as a distinct possibility that in other places, too, where there is no evidence to contradict it, i[1] and i[2] may have been working as scholars in their own rights, not as scribes.

I[1] notes Greek words in the margins of another manuscript, the 'Leiden Priscian' (*Leiden BPL 67*).[23] But far more interesting is his contribution to *Laon 24*: a letter addressed to a certain Winibert, who is probably the Abbot of Schüttern of that name. In the letter, the writer asks Winibert to send him his copy of Martianus Capella, which he promises to emend 'in those parts which we left aside when we were together'. He expresses his desire to spend time with Winibert once again, using an elegant poetic conceit and a Greek word. John Contreni attributes this letter to Eriugena, on the grounds that i[1] is his hand.[24] Contreni's conclusion *might* be correct, even if his grounds are mistaken. But there is no good, positive reason to attribute the letter to Eriugena; and every likelihood that i[1] himself composed it.

I[2]'s activities were more diverse. In two manuscripts he adds notes on the lives of Church Fathers: in *Paris BN 14088*, i[2] has copied four extracts from the Cassiodorean *Historia tripertita*, two of them concerning Basil, his brother Gregory Nazianzen and Gregory of Nyssa.[25] In *Bamberg Patr. 46*, one of the rare, early manuscripts of Marius Victorinus's *Adversus Candidum*, he adds a short extract from Jerome on the life of the author, as well as contributing some very brief glosses to the text.[26] Since there are also glosses here written by a Caroline scribe, it is quite possible that i[2] was working under super-

---

22 This note is edited in Jeauneau, *Quisquiliae*, p. 87. This article also contains a very full description of the Mazarine manuscript; for this manuscript, see also below, pp. 112–13.

23 These notes are recorded in the apparatus of M. Hertz's edition of Priscian in H. Keil, *Grammatici Latini* II and III (Leipzig, 1855/1859).

24 See J. Contreni, 'À propos de quelques manuscrits de l'école de Laon au IXe siècle: découvertes et problèmes', esp. pp. 9–14; and 'The Irish "Colony" at Laon during the time of John Scottus', esp. pp. 59–60.

25 These extracts have not, to my knowledge, been identified with their source before. They are (references to *MPL* 69): 1116B: 'Ergo Gregorius . . . Arrianus'; 1129CD: 'Distribuerunt ergo . . . Basilii(que) germano'; 1128AB: 'Si persecuti uos fueritis. . . Hierusalem requirant'; 'Ambrosii sententia . . . ratio potestatem'. I find it difficult to believe that a palindromic poem on the recto of the flyleaf, in Irish script, is in the hand of i[2] (or, for that matter, i[1]), despite Bischoff's evident opinion (cf. *Laon Conference*, p. 94) that i[2] wrote it.

26 The notes and the extract are printed in Hadot's edition of Marius Victorinus; see p. 48 for the Jerome extract, taken from his preface to the Epistle to the Galatians.

vision, but equally likely that the historical quotations in both these manuscripts were his own choice. Certainly, i²'s work on the second revision of the *Periphyseon*, B, might best be described as a mixture between independent and supervised activity. I² co–operated with a Caroline scribe in making corrections to the text and adding marginalia, a few of them lengthy and almost certainly the work of Eriugena. I² alone was responsible for adding lemmata – chapter headings and subtitles entered in the margin. Bishop has commented that in *B* 'the appearances of i² are all accountable as editorial – one of the functions of an editor being to record verbatim the latest authorized additions'.[27] There is no reason at all why i² himself should not have been responsible for the lemmata and even some of the shorter additions.

The most philosophically interesting of i²'s notes is found on the flyleaf of *Laon 55*. The contents of this passage have been analysed by Jeauneau.[28] He shows how the four biblical glosses which make it up echo Eriugenian themes and language: the procession of all things from God and their return to him; the unknowability of God as he really is. Two ideas he traces back to Maximus's *Ambigua*: an interpretation of the word *abyssus*, and an explanation of Christ's injunction to love one's neighbour as an order to love one's body, which will ultimately be transformed into a spiritual body and then return, along with the soul, to God. A feature of the second of these glosses is both reminiscent of the *Periphyseon* and yet strangely divergent from it. A fourfold division of Nature is proposed, just as in the *Periphyseon*; but the terms of this division – into that which is uncreated and unborn, that which is uncreated and born, that which is created and unborn and that which is created and born – are not those of Eriugena's masterpiece.

Are these glosses the work of John Scottus himself? Jeauneau leaves the question open, but there is evidence to suggest that Eriugena did not compose them. First, there is a somewhat facile quality to the reasoning, where no idea is thought through properly, which is typical of John's best followers, but not of the philosopher himself. Second, there are features of these glosses which are difficult

[27] Op. cit., p. 92.
[28] See B. Bischoff and É. Jeauneau, 'Ein neuer Text aus der Gedankenwelt des Johannes Scottus'.

to explain if John wrote them, whether he did so before or after completing the *Periphyseon*. If before, why did he not incorporate at least the second of the ideas taken from Maximus, the interpretation of 'Love thy neighbour', in his masterpiece? It would have been a very suitable addition to his discussion of spiritual bodies. If after he finished the work, why should he have elaborated a different, less searching, division of nature from that which he had worked out in the *Periphyseon*? The very position of these glosses on the flyleaf of a manuscript would suggest that they were composed by the man who wrote them down; and it would be perfectly consistent with the picture of i^2 gained from his other appearances that he should have invented these glosses.

Altogether, the notes of i^1 and i^2 reflect the interests which might be expected of two of Eriugena's closest associates. i^1's notes in the Leiden Priscian and the Paris manuscript of Hilduin's *Passio Sancti Dionysii* show an interest in Greek and some knowledge of the language. Music, a special interest of John's, is the subject of i^2's glosses in *Paris BN 13908* and of those to Martianus, since Book IX of the *De nuptiis* is devoted to music. The Church Fathers on whose lives i^2 copied extracts – Marius Victorinus, Basil, Gregory of Nyssa and Gregory Nazianzen – were all important sources for the *Periphyseon*. i^1's study of Martianus, as told in his letter to Winibert, might have been an offshoot of Eriugena's own work on the *De nuptiis*; and the Eriugenian nature of the glosses in *Laon 55* has already been illustrated. It is not therefore in the least fanciful to regard i^1 and i^2 as pupils of the Irish philosopher. They happened also to be expert scribes, who could help John in the business of revising his works; but they were capable of pursuing their own studies and thoughts, along the lines suggested by their master's interests and example.

II

Traube's enthusiasm over R, the earliest surviving manuscript of the *Periphyseon*, did not derive only from the thrill of discovering, as he believed, the very hand of Eriugena. He realized that from this manuscript, from B, the second revision of the *Periphyseon*, and from a group of manuscripts now at Paris, which preserve a further revision of John's work, it would be possible to see Eriugena in the process of changing and developing his work. I shall use the same material as evidence for a different but related enquiry: what can be learnt from the early manuscripts of the *Periphyseon* about the milieu in which John worked and the way in which his work was received by his contemporaries?

There is no final proof that the additions and corrections in *R* were made under John's orders, but their character is decidedly authorial. The marginalia fall into six categories: brief corrections and additions of words accidentally omitted; short additions which have the character of glosses (where, for example, the general reference to an author in the text is made specific to one of his works); reference forward to subjects discussed in later parts of the work; clarifications of an argument, often of a legalistically precise nature, which attempt to ensure that the meaning of the text could not possibly be misconstrued; elaborations of a train of thought which depend on discussions later in the work; and, very occasionally, a fresh development of an argument put forward in the original version.[29] Whilst the marginalia of the first four types could imaginably have been devised by someone other than the author, this would be difficult to believe of the two latter types, so thoroughly Eriugenian is their language and pattern of thought. The most economical hypothesis, therefore, is to suppose that the first revision of the *Periphyseon* was entirely authorial.

Eriugena is very often presented as an isolated thinker, who willingly ignored the impression which his idiosyncratic system would make on his contemporaries. The revision presented by *R* is alone enough to give the lie to this theory. Physically, it shows John working with considerable resources at his disposal: two pupils, who were also scribes, and a number of other copyists, are employed to

---

[29] I give just a few illustrative examples of each sort of addition:

Brief corrections: I, p. 46:20 *in* added; I, p. 106:22 addition of N(*utritor*); II, p. 172:18 *in* added.

Gloss-like additions: I, p. 116:9–10 Gregory of Nyssa's *Sermo de Imagine* is specified; II, p. 174:16 an example of qualities is given; II, p. 184:20 an argument referred back to is restated.

References forward: I, p. 114:19–20 reference to a discussion of the Return later in the work; II, p. 116:18–20 reference forward to the discussion of divine self-ignorance.

Clarifications: I, p. 130:31–4; I, p. 198:22–6; II, p. 100:6–7.

Elaborations dependant on later discussion: I, p. 98:2–7 addition on *locus* which reflects the theory of space as definition developed later in the book; II, p. 22:1–31 an anticipation of the discussion, which takes place in Book v, of God's intentions for Man if he had not sinned.

Substantial developments of argument: I, p. 152:17–30 a new theory of the relationship between *usia* and bodies (see above, Chapter 3, p. 81). But cf. I, p. 156:28.

help him revise a manuscript which cannot have been the first text of his work to have been made.[30] Intellectually, it reveals that John's fundamental concern in revision was with clarity; and not the sort of essential clarity of thought, which a philosopher cultivates with an eye to posterity, but a very down-to-earth clarity, which made his work more useful and comprehensible to his contemporaries.

The text and marginalia of *R* were copied out neatly to form the main text of *B*; and then the *Periphyseon* underwent a second revision in the margins of this manuscript. This revision was far less extensive than the first: there are very few additions of any substance, and one cannot be certain that all the minor corrections and glosses are Eriugena's own. *B* should be regarded as an edition of John's work, furnished with lemmata by i[2] for easier reading: as such, it suggests that the philosopher did not lack an audience.

Even in speaking of the second revision of the *Periphyseon*, there is need for caution. *B* is a manuscript of Books I–III alone: since this revision is constituted by the text and marginalia of *B*, it is impossible to reconstruct it for Books IV and V, or even to be sure that these books went through this stage.[31] Discussion of the third revision of John's masterpiece requires yet more care. A group of manuscripts now at Paris presents a text of *Periphyseon* Books I–III, which incorporates both the marginalia of *B* and some extra material. It is this additional material which constitutes the third revision. For Books IV and V matters are not so clear. One of the Paris manuscripts of the third revision, *BN 12964* (*P*), contains Book IV and part of Book V, as well as Books I–III. The text of Books IV and V in two further manuscripts of these two books alone, *BN 12965* (*F*) and Bamberg Ph 2/2 (*J*), is very similar to that of *P*. Can one therefore say that this is a text of the third revision of Books Four and Five? *R* contains part of Book IV, and there are some additions in the text of *P*, *F* and *J* for this section which are not merely the incorporation of marginalia in *R*; but whether they are the results of one or two further revisions is not to be determined. For the end of Book IV and the whole of Book V, there is even greater uncertainty about the nature of the revisions, since neither *R* nor *B* contains this part of the work. Perhaps it is no

---

[30] See Rand, 'The supposed autographa', p. 136.

[31] Articles by Jeauneau and Bishop, dealing with the important evidence for the revisions of Books IV and V provided by a twelfth-century manuscript, *Trinity College Cambridge o. 5. 20*, are to be printed in the near future.

accident that the marginalia in *R* become very sparse and insubstantial towards the end of the manuscript: the end of the *Periphyseon* may have been revised far less thoroughly and frequently than the earlier sections.

The third revision was not an extensive one. Its interest lies in the fact that it was almost certainly not authorial, but shows the efforts of John's followers to elucidate and, in certain cases, modify the philosopher's work.[32] They were not in general very successful. Some of the additions, admittedly, simply carry on the process, which John had begun in the first revision, of making sure that the text leaves no room for misunderstanding.[33] But two additions in which the revisers draw on external material – John's *Commentary on Dionysius's Celestial Hierarchy* and his translation of Maximus's *Ambigua*[34] – are not relevant to the argument of the text. In one case, at least, the reviser simply confuses John's ideas: remembering, presumably, that John treated formless matter, like God, as indefinable, and therefore not-being, he ascribes to it the not-being through excellence which is the property of God and the primordial causes.[35] John himself had very carefully distinguished these two types of non-existence. And the reviser makes two additions which seem to be intended to assert the *filioque* doctrine.[36] On one occasion alone is an addition relevant and sensible:[37] since this is also Eriugenian in language, perhaps it is a stray authorial suggestion which the reviser had gathered by some means. The unimpressive contents of the third revision do not detract from one aspect of its significance for the historian of John's influence. For the very fact that his followers should have troubled to revise his masterpiece, however poorly, shows that they studied his work in detail.

The manuscripts of the third revision can, by their physical characteristics alone, give some more valuable clues as to how the *Periphyseon*

---

[32] Sheldon-Williams provides a very useful table at the end of Volume I of his editions (pp. 247–69), in which the additions made in the various recensions are displayed; unfortunately, this feature is not retained in his second volume. I owe much in my account of the third revision of the *Periphyseon* to Sheldon-Williams's table and notes.

[33] E.g. I, p. 86:12. The text says that God is neither a genus nor a species; the reviser adds 'nor an accident'.

[34] At I, p. 42:4–6 and II, p. 112:29 respectively; see Sheldon-Williams's notes I, 26; II, 28.

[35] I, p. 38:23; see Sheldon-Williams's n. 14.

[36] II, pp. 82:24–5 and 188:14–15; see Sheldon-Williams's n. 279 and 507.

[37] II, p. 148:25–7. See Sheldon-Williams's n. 419.

was read.[38] This group of early manuscripts dates from the later ninth and early tenth centuries: *P*, I believe, was written in the 870s or 880s; and *F* bears so strong a resemblance in script and presentation to *B* and to the Mazarine manuscript of Eriugena's translation of the *Ambigua* (*Mazarine 561*) that a date c. 870 may be suggested for it. *Paris BN 12255* (*E* – Books I and part of II) was probably written before 900. All these manuscripts are written in a script which has the characteristics of that current in North France – the field of Eriugena's activities – at this time. The section of *Paris BN 12960* (*G*) containing the beginning of *Periphyseon* Book I has been said to be in the script of Corbie;[39] and there is good evidence that *P* was at this monastery shortly after it was written, if indeed it was not actually copied there.[40]

This relative similarity in date and place of origin contrasts with the wide variety of types of manuscript which constitute this group. *Paris BN 1764* (*D* – Books I and part of II) is a large, elegantly produced codex: a library copy of John's work which was never read with much attention, to judge from the lack of any attempt to correct the very frequent careless errors which mar the text. *P* is also a fine, large volume, and *F* is a manuscript *de luxe*: but both copies show signs that they were used as well as valued. In *P* there are some marginal notes (which I examine below, pp. 101–2); in *F* a contemporary hand adds in the margins passages accidentally omitted from the main text. Both these manuscripts contain regular lemmata which would help the reader to find his way through John's work. *J* is a less elegant manuscript than either of these, but its marginalia (see below, pp. 102–3) point even more firmly to its careful use. *E*, another less imposing codex, contains no such revealing signs of study; but the presence of a number of glosses entered by the text-scribes, some of them found elsewhere only in *B*, suggests that it too was a working copy.

All these manuscripts are devoted entirely to the *Periphyseon*. By contrast, *G* contains the beginning of John's work along with a collection of other texts. The section of the *Periphyseon* and a set of

[38] I have examined these manuscripts, which formed the basis for Floss's edition, personally; but I have been helped in describing them by Sheldon-Williams's remarks (I, pp. 13–17) and Lucentini's corrections to them.

[39] See M. Manitius, 'Zu Dunchad und Iohannes Scottus' Martiankommentar', *Didaskaleion* I, 1912, p. 138.

[40] See below, p. 101.

glosses to Books II and IV of the *De nuptiis*, related to John's glosses to this work and once attributed to a certain Dunchad, form a separate book. But the contents of the rest of the volume make it very probable that the whole manuscript was put together in the early Middle Ages. *G* is a text-book for the study of the Liberal Arts and dialectic in particular. As well as the 'Dunchad' glosses to Martianus, *G* contains a set of glosses to this work which derive from Eriugena himself, if not directly; and another set of Martianus glosses – those of Remigius of Auxerre.[41] There is also an incomplete copy of Boethius's first commentary to Aristotle's *De interpretatione*. This manuscript suggests that part of the *Periphyseon* at least (Book I?) was studied as a school-text at Corbie in the late ninth or early tenth century. The grouping of John's work with texts on dialectic and the Liberal Arts in *G* is paralleled by the use of the *Periphyseon* as an aid to the study of the *Categoriae Decem*.

Two of these manuscripts of the *Periphyseon*, *P* and *J*, contain marginal notes which give some indication of how Eriugena's masterpiece was read. The notes in *P* are few in number and meagre in content. Limited in each case to a 'Nota' sign, or to a word or two copied from the text, they must be the personal notes of an individual scholar, designed to recall his attention to passages which had particularly struck him. In this respect, they are like the notes which Martin of Laon left in a number of his manuscripts. At one stage, these notes were indeed thought to have been Martin's. But now John Contreni, the leading expert on Martin of Laon, has abandoned this view: rather, he implies, the annotating hand is from Corbie, since it appears in several other Corbie manuscripts.[42] *P* was certainly at Corbie in the later Middle Ages;[43] but, nevertheless, one cannot be sure that the annotations were made at Corbie. The library at Corbie built up a large collection of manuscripts written elsewhere: it is quite possible that a group of manuscripts with annotations in the same hand could have come to Corbie from elsewhere.

The notes in *P* do not bear witness to a sophisticated understanding of the *Periphyseon*. Often the annotator seems to be more interested in the interpretation of a specific word or phrase than in the course of

---

[41] On the various glosses to the *De nuptiis*, see below, pp. 117–19.

[42] See *The Cathedral School*, p. 96 n. 3.

[43] A note in the manuscript (printed by Sheldon-Williams, I, p. 13) records the book as the property of Corbie, and suggests that it was lent to the monks of Laon at some stage.

John's argument. For instance, he marks the passage in which the 'flaming sword' of Genesis 3.23 is said to signify the Word of God (that is, Christ).[44] In a passage criticizing those who believe that 'the Last Judgement will take place within the confines of this world', it is not John's daring theology, but rather the etymology of 'Iosaphat', that seems to have caught the annotator's attention.[45] Another passage, giving etymological interpretations of the word 'Cherubim', is also marked. Where the annotator does show interest in a theological passage, his emphasis remains different from the author's. He chooses to mark a passage in John's account of the return of all things to God which is least concerned with the metaphysics of this concept but which stresses, as Alcuin had done in his *De imagine Dei*, the possibility of Man's redemption through his moral rectitude.[46] Two other passages which are marked in this section of the *Periphyseon* suggest that the annotator was interested, not in John's overall use of the neoplatonic idea of the Return, but in detailed christological points. One of them asserts that Christ, when on earth, was not circumscribed in space or time;[47] the other discusses the ultimate unification of all things in God in terms of the unification of all men in Christ, the perfect man.[48] Altogether, the notes in *P* show that the *Periphyseon* was read with attention; but they suggest only a limited interest in Eriugena's characteristic ideas, and but a partial comprehension of them.

The two hands which annotated *J* belonged to far more sympathetic and intelligent readers. Two *Nota* signs appear by a passage proclaiming that all men, even the evil, will achieve final salvation;[49] and a passage arguing the incorporeality of hell is marked.[50] One of the annotators must have been interested in the conflicts of Latin and Greek authorities which occur so often as the *Periphyseon* approaches its conclusion. He notes a passage where Augustine's view, which Eriugena opposes, that after the resurrection of all men Christ's body will have a spatial position in the heavens, is discussed;[51] and, beside a passage where John says that 'almost all authors in both languages' (i.e. Latin and Greek) believe that the number of men who will enter

---

[44] p. 333 = 846D.   [45] p. 439 = 996CD.   [46] p. 331 = 862D.
[47] p. 436 = 994AB.   [48] p. 437 = 994BC.   [49] 967 CD. Hand One.
[50] f. 171r = 971 CD. Hand One.
[51] f. 184v = 990D: '*Nota* Augustinum affirmare corpus Domini post resurrectionem in caelo localiter esse.' Hand Two.

heaven is the same as the number of rebellious angels, he writes, 'the Roman Gregory does not agree with these things'.[52] *J* was clearly read with interest by men who could recognize the significance of some of John's audacious ideas, even if they would not subscribe to them.

The two final examples of early manuscripts of the *Periphyseon* have special value as evidence. They are not complete texts, but florilegia, and therefore indicate the sort of interest which his followers displayed towards Eriugena's work. One (*X*), preserved in *Valenciennes 167*, has been edited and discussed by Mathon;[53] the other (*Y*) has not, to my knowledge, been previously known to scholars. Details of this florilegium, preserved in *Paris BN 13953*, are given below (see pp. 171ff.).[54] The two florilegia may best be considered together: *X* begins shortly after *Y* breaks off towards the end of Book I; both florilegia derive from a very similar text of the third revision; and – as will emerge – the method and interests of the two compilers were very similar. Indeed, it is very possible that *X* and *Y* are the parts of a single florilegium, which perhaps stretched beyond the beginning section of Book II where *X* concludes.

Mathon believed that Hucbald of St Amand probably compiled *X*, but his evidence is not at all convincing. The manuscript was at St Amand in the twelfth century, but it is not among those recorded as donations of Hucbald's to his monastery.[55] There is no good reason to assume that the copyist of *X*, who wrote the rest of the manuscript, was Hucbald: probably he was a professional scribe.[56] The dates of the manuscripts – the beginning of the tenth century for *Y*, possibly slightly earlier for *X* – give the latest possible dates for the

---

[52] p. 195v = 1006C: '*Nota* Hiis non concordat romanus Gregorius.' Hand Two.

[53] 'Un florilège érigénien à l'abbaye de Saint-Amand au temps d'Hucbald'.

[54] A rather fuller discussion by me of this florilegium and its relations to *X* than I have been able to include here will be published in *Recherches de théologie ancienne et médiévale*, 47, 1980, pp. 271–7.

[55] The catalogue which records these donations is found in *Paris BN 1850* ff.199v–202; ed. L. Delisle, *Le Cabinet des manuscrits de la Bibliothèque Nationale* II (Paris, 1874), pp. 448–58, and by J. Desilve *De Schola Elnonensi Sancti Amandi* (Louvain, 1890), pp. 154ff.; cf. A. Boutémy, 'Le Scriptorium et la Bibliothèque de Saint-Amand d'après les manuscrits et les anciens catalogues', *Scriptorium*, 1, 1946–7, pp. 6–16.

[56] Mathon's surmise that the scribe of this manuscript was 'doué d'une certaine culture' is based on a false assumption: it is not the text-scribe, but another hand (perhaps of the eleventh century) which identifies Lucan and Virgil as the authors of the quotations on fol. 9r.

compilation of the florilegia. Both manuscripts are apparently from North France, and a few details suggest Auxerre, more precisely, as the place of origin for *Y*: *BN 13953* contains a set of glosses to Prudentius in continuous form which are related to the glosses of Remigius of Auxerre;[57] and Remigius uses John's dual etymology of θεός from θέω and θεωρῶ, which is excerpted in *Y* (no. vi), in no less than three of his commentaries.[58]

The compiler(s) of *X* and *Y* seem to have made enthusiasm for definitions a guiding principle in their choice of extracts. Wherever the text provides a definition, the florilegia will excerpt it; and where the text, read aright, is not defining anything, a passage will sometimes be lifted out of its context so as to give the appearance of a definition: this is the case with the two extracts in *Y* (xvii and xix) on ἐνέργεια, each of them misleading. A fascination for Greek terms, especially theological ones, is linked to this taste for definition; the compilers are keener on no type of extract more than one which takes the form of a gloss on a Greek theological term. Without knowing whether or not each florilegium is complete, it is difficult to draw firm conclusions from the sort of subject-matter they cover. Many of John's most characteristic and sophisticated logical ideas do not appear. For instance, the compiler of *Y* is interested in Eriugena's discussion of God, but not in God's transcendence over the Categories, which forms the central theme of that discussion; and he represents John's logical and scientific discussions almost solely by passages on the concept of space and its relationship to the body. Both *X* and *Y* have their importance precisely because of their shortcomings: they are testimonies to the interest shown in the *Periphyseon* by those not fully abreast of Eriugena's ways of thought.

Just as the examination of the notes in i¹ and i² suggested that Eriugena had closer and more intelligent followers than has generally been supposed, so the study of the early tradition of the *Periphyseon* suggests that the work was far more widely and variously read than has been imagined. Admittedly, these manuscripts do not provide

---

[57] See Courcelle (op. cit., pp. 264–7), who says that these glosses derive from those of Remigius. H. Silvestre argues, however, that the commentary is anterior to Remigius's and is used by him as a source: see 'Aperçu sur les commentaires carolingiens de Prudence,' *Sacris Erudiri*, 9, 1957, pp. 50–74 and note on p. 398.

[58] To the *De consolatione*, Augustine's *De dialectica* and to Caelius Sedulius: see Courcelle, op. cit., pp. 256–8; and *Sedulii Opera Omnia*, ed. J. Huemer (Wien, 1885) (= *CSEL* 10), p. 323:27–8.

evidence that John's masterpiece was read outside the region where the philosopher lived and worked. But within this area, the *Periphyseon* is found in elegant library copies, volumes which have been studied privately by scholars, and in school-books. The range of readers is as great as that of their codices: from the intelligent and well-informed through to those who valued the trappings of Eriugenian thought, although they could not comprehend the substance of it.

III

In the two preceding sections, I have gathered the concrete, anonymous evidence for Eriugena's influence on his contemporaries. Now I shall ask whether any of the known figures of John's time can be shown to have had contact with the philosopher, and, if so, what level of understanding they brought to his works.

Of the many Irishmen who worked on the Continent in the ninth century, Sedulius alone can lay claim to a level of culture, if not personal genius, equivalent to Eriugena's. His best poems display a self-conscious sophistication which is closer to the manner of the Archpoet than to any poet of his own age.[59] His *Liber de rectoribus christianis*[60] makes a skilled use of the prosimetric form which reveals a study of Boethius's *De consolatione* and, perhaps, of Martianus Capella. His short commentary on Jerome's prefaces to the Gospels reveals a knowledgeable, critical approach to Scripture;[61] and his *Collectaneum*[62] testifies to a very considerable range of reading. Moreover, Sedulius knew some Greek, although probably rather less than John.[63] However, there is no sign, in his surviving works, that Sedulius showed an interest in the fields where Eriugena excelled – philosophy and logic.[64] Is there any evidence to suggest that this

---

[59] Edited by L. Traube in *MGH Poetae Latini Aevi Carolini* III, pp. 151–237; cf. R. Düchting, *Sedulius Scottus: seine Dichtungen* (München, 1966).

[60] Edited in S. Hellmann, *Sedulius Scottus*, pp. 19–91.

[61] *Explanationes in praefationes S. Hieronymi ad Evangelia*, MPL 103, 331–52.

[62] See Hellmann, op. cit., pp. 92–146.

[63] See L. Traube, 'O Roma nobilis', esp. pp. 353–6.

[64] Traube (op. cit., p. 344) claimed to have found evidence in an eleventh-century library catalogue from Toul of a commentary by Sedulius on Porphyry's *Isagoge*. But Manitius (*Geschichte* I, p. 322) convincingly dismissed this idea as arising from a misinterpretation of a catalogue entry.

impression is misleading, and that the two men had intellectual contacts?

There is a group of manuscripts, all copied by Irishmen, which looks promising for this purpose.[65] In the margins are written the names of a number of people, among them the most outstanding intellectuals of the age. Many of them are Irishmen, including both John and Sedulius; but the non-Irish Ratramnus and Gottschalk are also named. Some of the names occur frequently and in more than one manuscript. Although Sedulius and John Scottus are each named in two manuscripts, there is only one, *Bern 363*, where the names of both occur, mostly separately, but in a few instances together by the same passage. *Bern 363* is a late ninth-century copy, glosses and all, of a mid-ninth-century original;[66] it was probably written at Strasbourg. Its contents are varied: Horace's poems, minor rhetorical works, Augustine's *De dialectica*, and a commentary on Aristotle's *Categories* not found elsewhere.[67] But most of the marginalia are found by the longest of the texts, a version of Servius's commentary on Virgil.

Before the value of these marginalia as evidence for contact between John and Sedulius can be assessed, one must try to resolve why the annotators of the exemplar of *Bern 363* decided to put the names of a number of their most eminent contemporaries by passages in the work of an antique commentator. The passages marked 'Ioh(annes)' – that is, John Scottus – will provide the best clues (as Traube recognized, though he did not pursue the enquiry), because more is known of John's work and opinions than of those of his contemporaries who

---

[65] This comprises *Bern 363* (Facsimile: H. Hagen, *Codices graeci et latini photographice depicti* II (Leiden, 1897)); a Greek text of the Gospels with Latin interlinear translation, *Sankt Gallen 48* (Facsimile: H. C. M. Rettig, *Antiquissimus quatuor evangeliorum Codex Sangallensis greco-latinus* (Turici, 1836)); and a Greek text of the Pauline Epistles also with interlinear Latin translation, *Dresden Bibl. Msc. A 145b* (*Facsimile*: A. Reichardt, *Der Codex Boernerianus . . . in Lichtdruck nachgebildet* (Leipzig, 1909). A Graeco-Latin Psalter, *Basel A. VII. 3*, which Bischoff adds to the group, does not contain the rich marginalia of the others. A manuscript of Priscian, *Sankt Gallen 904*, which Traube included in the group, is not thought to have been written in Ireland. See Traube, op. cit., pp. 346–53; J. F. Kenney, *Early Sources for the History of Ireland* (rev. edn, Shannon, 1968), pp. 556–60, 562–3; Bischoff, 'Irische Schreiber im Karolingerreich', esp. pp. 51–3.

[66] Both Lindsay (*Early Irish Minusucule Script* (Oxford, 1911), pp. 50–4) and Bischoff (as reported in Glauche, *Die Schullektüre im Mittelalter – Münchener Beiträge z. Mediävistik u. Renaissance-Forschung* 5 (München, 1970), pp. 39–40) agree on a ninth-century dating, Bischoff adding that it was written at Strasbourg. L. C. Stern ('Bemerkungen zu den Berner Glossen') showed on historical grounds that the manuscript must be a copy of a mid-ninth-century original.

[67] See above, pp. 18, n. 17.

are named.[68] There are a number of passages marked 'Ioh(annes)' which cannot be related to any piece of writing or idea known to be John's. Others, however, are more revealing. There are a number of correspondences with his glosses to the *De nuptiis*;[69] and at one point the annotator makes such a reference explicit, writing, 'de dialectica Ioh(annis)', that is, 'John's glosses on the Fourth Book of the *De nuptiis*, which is concerned with dialectic'.[70] Since both in *Bern 363* and in two other manuscripts of the group the name Gottschalk appears by passages which relate to his grim view of divine predestination,[71] it may be thought that the annotations in *Bern 363*'s exemplar were made early in John's career, when his fame rested on his teaching of the Liberal Arts and his polemic against Gottschalk. But some of the passages marked with John's name do not bear out this hypothesis. The note, 'Ioh(annes) de inferno', appears by a statement of Servius's that, according to Lucretius and others, the Underworld could not exist:[72] John argues that there can be no such thing as a corporeal hell in his *De praedestinatione*, the work which he wrote against Gottschalk, but also – and at greater length – in the *Periphyseon*. A passage marked 'Ioh(annes) contra Gregorium'[73] deals

---

68 The list of the occurrences of each name and the passages beside which it appears, which Hagen provides in the introduction to his facsimile, has proved invaluable to me in the course of the investigation which follows.

69 *f.90r* = Servius (ed. Hagen (Leipzig, 1878–1902) – all page and line references are to this edition) I, p. 309:20: 'Tritonia pallas . . .' cf. *Annotationes in Marcianum (Ann.)* (ed. C. Lutz (Cambridge, Mass., 1939) – all references are to this edition) p. 153:1 'TRITONIA id est Pallas'.

f.128v = Servius, II p. 29:20ff.: 'Ratio autem haec est styx maerorem significat unde ΑΠΟ ΤΟΥ ΣΤΕΓΕΡΟΥ [*sic*] d est a tristitia styx dicta est.' Cf. *Ann.* p. 8:14 'Stix vero tristitia . . .' *f.130v* = Servius, II, p. 46:13ff.: 'per flegetonta inferorum fluuium ignem significat. Nam phlox ignis est . . .'; cf. *Ann.* p. 22:5–6: 'flumen igneum in quo anime puniantur quod a Grecis πυριφλεγέθων id est ignis flagrans, nominatur . . .'. On John's authorship of the *Annotationes*, see below, pp. 117–19.

70 *f.79r* = Servius, I, p. 188:6ff.: 'Hymineus autem ut alii dicunt deus est nuptiarum . . .'; cf. *Ann.* p. 105:23–4: 'Ymen ipse est deus nuptiarum, filius Veneris . . .' (to Book IV of *De nuptiis*). P. Lehmann ('Von Quellen und Autoritäten Irisch-Lateinischer Texte', *Bayerische Blätter für das Gymnasienschulwesen*, 61, 1925, pp. 29–34 = *Erforschung des Mittelalters* 3 (Stuttgart, 1960), see esp. pp. 145–6) first noticed this reference to John's Martianus glosses, without, however making any textual comparisons with *Ann.*

71 The words 'contra godiscalcum' appear in *Bern 363* (f.61v) beside a passage of Servius (I, pp. 27:22–28:3) which suggests that human volition is at least one of the causes of things. Gottschalk's name appears in *Sankt Gallen 48* (facs. cit.) by Luke 13.24 (p. 263), a verse which says that few men will be saved; and by John 12.40 (p. 367) which refers to the blinding of men's eyes and the hardening of their hearts. In the Dresden manuscript of the Pauline Letters the name stands on fol. 4v by Romans 3.5, where a phrase which suggests that Man's evil recommends God's justice occurs.

72 *f.128r* = Servius, II, p. 27:11–15.   73 *f.55v* = Servius, III, p. 337:24ff.

with the return of all things to their origin, a physical counterpart to the metaphysical doctrine of the Return which John expounds in the *Periphyseon*. Also, the Greek term τὸ πᾶν used in this passage is a favourite expression in John's masterpiece. A couple of other passages marked with John's name take up the idea of a return of things to their origin.[74] The strongest indication, however, that the annotators of the exemplar of *Bern 363* knew of the *Periphyseon* is provided by a verbal echo. The name of John appears beside a passage reading, 'Nam nihil aliud est nox nisi umbra terrarum.'[75] It is hard to resist the conclusion that in making this reference the annotator was responding to the *verbal* similarity of the following passage from the *Periphyseon*: 'Ibi siquidem secundum rerum factarum considerationem *non aliud* tenebras *noctem*que accipimus *nisi umbram terrae.*'[76]

Traube suggested two possible explanations for the notes in *Bern 363* and its companion manuscripts: either the notes refer to subjects which the annotators wished to raise with the scholars named when they had a chance to meet them in person; or they refer back to the writings of those named. It is the latter alternative which the investigation above suggests as the more probable; and it appears, also, that these marginalia were not written earlier than the late 860s, by which time the *Periphyseon* was complete. With this in mind, one may turn to consider the passages marked with the names of both John and Sedulius Scottus.[77] A considerable number of these are concerned with grammatical and etymological questions; but a couple of the passages bear a relation to John's Martianus glosses;[78] and a couple to John's philosophical ideas: one discusses man's composition from the elements, another treats the punishment of the dead as purgative and

---

[74] *f.128r* = Servius, II, p. 28:5–9; *f.137v* = Servius, II, p. 97:4–8.

[75] *f.130v* = Servius, II, p. 44:18–20.

[76] I, p. 170:22–3.

[77] Not all the passages listed by Hagen as being marked with the names of both John and Sedulius can be accepted as such: for instance, at f.94v (Servius, I, p. 357:3–12) the names of John and Sedulius are separated by that of Turchelsach.

[78] *f.71r* = Servius, I, p. 110:5 'Maiae genitum idest mercurii . . .': cf. *Ann.* p. 8:23–4: 'Matrem autem Mercurii Maiam, id est nutricem . . .'
f.139r = Servius, II, p. 105:26, 27 and p. 106:1, 2: 'aetherium sensum ΠΥΡΝΟΕΠΟΝ ignem sensualem idest deum per quod quid sit anima ostendit. Aurae simplicis ignis non urentis. Simplicis autem nostri comparatione qui constat de ligno et aethere'; cf. *Ann.* p. 50:16–23: 'Vulcanum dicit ignem videlicet terrenum, qui quasi claudus dicitur, quoniam terreni ignis nimiam temperat celeritatem . . . Inter Vulcanum et Iovam et Vestam hoc interest: Vulcanus est ignis devorans et consumens omnia, Vesta est ignis accomodatus in usus hominum, Iovis est ignis innocuus qui in celo est.'

so transitory.[79] Did John and Sedulius co-operate in writing a philosophical work, or, at least, in teaching philosophy and grammar? Did Sedulius help John to annotate Martianus? And, if the answer to this latter question is positive, why does the annotator refer to *'John's* "de dialectica"'? One could go on raising possibilities and pointing out difficulties; but it would be credulous to place much trust in these enigmatic notes, composed perhaps after John's lifetime. As evidence, rather than material for conjecture, the notes in *Bern 363* merely add weight to the idea that John was an author closely read by his own and the next generation: they do not prove that he was in contact with Sedulius.

It is no longer thought by most scholars that the town of Laon enjoyed a special connection with Eriugena. The evidence indicates that the Cathedral School of Laon and the Palace School of Charles the Bald were distinct entities, even if John and his colleagues were frequent visitors to Laon.[80] The master of the Cathedral School in John's heyday was another Irishman, Martin. He is a figure who has left very little in the way of writings; but, thanks to Contreni's patient examination of the manuscripts which he marked, it is possible to form a picture of Martin's intellectual character.[81] He emerges as a schoolmaster, interested in the Liberal Arts, grammar, and also in the canonical life. Greek obviously fascinated him, and his knowledge of the language may have been second only to John's in Charles's kingdom; but philosophy seems not to have been a major enthusiasm.

Nevertheless, there is some indication that Martin was acquainted with the *Periphyseon*. All the works that can be reasonably credited to Martin are found, written by Martin himself, in a single manuscript, *Laon 444*.[82] They include a couple of Latin poems,[83] a letter probably to Servatus Lupus,[84] and a lengthy grammatical section, containing

---

[79] f.55v = Servius, III, p. 337:3–7; and f.139r = Servius, II, p. 104:11–15 respectively.

[80] See esp. Contreni, *The Cathedral School*, pp. 83–7.

[81] Ibid., pp. 95–134.

[82] Considerable extracts from this manuscript are printed by M. Miller, 'Glossaire Grec-Latin de la Bibliothèque de Laon'.

[83] *De Octo Vitiis* (f.4r) (ed. *MGH PLAC* III, pp. 692–3); and a dedicatory poem to – in Contreni's opinion – a certain Hartgarius (ed. ibid., p. 686, and cf. Contreni, op. cit., pp. 60–1).

[84] See Contreni, op. cit., pp. 103–9 for an edition and discussion of this letter.

some poems in Greek.[85] There is also a series of philosophical remarks which forms a preface to the manuscript as a whole. A reference
which may be either to the *Periphyseon* or to John's translation of the
pseudo-Dionysius has been noted by both Contreni and Cappuyns:
it recalls, using both the Greek and Latin terms, the pseudo-Dionysius's
description of God as more-than-good, more-than-true, and even
more-than-God.[86] But there are two further allusions to John's ideas
in this manuscript, both of which must be taken from the same passage of the *Periphyseon*: one of these was noted by Sheldon-Williams,[87]
but the other seems to have escaped the attention of scholars. In each
case Martin refers to John s dual etymology of the Greek word for
God, θεός, from θέω ('I run) and θεωρῶ ('I see').[88] However, in each
case, Martin blunders with his Greek, taking θέω to mean both 'I see'
and 'I run'. Since, in the uncorrected version of *R*, a scribal error
gives θέω these two meanings, it would be fair to assume that Martin
had access to this manuscript or its exemplar; and, therefore, to the
Periphyseon at a very early stage in its dissemination. The first of these
references to John's etymology is of particular interest. It ends the
philosophical preface, following quotes from John Chrysostom on
the dignity of Man as a rational animal, and Servius on the trans-
mutation of a human into a God:[89]

> deum   uidendo et   circumcurrendo
> ΘΕΟΝ ΑΠΟ ΤΟΥ ΘΕΙΝ ΚΑΙ ΠΕΡΙΤΡΕΧΕΙΝ
>
> nusquam   stando   sed   omnia   implendo
> ΜΗΔΑΜΗ ΕΣΤΑΝΑΙ ΑΛΛΑ ΤΑ ΠΑΝΤΑ ΠΛΗΡΟΝ
>
> i. uideo. curro.
> ΘΕΩ

Either Martin is here glossing an undiscovered Greek source for half
of Eriugena's etymology, mistakenly believing that it puts forward a
double meaning for God's name; or the Greek is his own composi-

---

[85] Ed. *MGH PLAC* III, pp. 696–7.

[86] f.298v – p. 199 in Miller's ed.; I have checked all the quotations from *Laon 444* with
the manuscript itself: 'Vt Dyonisius Ariopagita dicit ΥΠΕΡΘΕΟΣ est superdeus et
ΥΠΕΡΑΓΑΘΟΣ superbonus et ΥΠΕΡΑΛΗΘΗΣ id est superuerus'; cf. *Periphyseon* I, pp. 76:34–78:12.

[87] Ed. cit., I, n. 62: it occurs on fol. 282vb of *Laon 444* = Miller, ed. cit., p. 152.

[88] Cf. *Periphyseon* I, p. 60:20–5.

[89] Printed by Miller, ed. cit., p. 11 = *Laon 444* f.2v. Jeauneau ('Quisquiliae . . .', p. 109)
identifies the quote from Chrysostom as being taken from his Homily 7 on the Epistle to
the Philippians; and (*Quatre thèmes érigéniens*, p. 131, n. 64) gives a number of passages in
Servius which may have acted as Martin's source.

tion, a free variation on an idea of John's, a learned *jeu d'esprit* which turns out to betray its author's ignorance.

Martin, then, certainly read some of the *Periphyseon* at an early stage; and the subject-matter of the quotations from John Chrysostom and Servius in his preface to *Laon 444* would have appealed to Eriugena. And there is evidence in this manuscript to suggest that Martin had read the *Categoriae Decem*,[90] but not that he had explored their logical problems as John did. The differences of interests and intellectual temperament between the two Irishmen appear to have prevented Martin from being more than mildly influenced by John.

For many of the other intellectuals of the later ninth century, there is not even the slight evidence of contact with Eriugenian thought which is to be found in the cases of Sedulius and Martin. Prudentius of Troyes, Florus of Lyon and Hincmar of Reims were all eager to condemn John's brilliant but tactless contribution to the debate aroused by Gottschalk's views on predestination, his *De praedestinatione*.[91] But none of these writers showed themselves at all interested in the metaphysical system which John sketched in this early work; and there is no evidence that they followed the progress of Eriugena's thought as it emerged in the *Periphyseon*. André Wilmart has suggested a rather lesser figure, Almannus, a monk of Hautvillers in the diocese of Reims (†882), as a thoroughgoing follower of John's.[92] A more critical examination of Almannus's 'philosophical letter' suggests, rather, that the monk of Hautvillers was interested in philosophical ideas more as stylistic ornament than for their own sake. Only two of the themes which Wilmart instances as examples of Almannus's Eriugenianism did not have wide currency outside the work of John: the description of God as 'superessential', and the division of Man into six parts, three interior and three exterior. If Almannus had read the *Periphyseon*, he cannot have done so with much interest or understanding.

There remain two connected figures whose contacts with John Scottus and his work *can* be shown to have been substantial. The one, Wulfad,[93] is a shadowy figure, whose writings have been all but lost,

[90] ff.290–291r = Miller, ed. cit., pp. 181–5.
[91] See Cappuyns, *Jean Scot Erigène*, pp. 102–27.
[92] 'La lettre philosophique d'Almanne et son contexte littéraire'.
[93] I tried to assemble all the various evidence for Wulfad's intellectual biography in a paper

if they ever existed; the other, Heiric of Auxerre, has left a large body of work.

Wulfad was a protégé of Charles the Bald, to whom the king entrusted the education of his son, Karlomann. Charles wished to make him Archbishop of Bourges, an ambition in which, after a fierce struggle with Hincmar of Reims, he succeeded in 866. Until this time, Wulfad occupied a number of abbacies, including that of St Médard of Soissons, frequented the court, and enjoyed the friendship and respect of the Palace philosopher, John Scottus. The *Periphyseon* itself provides the testimony to this comradeship. At the end of the final book, having dedicated his work first to God, John adds a more immediate dedicatee: Wulfad, his 'collaborator in philosophical pursuits' (*in studiis sapientiae cooperator*). The work, John says, was begun at Wulfad's instigation and brought to completion by his concern. John then asks Wulfad to go through the book, making a note of any instance where he has failed to return to a subject which he had promised, earlier in the work, to treat. With Wulfad's list in hand, John will then go through the *Periphyseon* chapter by chapter, repairing his omissions.[94] This very detailed evidence of the way in which John wished Wulfad to help him suggests that it was no mere rhetorical compliment, when he credited Wulfad with instigating and sustaining his labours on the *Periphyseon*.

There is further evidence of Wulfad's Eriugenianism. A list of Wulfad's books has survived[95] which indicates that he had a private library well stocked with theological works and books on sacred history, and containing an exceptional collection of works by John Scottus: Eriugena's translations of the pseudo-Dionysius and Maximus the Confessor's *Ad Thalassium* are listed, as well as the *Periphyseon*; and the list is written on the penultimate leaf of a volume containing John's translation of Maximus's *Ambigua*. The entry for the *Periphyseon*, 'libri perifiseon II', was interpreted by Cappuyns to

given to a conference on Charles the Bald held in London in March 1979: 'Wulfad, John Scottus Eriugena and Charles the Bald'. Proceedings of the conference are forthcoming in *British Archaeological Reports*. Accounts of Wulfad's political importance are provided by H. Schrörs, *Hinkmar, Erzbischof von Reims* (Freiburg im Breisgau, 1884), pp. 273–92; F. Lot, 'Une anné du règne de Charles le Chauve', *Le Moyen Âge*, 6, 1902, pp. 393–438, esp. pp. 407–18; and J. Devisse, *Hincmar, Archevêque de Reims 845–882* (Paris, 1975), pp. 91–100, 603, 611–28.

94 *Periphyseon* v, 1022AB.

95 Published with commentary by M. Cappuyns, 'Les "Bibli Vulfadi" et Jean Scot Erigène'.

mean 'the *Periphyseon* in two volumes'. But two other interpretations would be more consistent with the general usage in ninth-century library catalogues: either that Wulfad possessed two complete copies of the *Periphyseon*; or that he owned just two books (presumably the two first) of the five which make up the completed work. Each of these interpretations suggests Wulfad's very close involvement with Eriugena: the former makes it probable that he owned two recensions of the *Periphyseon*; the latter, that he had copies made of the individual books of John's masterpiece as and when they were composed.

The final page of the manuscript, *Paris Mazarine 561*, which contains Wulfad's book-list is occupied by some notes which have recently been edited and discussed by Edouard Jeauneau.[96] Three of them – a definition of *scoliae*, a quotation from John Chrysostom and a quote which, in fact, derives from Ambrosius Autpertus, but is attributed by the scribe to 'the same John'[97] – have nothing in especial to link them to Eriugena. But the fourth, probably written at a different time from the others, presents an imaginative extension of John's thought which is typical of his best followers. The passage describes the four dimensions of God: his length, which stretches from the highest creature to the lowest; his width, which is his appearance in visible and invisible things; his height, by which he excels all that may be said or understood; and his depth, by which, as the essence of all things, he exists incomprehensibly in his creatures. All these descriptions of the deity derive from the *Periphyseon*; but the use of the conceit about the dimensions of God to epitomize them is original. All four notes at the back of *Mazarine 561* must, presumably, have been written by someone from Wulfad's circle; and the intelligent Eriugenianism of the last is exactly what might be expected of Wulfad himself.

Wulfad's greatest service to John Scottus may, however, have been an indirect one. It now seems extremely probable that Heiric of Auxerre came to know Eriugena's work – and possibly the philosopher himself – during the period which he spent at Soissons be-

---

[96] 'Quisquiliae.'

[97] Jeauneau argues that, by this, the writer of the notes meant to refer to John Scottus (ibid., p. 117). But it seems to me clear that the reference is to Chrysostom, the *same* John as the author of the first quotation; and I would suggest that a homily by Ambrosius Autpertus had been mistakenly attributed to Chrysostom in a collection used by the writer.

tween 863 and 865.[98] Almost certainly, it was Wulfad who helped him to make this contact, for there is one piece of evidence beyond the circumstantial to link the Abbot of St Médard with Heiric. Among Wulfad's books was a copy of Petronius; and, as Contreni has pointed out, Heiric is unique among early medieval writers in his use of this author.[99]

The most striking piece of evidence for Heiric's assimilation of John's thought is presented by his homily I, 11.[100] Not only does this work make extensive use of Eriugena's *Homily on the Prologue to St John*; it also bases a couple of passages on sections of *Periphyseon* Books IV and V. Nor is it a matter of passive, literal copying. At times Heiric is, in Jeauneau's words, 'more Eriugenian than Eriugena himself', using, for instance, an Eriugenian expression to describe a concept mentioned in the *Homily*, where John had expressed himself less characteristically. This homily is unique among the published sermons of Heiric's in showing such unmistakable signs of Eriugena's influence; but further work on Heiric's unpublished homilies might reveal additional borrowings from John Scottus.[101]

Heiric also showed his fascination for Eriugenian terms and ideas in his long poetic life of St Germanus.[102] The main narrative of Germanus's life gave little opportunity for quasi-philosophical comment; but Heiric compensated himself in his invocation, which is studded with terms and ideas taken from John Scottus. Heiric seems to have been especially enthusiastic about Greek philosophical terms: he builds his philosophical allusions around the Greek terms which he borrows, rather than simply using these terms to state an argument. Nevertheless, unlike Almannus of Hautvillers for instance, he does demonstrate his understanding of a number of important Eriugenian doctrines, such as John's ideas on the Trinity and his concept of theophany.[103] This understanding had its limits. Heiric seems to have taken

---

[98] See R. Quadri *I Collectanea di Eirico di Auxerre*, pp. 18–24.

[99] *The Cathedral School*, p. 146.

[100] Jeauneau edits and discusses this homily in 'Dans le sillage de l'Érigène: une homélie d'Héric d'Auxerre sur le Prologue de Jean'; and he gives a fuller consideration of the homily's Eriugenian borrowings in 'Influences érigéniennes dans une homélie d'Héric d'Auxerre'.

[101] For the identification of Heiric's homilies published pseudonymously, see H. Barré, *Les homéliaires carolingiens de l'École d'Auxerre* (Città Vaticana, 1962), pp. 71–93, 160–79.

[102] Edited L. Traube, *MGH PLAC* III, pp. 427–517.

[103] *Invocatio* ll.7–18 and 43–8 respectively.

little account of Eriugena's 'negative ontology': in the same stanza, he can say that God 'is not for he more-than-is' (*non est nam superest*) and yet also describe the divinity as 'the being which creates substance, the place of things, goodness-in-itself, the Idea of the world'[104] – a description which, incidentally, confuses God with the primordial causes. But on a subject where John was so far from clear in his own mind, such as the relationship between negative theology and an ontology of participation, perhaps Heiric might be forgiven a certain muddlement. The ideas of the *Periphyseon* are again introduced towards the end of the work, first in the preface to Book VI, and then in the account of Germanus's death. The saint is said, at his death, to experience θέωσις, unification with God.[105] But Germanus does not enter a strictly Eriugenian heaven: he 'perceives all things below him, and Christ above all things'[106] – yet he would not, according to John, have perceived the Godhead at all. In the Paris manuscript of the *Vita S. Germani* (*BN 13757*) there are extensive annotations, some of which quote the *Periphyseon* and Eriugena's poem on the Incarnation where Heiric had used these works as sources.[107] Neither the text nor the glosses are in Heiric's own hand.[108] Whether the glosses were written at Heiric's direction remains uncertain; if not, their author was one who well understood Heiric's debt to Eriugena.

However, it is neither the homily I, II nor the *Vita S. Germani* which constitutes Heiric's most impressive claim to be the follower of Eriugena and his interpreter to subsequent generations of scholars, but rather a variety of sets of glosses on school-texts. Yet glosses are notoriously difficult to attribute; and often it is misguided to look for a single author of material so subject to change, amplification and compilation. Heiric's known interest in the thought of John Scottus makes him a promising candidate for the authorship of Eriugena-inspired glosses; and, certainly, when he returned to Auxerre in 865, he became one of the main channels through which John's ideas were transmitted to the tenth century and beyond. How far Heiric himself was responsible for the rich harvest of Eriugenian school-material will be one of the questions to be considered in the following chapter.

---

[104] Ibid., ll.25–30.   [105] Book VI, ll.300–1.   [106] Ibid., l.431.
[107] These are printed and identified by Traube in the apparatus to his edition.
[108] See G. Billanovich, 'Dall'antica Ravenna alle biblioteche umanistiche', esp. p. 336.

Chapter 5

EARLY MEDIEVAL GLOSSES ON THE
PROBLEMS OF THE CATEGORIES

I

The best sources for late ninth- and early tenth-century discussion of the problems of the Categories, Universals and essence are the sets of glosses to three works: Martianus Capella's *De nuptiis*, Boethius's *Opuscula Sacra* and, by far the most important, the *Categoriae Decem*. It is no accident that these glosses, especially those to the *Categoriae Decem*, also provide some of the fullest testimony to Eriugena's influence on his immediate successors. Each of these sets of glosses poses problems of authorship, which cannot even be formulated correctly, unless careful attention is paid to the nature of glosses, as opposed to literary texts.

Early medieval glosses are evidence for the methods and concerns of teaching and learning, not their conscious finished products. Sets of glosses may, in some cases, have been copied into manuscripts by pupils at their teacher's dictation;[1] or they may all have been copied from one manuscript to another by the teachers or their scribes. At all events, each glossed manuscript of a school-text is the record of the interests of a particular centre at a given time. Different copies of the 'same' set of glosses vary, not simply in their selection of glosses, but in the very level of interpretation they lend to their text. In one, all difficult, controversial or lengthy glosses will be condensed or omitted, whilst the interlinear verbal glosses will be particularly numerous; in another, few purely verbal glosses will be included, and some of the comments will be extended so as to form miniature philosophical treatises. I have tried to give an impression of the variations of material in one tradition of glossing, that of the *Categoriae Decem*, in my Preface (below, pp. 173ff.) to an edition of a selection of these glosses. There

---

[1] A powerful exposition of this view is given by G. Schrimpf, 'Zur Frage der Authentizität unserer Texte von Johannes Scottus "Annotationes in Martianum"', esp. pp. 132–4.

is a temptation for the scholar, faced with a group of manuscripts containing different, overlapping selections of glosses to the same text, to treat the material in each manuscript as an imperfect witness to a putative, perfect original. He will then edit the glosses as if he were reconstructing a literary text from a number of variously corrupt copies. As a result, he will have imposed a purely imaginary unity on the informative variety of early medieval sets of glosses.[2] I have tried to avoid this hazard in my edition and discussion of the *Categoriae Decem* glosses.

Besides instability, another characteristic of early medieval sets of glosses is their anonymity. However, the celebrity of a very few teachers, such as John Scottus or Heiric of Auxerre, led to certain exceptions to this rule. Not that even these masters would sign their schoolroom glosses; but eager followers would note such and such a comment as being John's, or a certain set of glosses as having been composed by Heiric. This is the problematic background against which attempts to attribute the early medieval glosses to the *De nuptiis*, the *Opuscula Sacra* and the *Categoriae Decem* have been made.

In Remigius of Auxerre's commentary to the *De nuptiis*, there are a few remarks which are said to be taken from John Scottus.[3] These remarks are present in a set of glosses to Martianus found in *Paris BN 12960*. But this does not prove that *BN 12960* contains Eriugena's glosses to the whole of the *De nuptiis* in their original form: Remigius refers to John only in the first three books of his commentary;[4] and a

---

[2] Cf. the critique of Courcelle's work on glosses to Boethius's *De consolatione* in F. Troncarelli, 'Per una ricerca sui commenti altomedievali al *De Consolatione* di Boezio'.

[3] I attempt merely to summarize what, in view of the most recent researches, may be safely said about John's glosses to the *De Nuptiis*: a history of the scholarship on this subject would require a chapter to itself. The most important contributions to the debate have been the following:
Editions: C. Lutz, *Iohannis Scotti Annotationes in Marcianum* (I–IX from *BN 12960*); E. Jeauneau *Quatre thèmes*, p. 91ff. (I from *Bodleian Auctores T. II. 19*).
Discussion: B. Hauréau, 'Commentaire de Jean Scot Erigène sur Martianus Capella, Manuscrit de Saint-Germain-des-Prés Nº 1110', *Notices et extraits des manuscrits de la Bibliothèque Impériale*, 20, 1862, pp. 1–39; E. K. Rand, 'How much of the *Annotationes in Marcianum* is the work of John the Scot?'; L. Labowsky, 'A new version of Scotus Eriugena's Commentary on Martianus Capella'; C. Lutz, 'The Commentary of Remigius of Auxerre on Martianus Capella', *Mediaeval Studies*, 19, 1957, pp. 137–56; and article on Martianus Capella in *Catalogus Translationum et Commentariorum* II, ed. O. Kristeller (Washington, 1971), pp. 367–81; H. Liebeschütz, 'Zur Geschichte der Erklärung des Martianus Capella bei Eriugena'; and 'The place of the Martianus *Glossae* in the development of Eriugena's thought'; G. Schrimpf, 'Zur Frage der Authentizität'; C. Leonardi, 'Glosse Eriugeniane'.

[4] These references are listed by Schrimpf, op. cit., p. 138, n.26.

manuscript in the Bodleian at Oxford, *Auctores T.II.19*, contains a set
of glosses to Martianus similar to those in *BN 12960*, but with substantial variations in the first book. These variations, some of which
are strikingly Eriugenian in character, seem to have been present in
part in the manuscript which Remigius used as a source.[5] From this
evidence it appears that John composed glosses to at least the first three
books of the *De nuptiis*; and that the glosses in *BN 12960* and *Bodleian
Auctores T.II.19* are based on those of Eriugena, although they may
not preserve faithfully, exclusively or entirely what he composed. The
marginalia in *Bern 363* suggest that John also composed glosses to
Books IV and VI of Martianus, since they put John's name by passages
in Servius which correspond to glosses in *BN 12960* to these books of
the *De nuptiis* as well as to Book I. In *Leiden BPL 88*, i^2 is one of the
hands which enter glosses to *De nuptiis* Book IX which are very similar
to those in *BN 12960*; this fact, together with the Eriugenian themes
and language of some of these glosses suggests that John was the
originator of these comments. Altogether, the most probable hypothesis is that Eriugena glossed the whole of the *De nuptiis*, but that the
text in *BN 12960* is not a consistently trustworthy witness to his
thoughts – good for Book I (where *Bodleian Auctores T.II.19* can
give additional material) and for Book IX, and poor for Books
V–VII.

BN 12960 contains two more commentaries to the *De nuptiis*. One
has been reliably attributed to Remigius of Auxerre. The other, to
Books II and IV only, was thought by Cora Lutz, its editor, to be the
work of Dunchad.[6] More recently, the evidence on which Miss Lutz
based her attribution has been shown to be groundless;[7] manuscripts
containing the whole of the set of glosses have been found;[8] and it has
been argued that the commentary was the work of Martin of Laon.[9]
But this attribution is not much better grounded than that to Dunchad
had been.[10] The glosses show every sign of having used Eriugena's

---

[5] Cf. ibid., pp. 128–30.

[6] She edits them under this attribution: Dunchad *Glossae in Martianum* (*Philological Mono-
graphs of the American Philological Association* XII) (Lancaster, Pa., 1944).

[7] See J. Préaux, 'Le Commentaire de Martin de Laon sur l'oeuvre de Martianus Capella',
esp. p. 440.

[8] See C. Leonardi, 'I codici di Marziano Capella'; and Lutz in *Catalogus Translationum*.

[9] By Préaux, op. cit.

[10] See J. Contreni, 'Three carolingian texts attributed to Laon:Reconsiderations', esp. pp.
808–13.

commentary as a source, rather than having been composed independently; and it is even possible that their compiler had access to some Eriugenian material not in *BN 12960*.[11] This set of glosses was used by Remigius as a source, along with those of John Scottus. Contreni has suggested Heiric of Auxerre as their author[12] – a plausible idea, though based only on circumstantial evidence. In discussing individual glosses on logical problems, it will be safe to assume that what can be found in the *BN 12960* 'John Scottus' commentary and in the pseudo-Dunchad commentary was current in Eriugenian milieux in the late ninth century, but not necessarily composed by the philosopher himself.

When Rand edited a set of early medieval glosses to Boethius's *Opuscula Sacra*, he argued that they had been written by John Scottus.[13] Rand's evidence was entirely internal: the knowledge of Greek and subtlety of thought displayed in the glosses supposedly marked them as John's; some of their ideas were Eriugenian, and, where they contained opinions markedly different from those of the *Periphyseon*, this, said Rand, was the expression of John's conservatism as he grew old. Not surprisingly, scholars were quick to question such flimsy argumentation. Cappuyns suggested that the nature of the glosses made them more probably the work of Remigius of Auxerre than that of Eriugena;[14] and he backed up this assertion with evidence from the manuscript tradition, which pointed towards Auxerre as the place where the glosses originated. Schrimpf remained sceptical as to whether any definite attribution of authorship could be made.[15] And Rand modified his earlier view. The glosses, he argued, are the work of John Scottus, but not directly so: 'the original Commentary derives from a set of notes that (John) drew up on the *Opuscula Sacra* . . . He may not be responsible for all that extant collections of glosses

---

[11] As, for example, the long gloss on 'accident' at ed. cit., pp. 22:27–23:21, which seems to expound a distinctly Eriugenian theory of the Arts.

[12] In a note in *Catalogus Translationum et Commentariorum* III, ed. F. E. Kranz (Washington, 1976).

[13] *Johannes Scottus*. Rand thought the glosses to Tractate IV the work of a different author, whom he identified as Remigius and who had also prepared an impoverished and abridged version of John's glosses to the other tractates. Later, however, Rand admitted, following Cappuyns, that the glosses to Tractate IV also existed in both recensions.

[14] 'Le plus ancien commentaire des "Opuscula Sacra" et son origine'.

[15] *Die Axiomenschrift des Boethius*, pp. 37–8.

contain.'[16] I would query Rand's implication that the glosses derive from a complete, substantial commentary of John's: but Eriugena may possibly have begun the tradition of commentary by contributing a stimulating but sparse collection of glosses. Cappuyns's study of the manuscripts suggests that it was in the School of Auxerre, under the aegis of Heiric or Remigius, that the glosses reached the form in which they circulated most widely.[17]

---

[16] 'The supposed commentary of John the Scot on the "Opuscula Sacra" of Boethius', pp. 76–7. One of Rand's assertions in this article is misleading. He remarks (p. 69) that one of the manuscripts containing glosses to the *Opuscula Sacra*, Bamberg Q. *VI. 32* (= *Patr. 46*) contains notes in the hand i[2]. These notes, however, are in a part of the manuscript which forms a separate book, and that has been simply bound together with the book containing the *Opuscula Sacra*. See above, pp. 94–5.

[17] An additional piece of evidence may throw some light on the origins of the *Opuscula Sacra* glosses. In an eleventh-century manuscript there is a gloss to Porphyry's *Isagoge* which – as a comparison makes evident – borrows material from the early medieval *Opuscula Sacra* glosses:

Materia est forma ipsa uel
substantia. Vnum est id
aliquid quod est uel unum
habet suum esse, sicut et   ... ergo esse hominis
corpus est esse hominis a   anima et corpus est a
quibus (*sic*) homo accipit   quibus homo accipit
ut sit. Et ipsum aes metal-   ut sit. (4–5) ... aes metallum
lum quod ex terra sumitur,   quod et ex terra sumitur
rubicundi coloris, non   rubicundi coloris. (9–10)
dicitur secundum terram,
quod est eius materia, sed
secundum aeris figuram, id   Figuram. id est
est colorem. Dicit autem   colorem. (12) ... dicit
Iohannes Scotus, 'Ferrum de   Iob: ferrum de
terra tollitur, et lapis,   terra tollitur et lapis
calore solutus, in aes   calore solutus in aes
conuertitur. Ideo autem eius   vertitur. (10–11)
materia est terra uel lapis.'
(*Firenze Laurenziana Gadd.*   (Glosses to *Opuscula Sacra*,
plut. 89. sup. 80, f.7v, gloss   ed. Rand. Figures in brackets
to Porphyry *Isagoge*, ed. cit.,   refer to the lines of p. 36).
p. 18:9–10)

Particularly interesting is the attribution in the Porphyry gloss of a statement to John Scottus. Does this mean that, in the eleventh century or earlier, a copy of the *Opuscula Sacra* glosses circulated with an attribution to Eriugena? This is possible, but there is also another way of explaining the reference to John in the Laurenziana manuscript. The statement attributed to Eriugena is one which the *Opuscula Sacra* glosses take from and attribute to Job: the word 'Iob' could have been misread, at some stage, as 'Ioh' and then expanded to 'Iohannes Scotus'. (Minio-Paluello notes this reference to Eriugena in the Laurenziana manuscript (*Aristoteles Latinus: Codices supplementa altera*, p. 139) but does not give its full context or notice the use of the *Opuscula Sacra* glosses. For this manuscript see also below, p. 179.)

In the Preface to my selection of glosses to the *Categoriae Decem* (below, pp. 173 ff.) I present and explain some of the detailed evidence relating to this tradition of glosses. Here I will summarize these results and their bearing on the question of authorship.

In some nineteen manuscripts of the ninth to twelfth centuries there are glosses to the *Categoriae Decem* which include part or most of what I call the 'standard' set of glosses to this work. A gloss is standard simply if it appears in a considerable number of these manuscripts. No manuscript contains all the standard glosses; and none of these manuscripts lacks at least a few of what I call 'eccentric' glosses – glosses found in just one (or, occasionally, two) manuscripts. One late ninth-century manuscript, *Milano Ambrosiana B 71 sup.* (*M*), contains just a very few standard glosses to the *Categoriae Decem*, but also a large collection of fascinating glosses to this work, many of which show very clearly the influence of John Scottus's *Periphyseon*. Some of these mostly Eriugenian glosses are present also in one or both of two other manuscripts, *Paris BN 12949* (*H*) (s. x) and *Sankt Gallen 274* (*G*) (s. ix ex.), which also contain many of the standard glosses. A traditional way of analysing this evidence would be to postulate two separate sets of glosses: the standard set, represented more or less well by the various manuscripts containing mostly standard glosses; and the Eriugena-inspired set, which is to be found in its least contaminated form in *M*, and combined with the standard set in *H* and *G*. Such an analysis might possibly accord with the truth, but it goes beyond its evidence. Moreover, it does not fit neatly with all the facts. Among the standard glosses are several inspired by the *Periphyseon*: must they be considered 'contaminations' from the Eriugena-inspired set? And how does this analysis explain the richness of eccentric glosses in *G*, or the presence in *Paris BN 1750* (*Q*) (s. x ex./xi in.) alone of one gloss obviously based on the teachings of John Scottus? The tradition of early medieval sets of glosses is too complicated to be explained by simple formulations.

Previous discussion of the authorship of the glosses to the *Categoriae Decem* has been based on the mistaken assumption that the collection of glosses in *H* was the original from which all other copies were derived.[18] In *H*, there is a note in one of the glossing hands ascribing

---

[18] See Cousin, *Ouvrages inédits d'Abélard*, pp. 618–24; Hauréau *Histoire* I, pp. 184–96; Barach,

the *Categoriae Decem* glosses to 'Heiric, Remigius's teacher'. Scholars have accepted this uncritically; and Minio Paluello even went so far as to make the demonstrably false statement that the glosses were written down in *H* by Heiric himself.[19] In fact the note of attribution was most plausibly composed, as Courcelle has suggested, by a member of Remigius's circle.[20] There is no reason to question its veracity as such: but to which of the glosses in *H* to the *Categoriae Decem* does it refer? *H*'s *Categoriae Decem* glosses were entered by a number of hands, at more than one time, and, probably, from more than one source. Did Heiric compose (or compile) all of them, or just one layer of the material?

A tentative answer to this question is suggested by *M*. One of the main glossing hands in this manuscript is, in my opinion, very similar, if not identical, to one which glosses a copy of the *Liber Glossarum* in the British Library (*Harley 2735*). According to Bischoff, this hand is found in a number of manuscripts from Auxerre and belonged to a scribe associated with Heiric.[21] One of the glosses[22] in *M* lends some further support to the idea that this manuscript was glossed at Auxerre, perhaps under Heiric's direction. As examples of accidental attributes which can be added to a proper name it gives 'older', 'more powerful' and 'of Auxerre' (*autisiodorensis*). In the same gloss, 'Germanus' is given as an example of a proper name: is it simply coincidence that Heiric's major poem was a life of St Germanus?[23]

One may, therefore, conjecture that the mostly Eriugena-inspired material in *M*, *G* and *H* was composed or compiled by Heiric, al-

---

'Zur Geschichte des Nominalismus . . .'; Minio-Paluello, *Aristoteles Latinus* I, 1–5, p. lxxix (and n. 3).

[19] None of the glossing hands in *H* resemble the hand reliably identified as Heiric's by Billanovich, 'Dall'antica Ravenna', p. 336.

[20] *La Consolation*, pp. 251–9. The suggestion had already been made by Traube, 'Computus Helperici', *Neues Archiv*, 18, 1892, pp. 73–105, esp. pp. 104–5.

[21] See 'Paläographie und frühmittelalterliche Klassikerüberlieferung', *La cultura antica nell'occidente latino* I, pp. 59–86, esp. p. 77.

[22] f.38r; rt. margin.

[23] After I had reached the above conclusions about *M*, Professor Bischoff most kindly provided me with the following note about the manuscript, which confirms my suggestion that it was possibly written and glossed at quite an early stage of the School of Auxerre: 'Der Text kann m.E. in das III. Viertel des IX. Jhs. gesetzt werden, und die Glossen, von mehreren Händen, sind praktisch gleichalt. Besonders aufschlussreich, als direktes Zeugnis für die Schule von Auxerre, ist ja die Note "Consequenter . . ." auf fol. 38R. Ich halt es nicht für ausgeschlossen, das die Hs. im Germanus-Kloster geschrieben und benützt wurde, nicht zuletzt wegen des gleichen Besitzganges mit der Auxerre-Hs. D 23 inf. (Beda).'

though no extant manuscript may preserve the exact form of his teaching. It does not seem probable that Heiric had a set of Eriugena's own glosses to follow: the glosses in *M* seem to be the work of an imaginative thinker who has read the *Periphyseon*; they lack the logical thrust of John's own work and his characteristic traits of expression. Whether the standard glosses are also the products of the School of Auxerre, or whether they derive from a quite independent tradition of glossing, remains uncertain. For a working hypothesis, as distinct from conjecture, however, it is best to limit oneself to the internal evidence of the varying sets of glosses in each manuscript. Those in *M*, *G* and *H* certainly derive from centres in which Eriugena's thought was valued and, in some measure, understood. The lesser amounts of Eriugenian material in the other manuscripts can be used as an index of the spread and decline of John's influence; and the selection of standard material and inclusion of eccentric glosses in each of these manuscripts provide a clue to the interests and intellectual level of the centres and periods at which they were produced.

II

The treatment of *Usia* in the glosses to the *Categoriae Decem*, the *De nuptiis* and Boethius's *Opuscula Sacra* reflects the development which has been traced from Aristotle, through his antique and patristic commentators and users, to Ratramnus of Corbie and John Scottus. A standard gloss to the *Categoriae Decem* paraphrases and makes more explicit a passage in the pseudo-Augustinian text which places *Usia* at the top of the generic table.[24] The genus of Cicero is Man, of Man animal, and animal *Usia*; but *Usia* has nothing above it and so is called – some manuscripts specify – the *genus generalissimum*. In the glosses to Martianus deriving from John Scottus (which I shall call the 'Eriugenian Martianus glosses') the same idea of *Usia* as *genus generalissimum* appears: *Usia* is that beyond which no intellect may ascend and which comprehends all natures.[25] *Usia* is thus at the very opposite end of the generic table from the individual. The Eriugenian *De nuptiis* glosses attempt to reconcile this notion with Martianus's more Aristotelian exposition by making a distinction between *Usia*, which is above all

[24] To ed. cit., p. 145:28. In *MHACLNOPQRSVW*.   [25] Ed. cit., p. 93:11–15.

the Categories and has no accidents, and substance (*substantia*) which is the first of the Categories and is subject to accidents.[26]

From such a concept of *Usia*, it is but a small step to an ontology of participation. Such a theory is proposed succinctly in the Eriugenian Martianus glosses. A standard gloss to the *Categoriae Decem* (IIIa)[27] develops this idea. God is 'true being', and the being which derives directly from him lasts for ever without deterioration: the soul and the four elements are examples of things which have this sort of simple, indestructible essence. For this reason, whilst bodies decompose, the four elements to which they return remain entire. The theory that it is from God, true being, that the limited being of other things derives, is also expressed, in more Boethian language, in an *Opuscula Sacra* gloss.[28]

Among both the *Categoriae Decem* and the *Opuscula Sacra* glosses attempts are found to clarify in theological terms the relationship between true being and the being which derives from it. One of the *Opuscula Sacra* glosses bases itself on a distorted interpretation of Boethius's complicated discussion of *esse* and *id quod est* in the *De hebdomadibus*.[29] According to the glossator, Man or anything else made of parts *is not yet* (*nondum est*) before it has been created in its genera and species but lies hidden in the foreknowledge of God. This is a clear echo of a doctrine which John Scottus elaborated from Augustine and made into one of the governing ideas of his *Periphyseon*. The same idea, and one of the same biblical quotes, appear in a gloss to the *Categoriae Decem* (XIX) found in *M* only. 'God, who lives in eternity, created all things at once', says *Ecclesiastes*: but how can this be? Were the animals created all together, at the same time as earth and heaven? The answer to the question is Augustine's (and Eriugena's): God created all things simultaneously in the 'causes of the elements', but only gradually did they come forth from these causes.

Another *Categoriae Decem* gloss, found in *H*, *A* and *C* only (IC), attempts to link a theology based on an ontology of participation to one founded on an Eriugenian negative ontology. *Usia* and its nine

---

[26] Ibid., p. 95:1–4.

[27] Roman numerals refer to the glosses edited below, pp. 185ff.

[28] Ed. cit., p. 37:32–5: 'A b u t i m u r. Sicut nostrum esse non est verum esse, quia non est id quod est, sed esse dicimur, quia a vero dei esse accepimus, ita et formae quae in corporibus sunt non sunt verae formae, sed quia ab illis aeternis formis veniunt, formae vocantur abusive.'

[29] See above, Chapter I, p. 27.

accidents (that is, the other nine Categories) are found in everything that can be touched or sensed. But God has no substance, and is therefore called 'nature'. God's nothingness is that of supreme excellence; and this is clearly distinguished from the nothingness of evil, which is a nothingness by privation. A standard *Categoriae Decem* gloss (1b) expounds John's negative ontology more directly. Nature is the general name for all things which are or which are not. Things are said not to be, not because they have no existence, but because they excel all bodily or mental perception.

In *M* and *H* alone, there are found glosses which further elaborate an Eriugenian ontology. *M* and *H* share a gloss (XIII) which is entitled, 'On *Usia*'. Understanding *usia* is beyond human capacity; *usia* is better described as nothing than by any positive characteristics. This idea is another, more paradoxical aspect of John's negative ontology.[30] *Usia* is impossible to describe, therefore it is not: not only is not-being more excellent than being, but being itself may be said not to be. The glossator of *M* emphasizes his interest in this area of John's thought by using as a gloss a direct quote from the *Periphyseon* – in its turn based on Maximus – which states that, just as God cannot be understood, so every *usia* is incomprehensible: it may be known *quia est*, but not *quid est*.[31] Gloss XIII continues, however, by giving Gregory the Great's formula of divine omni-presence, a distinctly cataphatic utterance which, nevertheless, enjoyed a certain popularity among the followers of John Scottus. It had been a feature of discussions of the relationship between God and *usia* since the time of Augustine that they should be turned into statements of divine supereminence.

A long gloss in *M* only, unfortunately badly damaged, illustrates the theological exuberance which a follower of Eriugena could bring to ontology (111b). It begins by setting out a hierarchy of the species and genera, using a strange terminology developed from the *Categoriae Decem* under the influence of John Scottus. Primary *usia* is called a 'simple hierarchical homonym'; and secondary *usia* – that is, a species like Man – is described as a 'homonym by derivation'. Presumably the reasoning behind this is that 'man' stands for just *one* thing when it is used to denote primary *usia* – this or that particular man; and that it

---

[30] See above, Chapter 3, p. 83.
[31] f.34r, to ed. cit., p. 134:19, quoting *Periphyseon* I, pp. 38:27–40:7. *M* also contains another, longer quote from the *Periphyseon* (I, p. 102:31–104:35 with minor variations) (f.43v) which puts forward the theory of the unknowability of *usia*.

stands for just *one sort of* thing when it is used to describe secondary *usia* – a species like Man. More general classes are described as 'trionyms by augmentation' and 'quadrionyms by collection', according to the number of ranks of more specific classes which they embrace. But at the top of the hierarchy is 'the most general *usia*', and this, like primary *usia*, is considered to be a homonym. The glossator then proceeds, in a way he could have learned from the *Periphyseon*, to make an 'analytical' descent from the most general *usia*, down through the genera and species, to primary *usia*. From the point of view of the descent, genera are not 'quadronyms' but 'bionyms by procession', since they are the second rank down in the order of analysis. From all this, the glossator argues that primary *usia* contains the *usia* which is most general, as well as the genera and species. And so, he adds, quoting from the parable of the workers in the vineyard, the last shall be first; and then, clearly thinking of Eriugena's scheme of procession and return to God, the glossator states that all things at first and at last were and will be one. Absorbed by his theological theme, the writer finally equates simple *usia* not with the individual, but with Christ, in whom all things were created and became life. And Christ's final appearance at the end of time is seen as the manifestation of *usia* at all levels of the generic hierarchy, right up to the *genus generalissimum*. This, at least, appears to be the general sense of this fantastic mixture of Aristotelian logic with Neoplatonic theology. It is one of the many instances in *M* where the glossator's enthusiasm for scriptural comparisons leads him far away from the logical content of the passage he is discussing.

After so many extravagantly metaphysical statements of ontology, another gloss found in *M* only (XXIII) comes as something of a surprise. *Usiae*, it says, are visible and can be understood without accidents; but accidents can be understood only when abstracted from bodies by the mind. This concept of accidents can only be explained as the result of an understandable confusion between individual accidents (this white in this sheet) and their universals (white in general): it makes sense to say of the latter, but not of the former, that they can only be understood by abstraction. The notion of *usiae* as visible goes completely against an ontology of participation and the theory of the unknowability of *usia*. However, it does come close to a different, rarer strand in John's thinking, by which real bodies are distinguished from geometrical figures because they have *usia*. And the gloss continues by expressing, though unclearly, John's theory that the mind creates the human body.

A look at a few of the eccentric glosses on *usia* in tenth-century manuscripts of the *Categoriae Decem* is informative. Two (xxvi – *A* only; and xxvii – *C* only) present the idea of *usia* as the topmost member of the generic table. Another gloss, in *A* only, adds a note of caution.[32] Although, as the *Categoriae Decem* says, *usia* is the broadest of all terms, beyond which nothing can be thought or found, a proper name, such as Cicero, is better and more informative, because it gives one all the information one needs: I will not know who you are talking about, if you just describe him as 'a man' or 'a large animal'. There is no indication in later tenth- (or eleventh-)century eccentric glosses of the Eriugenian or wildly metaphysical approach to ontology pursued by the scholars of the ninth century.

For Hauréau, Barach and Prantl,[33] the chief interest of the glosses to the *Categoriae Decem* was their markedly nominalist tendency. By 'nominalism' these scholars appear to have meant what might better be described as conceptualism. According to such a theory, genera and species are merely the products of the mind, which collects and compares the information provided by the senses. To go on to say, as these nineteenth-century scholars do, that genera and species are therefore just names, is rather confusing. A name which designated nothing would not be a name at all: the consequence of conceptualism is not that the names of genera and species designate nothing, but that they do not correspond to sensible objects in the manner of the names of individuals. It seems unlikely, however, that such a conceptualist position should be expressed in a set of glosses so markedly influenced by the work of Eriugena. How prevalent is conceptualism in the *Categoriae Decem* glosses and the other logical sets of glosses compiled by the followers of John Scottus?

There is no detailed discussion of the problem of Universals in the *Categoriae Decem* glosses examined by Hauréau and Barach. These two scholars base their argument on incidental references of two kinds to the subject: discussion of species and genera in linguistic, rather than conceptual, terms; and passages which treat perception in a fairly

---

[32] f.195v to ed. cit., p. 134:19.
[33] Hauréau, op. cit., I, pp. 184–96; Barach, op. cit.; Prantl, op. cit., II, pp. 40–1.

empirical way. I shall try to show how neither of these two types of material shows that the glossators held a conceptualist theory of Universals.

Hauréau and Barach both print a gloss which is, in fact, standard.[34] This gloss is based on the opening section of the *Categoriae Decem*. There the paraphraser runs upwards through the generic table, from individuals to *Usia*, describing each of these items as names. This procedure involves no taking of position on metaphysical issues. 'Cicero' is the name of an individual; 'Man' is the name of the species to which he belongs; 'animal' is the name of the genus animal; and 'Usia' is the name of what is considered to be the *genus generalissimum*. If simply to call a particular genus or species a name implies that it does not really exist, then this passage from the *Categoriae Decem* would imply that neither *usia* nor individuals really exist. The gloss merely abbreviates the argument of this passage. Another gloss cited by Hauréau simply states that to mention a quality, such as white or black, without stating the substance in which it is contained, is not sufficient to indicate a given object precisely. This in no way amounts to the statement of a conceptualist position.

More difficult is another of the glosses printed by Hauréau, in which the assertion in the *Categoriae Decem*, that whatever may be predicated of an animal may be predicated of Man, is examined (vIc). Someone might object, the glossator says, that genus may be predicated of animal, but cannot be predicated of Man, since Man is not a genus but a species. The glossator answers this anticipated objection by distinguishing between what is predicated of a class *secundum rem*, that is, characteristics that are defining of the class; and terms, such as genus or species, which describe a class according to its nature as a class. In a slightly clumsy way, the glossator is making a distinction between levels of discourse: terms such as 'having a mind' and 'having sensation' describe the members of a class; terms such as 'species' and 'genus' describe the class. Only of the members of the class will it be true that they exemplify all the characteristics of hierarchically superior classes. From this distinction it in no way follows that, as Hauréau interprets the gloss, 'neither genus nor species, taken absolutely, are things: they

---

[34] Hauréau, op. cit., p. 194, n. 1; Barach, pp. 7–8; to ed. cit., 133:17 PER GRADVS, CVNCTA QVAE SVNT (cf. my Table I).

are words by which one distinguishes what belongs to the definition of Man, what to that of animal'.

Hauréau also brings forward a gloss dealing with perception to support his view that the glossator was a conceptualist. He does not notice that this gloss is in fact a literal quotation from Boethius's first commentary to Aristotle's *De interpretatione* and so is suspect as a guide to the glossator's own ideas.[35] More important, Boethius does not here express anything amounting to a conceptualist theory of Universals. He merely distinguishes between objects on the one hand, and, on the other, the understanding of objects and their description in speech and letters. Objects and understanding are recognized to be natural; speech and letters to depend upon human beings. Nor may any support be gained for Hauréau's position from a gloss which follows this one and is printed by Barach.[36] This describes the process of sense-perception, followed by cogitation leading to expression by words. Barach also prints a gloss distinguishing between speech, words and mental concepts;[37] and one distinguishing between signs and things.[38] No more than Hauréau's examples, are these evidence for the glossator's conceptualism.

The only one of the standard glosses which argues at all in favour of a conceptualist viewpoint on the part of the glossator of the *Categoriae Decem* is a brief note, printed by Barach, which reads: 'Intellectus generalium rerum ex particularibus sumtus est.'[39] This is a phrase of Boethius's which Ratramnus quotes frequently in support of his conceptualism. It implies, however, only the epistemological priority of individuals. So brief a gloss, culled from a favourite authority, can hardly be used to prove a thoroughgoing conceptualism on the glossator's part. A gloss found only in one tenth-century manuscript (v1b) might be used as evidence of nominalism, although it may simply be a careless phrasing of an uncontentious position: it says that Animal is the genus of all animals when it includes them under a single *name*.

There is definite evidence of realism, as opposed to conceptualism, in the Eriugenian Martianus glosses. Martianus had glossed *genus* as

---

[35] Ibid., p. 195, n. 1; to ed. cit., p. 137: 14 PRIMO DE HIS QVAE SVNT (cf. my Table 1 and n. 12 to the *Preface* to my selection of *Categoriae Decem* glosses).
[36] Op. cit., p. 12.   [37] Ibid., p. 9.   [38] Ibid., pp. 9–10.
[39] Ibid., p. 12 (in *HNR W*); cf. above, Chapter 3, p. 68.

'the collection of many forms by one name', a definition which might suggest, though it does not necessarily imply, that genera do not really exist. The glossator, by contrast, defines genus as 'the substantial unity of many forms' (*multarum formarum substantialis unitas*), thereby asserting the ontological claims of Universals.[40] Another of these glosses is a little problematic. It states that, according to Augustine (presumably, in the *Categoriae Decem*) *forma* and *species* are to be distinguished, because 'form can become a genus whereas species is properly understood through an individual' (*proprie individua intellegitur*).[41] This distinction may perhaps be a concession to the epistemological priority of individuals; but it certainly has no basis in its alleged source: the *Categoriae Decem* states that *forma* and *species* denote the same thing.[42] The glosses to the pseudo-Augustinian work are far more accurate in referring a discussion of genus and species, and how the same term may be one or the other, back to the *De nuptiis* (vIa).

In glossing a rather confused passage from Boethius's *De Trinitate*, the ninth-century commentator fails to get to the heart of the problem, but uses the opportunity to demonstrate an extreme realism in his approach to the problem of Universals.[43] The forms of all things, he says, following Boethius, are eternal and incorporeal: the forms which are in bodies are merely their similitudes. The glossator then brings this notion of form together with one which he could have learnt from the *Categoriae Decem* where forms, as I have said, were identified with species, but not with genera. Things are called according to their forms, the glossator argues, because it is easier to know something by its species than by its genus or by its matter. Easier than by its genus, because species are more limited in their scope; easier than by its matter, first, because matter is common to all things, but second, also because form, being eternal and immutable, is better than matter. This gloss suggests the same scepticism about the possibility of knowing individuals through the individuals themselves as Plato had expressed

---

[40] Ed. cit., p. 93:10.   [41] Ibid., p. 93:23-4.   [42] Ed. cit., p. 143:11.

[43] Ed. cit., p. 37:5-13: 'Formae omnium rerum aeternae sunt et incorporales, et illae verae formae sunt, ad quarum similitudinem hae, quae in corporibus sunt, productae sunt. Quia ergo illae aeternae formae meliores sunt, quam materia corporalis, cum tempore, quia aeternae, cum stabilitate, quia inmutabiles, satis congrue ea quae sunt secundum illas potius quam secundum materiam nominantur; vel quia materia plerumque communis est multorum, forma vero specialis singulorum generum vel hominis vel equi et facilior est rerum cognitio in specie quam in genere, ideo secundum formam vocantur.' For a discussion of the Boethian passage being commented, see above, Chapter 1, pp. 27-8.

in the *Philebus* and Porphyry had alluded to in his *Isagoge*.[44] The surest route to the knowledge of individuals is provided by the classes of the least generality, since they, at least, are immutable, unlike the infinity of ever-changing individuals.

Realism, rather than conceptualism, has been prevalent in the early medieval glosses so far examined; but none of them has expressed the hyper-Realism characteristic of Eriugena. As might be expected, it is in *M* alone, the most Eriugenian of the glossed *Categoriae Decem* manuscripts, that glosses are to be found expounding this point of view. One (xvi) states that in any man or horse there should be considered all the men or horses which were, are or will be. Another quotes the passage from the *Periphyseon* which states that there is no difference between a subject and something said *of a subject*, and, consequently, no difference between individuals and their species.[45] Another of these glosses (xxiv), quotes from the same passage and examines the problem from a characteristically theological point of view. When Christ says, 'I am the good shepherd', *shepherd*, which is a secondary *usia* (that is, a species) requires (*desiderat*) simple *usia*, which is Jesus. There is no difference, it goes on, between primary and secondary *usia* except in nature, species and number. The ingenious sophistry which follows defies paraphrase: 'We can see clearly that "species is the unity of numbers, and number the plurality of species", because the nature of this shepherd, which in species is the unity of numbers, is naturally distinguished by the unity of his goodness from all other good shepherds, whose goodness is not essential but accidental.' It is difficult to say what view of Universals, if any, is expressed by this fantastic mixture of the Aristotelian distinction between primary and secondary substances, the idea that God alone has true being, and the Boethian notion that God alone is essentially good.

Quantity, place and time are subjects not much discussed in the early medieval glosses to Martianus or to Boethius's *Opuscula Sacra*: but they receive extended, interlinking treatments in the glosses to the *Categoriae Decem*. Just as the author of the *Categoriae Decem* showed a greater interest in place and time than Aristotle had done in the *Categories*, so the glossator puts a greater emphasis on these two categories than he found in the pseudo-Augustinian text.

[44] See above, Chapter I, p. 23.   [45] f.44r quoting *Periphyseon* I, p. 102:15–21.

It may well be that John Scottus took from the *Categoriae Decem* the term 'quantum' to designate a quantity in its sensible manifestation. But the explicit distinction between *quantitas* and *quantum* was John's own; and it is from the *Periphyseon*, as Barach has noted,[46] that the glosses take this idea. VIII thus describes *quantitas* as something immutable, echoing a phrase from Boethius's *De arithmetica* which Eriugena frequently uses to describe unchangeability. The glossator goes on to point out that the text is not here concerned with natural *quanta*, but with geometrical *quanta* which alone contain such things as the line in the abstract, length-in-itself. Another standard gloss (VII) elaborates this idea. The dimensions of a body – length, breadth and height – are seen as accidents of the natural body, which confer measurement on it. The distinction which this gloss makes between the *corpus usiadis* and the *corpus mensure* is reminiscent of the passage in the *Periphyseon* where it is the possession of *usia* which is said to distinguish a real body from a geometrical figure. A gloss found in two tenth-century manuscripts only (VIII additional element) takes this distinction further. *Quantitas*, by which a body may be measured, is an accident; *quantum* is the solid reality of the body. Here Barach is right to suggest that the glossator adopts a far more empirical view than is generally Eriugena's. However, the next part of the gloss does not bear out this empirical approach: 'All figures are incorporeal when they are understood in themselves by the mind. But when they attach themselves to bodies, they then become like bodies . . .' Here it is as if the incorporeal figures were something quite separate from bodies, to which they can at times become attached.

The concept of place found in the glosses (e.g. Gloss v and b) is the unmetaphysical one of the *Categoriae Decem*, in which place is the boundary of bodies, modified by certain emphases which seem to derive from John Scottus.[47] For example, a standard gloss (va) states that every *usia* is in place and place is outside *usia*; but another gloss (vb) says that 'there can be no *usia* without place, nor any place without *usia*, because place is nothing but the boundaries of a body'. This suggests that the glossator has not understood John's theory of place at all, and has equated *usiae* with natural bodies. Apart from a

[46] Op. cit., p. 17.
[47] A gloss to LOCVS AVTEM (ed. cit., p. 150:16) in *CLQW* quotes nearly literally a phrase from John's account of place (*Periphyseon* I, p. 110:9–10).

long piece on the subject in an eleventh-century manuscript (*S*), time receives briefer treatment. Short alternative definitions, such as 'the fastest succession of things', or 'the rational attention of every mind concerned with the action of a creature', or 'the perception of pauses, that is, of the space which any substance spends in the performance of its action',[48] do not explore the complications of the subject.

A gloss found in four ninth- and tenth-century manuscripts[49] extends the treatment of place and time to ask some simple metaphysical questions. The author of the *Categoriae Decem* does not decide whether place and time are corporeal or not; but, 'as it appears to wise men', they should be thought incorporeal. Whereas a body placed in space can be seen, the space itself is invisible if the body is taken away. Time, the glossator continues, is simply the course of the sun, and since that is incorporeal, time must be incorporeal too. The various terms which the pseudo-Augustinian text uses in its fleeting mention of the problem of time's corporeality are the subject of contradictory attempts at interpretation in a number of manuscripts (x). The little treatise *De loco*, found in *H* and *S* (xxxi) starts at the simplest level by recalling the common use of the term 'locus' to describe bodily objects and material areas. But the glossator suggests that, despite this usage, space may be thought incorporeal: place is not a body but bodies are in place.

There is only one short gloss in one manuscript, *H*, which shows a definite knowledge of Eriugena's idiosyncratic theory of place. It reads: 'Unaneu, id est, quibus sine; plus esse quam cathegoria. Teste Iohannis.'[50] By 'unaneu', the glossator means to indicate John's phrase (borrowed from Maximus), 'ὧν ἄνευ τὸ πᾶν', by which the necessity of place and time for the existence of the universe is expressed. Given this direct reference to John, it seems possible that the ending of the piece *De Loco* (which is also found in *H*), where the indestructibility of place is emphasized, may be echoing the lengthy statement of this position in *Periphyseon* Book v.

Among the glosses to the *Categoriae Decem*, there is a considerable number of discursive comments on metaphysical, moral and

---

48 These definitons occur in a gloss to ed. cit., p. 167:16, LOCVS ET TEMPVS ESSE, in *GHLW*.

49 To the same lemma as above, in *MNVW*.   50 f.23 bis v.

theological matters. These point both to the range of the compiler's interests and to the way in which the study of logic was combined with speculation on a far wider range of topics. Of the standard glosses, one (IX) is concerned with the triad οὐσία, δύναμις, ἐνέργεια; but it does not refer directly to the discussion of these concepts in the *Periphyseon*. Another distinguishes those types of actions which can be said to be neither good nor evil.[51] One links a discussion of privation with a passage from Gregory the Great's *Moralia in Iob*;[52] and another states that the right way of acting is to pursue a mean between extremes, neither failing to perform good actions, nor attempting more than one puts into practice.[53] Two discursive standard glosses are probably influenced by the teachings of John Scottus. One says that there is nothing contrary to the faith in believing that there are dwellers in the antipodes.[54] These men live in the manner of the Persians (*Persarum*) – or so the gloss reads in every manuscript except *G*, which (more plausibly?) has the Antipodeans living like wild beasts (*ferarum*). The other gloss (IV) mentions the characteristically Eriugenian term 'theophanies'. These, it says, are in God and divine things: a distortion, it seems, of John's idea that God cannot be known directly but only through his theophanies.

A continuation of IV is found in *M*, *G* and *H* only (XI). This gloss begins with a reference to the *Solutiones ad Chosroem*, a Greek work by Priscianus Lyddus, which has had strong claims made for it, particularly by Mlle d'Alverny,[55] to have been translated by John Scottus or within his circle. The gloss, however, does not follow Priscianus closely or for long: in its development it owes more to the *Periphyseon* than to any other source. Having distinguished between a *fantaston*, an object of sense-perception, a *fantasia*, a sense-datum, and a *fantasma*, a sense-impression stored in the memory, the glossator proceeds to parallel these three concepts to the three heavens, the third of which

---

[51] To NVNC EA OPPOSITA (ed. cit., p. 170:12–13) in *HGANSVW*.

[52] To SIQVIDEM PRIVATIO (ed. cit., p. 170:23) in *HLNQSVW*, abbreviated *A*. This gloss is very similar to one in Remigius of Auxerre's commentary to the *De Nuptiis* (in ed. Lutz II (Leiden, 1965), p. 46:13–15).

[53] To HANC RATIONEM PERIPATETICI (ed. cit., p. 171:11) in *HNQSVW*, shortened *L*.

[54] To NAM ET ANTIPODES (ed. cit., p. 152:19) in *GHCNSVW*; cf. John Scottus *Annotationes in Martianum* ed. cit., p. 143:22–144:3; and P. Delhaye *Le Microcosme de Godefroy de Saint-Victor: Étude théologique* (Lille/Gembloux, 1951), Note S, pp. 282–6: 'La théorie des Antipodes et ses incidences théologiques'.

[55] 'Les "Solutiones ad Chosroem" de Priscianus Lydus et Jean Scot'.

Paul was taken to in his ecstasy. The first heaven is those things that are, that is, which have bodies (*fantasta*); the second heaven is *mentuale* and consists of those things which are perceived (*fantasia*). The third heaven is made up of those things that are said (*fantasma*) and is 'intellectual'. The gloss goes on to quote Paul's phrase from the Bible: 'siue in corpus, siue extra corpus, nescio; Deus scit'. *H* here has an oddly corrupt text, ending 's. c. o. Deus sit'. The abbreviation could well stand for 'sed cum omnia Deus sit' – a reference of a distinctly Eriugenian kind to the state of affairs after the Return; although what the exact relevance of the remark to the rest of the gloss may be, and what led the scribe to choose so odd a reading, are matters for speculation.

A final section of this gloss talks of the image of God, ineffably reflected in Man as if in a mirror. Another gloss in *M*, *G* and *H* only (XII) is also concerned with the doctrine of similitude. It simply mixes the ideas of Augustine's, which appear in more direct citation in the passage on similitude included after the text of the *Categoriae Decem* in *H* and *S*, with those of the pseudo-Augustinian text. There is a continuation to this gloss in *M* and *H* only, which is interesting because it states the most pantheistically inclined aspect of Eriugena's doctrine in the strongest terms. All things are in God causally, and everything in God is God. All things are united in God, and God is spread through all things so that he is everything in all things (a favourite biblical phrase of John's): 'a creature is nothing but the infinite unification of God in himself by himself'.

M is especially rich in discursive glosses of a metaphysically daring nature. Especially interesting are those which take straightforward logical ideas from the *Categoriae Decem* and transform them into principles of Eriugenian theology. One of these (XX) interprets the notion of *polionima* in terms of cataphatic theology. God has many names. Some, like 'king' or 'uncreated creator' 'clothe and adorn him'; others, like 'lamb', 'ox' or 'lion' are improper and 'strip' (*denudant*) him. The reference here is to the idea of teratological symbolism, which Eriugena developed from the pseudo-Dionysius. Since no description can properly characterize the deity, it is better to represent God by symbols which are obviously unsuitable to him, because these present the least possibility of confusion. Synonyms and homonyms too come in for metaphysical treatment in another gloss (XIX).[56]

[56] Another gloss in *M* only (f.40r) takes up the same theme: 'Omonima nec sinonima nec

Homonyms, the glossator understands correctly, are things which have the same name although they are different. As an example, he chooses 'Jesus', the name both of Christ, who was God and man, and of other ordinary men. For this reason, Jesus both is and is not Jesus; and this – the glossator claims – is an example of cataphatic and apophatic theology. In interpreting the notion of synonyms, the glossator appears to follow the *Categoriae Decem*, which says that 'animal' is a synonym, because it can rightly be used to describe a man, a horse or a wild beast. In the gloss, the example is *animal* again, here because it can describe both men and other animals. But the glossator passes on from this point to the interpretation of a biblical passage in which the phrase 'all things' both does and does not include animals.

Other discursive glosses in *M* show further borrowings from the *Periphyseon*. On two occasions (xiva and xvii) John's etymology of θεός is quoted, once in rather garbled form. *M* is especially remarkable because, whereas most of the Eriugenian borrowings in the *Categoriae Decem* glosses could be explained by a reading of Book I of the *Periphyseon* alone, the glossator of this manuscript was equally familiar with the later books of John's masterpiece. Gloss xxi discusses the Return of all things to God, which forms the subject of *Periphyseon* iv and v. The elements are permanent and unchangeable, it says; and, at the Return, all men will be restored to their former bodies, recompounded from their constituent elements, but purified and made spiritual. There is a little confusion in this gloss, however, since the glossator does not properly distinguish between the elements and ideas. Gloss xviii is a rather rambling collection of ideas from various sources, but, in its final lines, it contains a probable recollection of Eriugena's description of the human intellect, which, by the power of grace, is allowed to escape the confines of human existence and circle ineffably around the deity.

A gloss which *M* shares with *G* (xv) is less rambling in its progress of ideas; and, unlike so much of the material in *M* only, it does not appear to be based on any typically Eriugenian ideas. Invisible things, the glossator says, attach themselves to other invisible things, in such a way that, for example, wisdom really is *in* the individual mind to

paronima recipit Deus, sed tantummodo polionima . . .' On teratological symbolism in John's work, see R. Roques, *Libres sentiers vers l'érigénisme* (Roma, 1975) (*Lessico intelletuale europeo* IX), chapter 1, pp. 13–43.

which it is attached. The glossator contrasts this inherence with the relationship between one material thing and another: the finger, which is part of the body, is not in the body as a subject but *de subiecto* with regard to the substance of the body. This is a serious misuse by the glossator of the term *de subiecto* as defined in the *Categoriae Decem*, since a finger is in no way the species of the substance of the body. If one says of wine or water, the glossator continues, that it is in a jug, then this is not a case of being *in a subject*: the jug, the wine and the water could be elsewhere. The idea of being *in a subject* which has now been defined is then applied to a quotation from *John:* 'That they all may be one; as thou, Father, art in me, and I in thee, that they also may be one in us.' By 'in us', says the glossator, the evangelist meant the same relation of inherence as wisdom in the mind. They will be one, not in substance, but because they will shine with virtues in the Father and the Son. The glossator applies the same analysis to another passage in *John,* and he goes on to elaborate that when virtue (*uirtus*) has become so constant that it embraces all parts of the soul, then its possessors will become 'in God that which God is'.

The glosses in G only are a great deal clearer, simpler and more down-to-earth than *M*'s eccentric material. Among G's discursive glosses on philosophical subjects, one treats the Platonic theory, espoused by Augustine, that various abstract types of knowledge have an eternal existence apart from anyone's possession of them (xxviii); another speculates on the possibility of knowledge about purely imaginary beings like a chimaera or a centaur (xxix). Especially interesting is gloss xxv, which proposes a triple etymology for the word *elementa*: from *yle*, the Greek word for formless matter; from *elimo*, because bodies are formed from the elements; and from *eluo*, because, when the elements properly manifest themselves, the bodies which they form are purified. Could this possibly be a reference to the formation of pure, spiritual bodies from the elements after the Return?

Finally, there is just one eccentric gloss in an eleventh-century manuscript, Q, which is of great interest (xxx). It gives a brief but accurate paraphrase of the views on divine punishment which John Scottus put forward in his *De praedestinatione* and elaborated in the *Periphyseon*. God does not inflict punishments on a substance. But impressions of grief and bitterness, qualities which were not created by God, assail the soul, just as thirst is not in Man by nature, but, by the power of nature afflicts Man or leaves him. God is the life of the living and the death of the dying; or rather, the glossator adds, citing a biblical passage dear to Eriugena, he is the death of Death.

There is hardly any evidence, in the standard glosses to the *Categoriae Decem* or elsewhere, of the nominalism which Hauréau and Barach claimed was to be found. In the glosses to the pseudo-Augustinian work, to the *De nuptiis* and to Boethius's *Opuscula Sacra, usia* is firmly established as the *genus generalissimum* and an ontology of participation is, at times, set forth. However, in none of the standard sets of these glosses is there a complete adoption of John Scottus's most characteristic ideas about the Categories, such as his negative, apophatic ontology, his hyper-Realism and his theory of place and time. The standard glosses to the *Categoriae Decem* adopt a point of view on the theory of place mid-way between a naive materialism and the arguments of the *Periphyseon*; and, like the other two sets of glosses, they pick up certain of Eriugena's other ideas, without developing them into a coherent theory of the Categories. In *M*, and to a lesser extent in *H* and *G*, there is a great deal more material inspired by the *Periphyseon*; but, despite a sympathy for some of John's most unusual conclusions, the author of these glosses does not try to grasp John's thought on the Categories as a whole. This may be due to what I have argued is the ultimate incoherence of John's theory of the Categories. The gradual standardization of the glosses was accompanied by a move away from metaphysically extravagant interpretations; and this is also illustrated by the eccentric glosses to *O* and, at an early stage, by some of the material peculiar to *G*. The work of the School of John Scottus proved most enduring where it was least characteristic of its founder.

CONCLUSION

Many a reader will doubtless dissent from some of the arguments I have advanced, and disagree with some of the interpretations I have given. But no one, I hope, who has read these pages will think that the early medieval period was the philosophical desert, watered by the fewest oases, which some historians have portrayed. At the courts of Charlemagne and Charles the Bald, and in the monasteries of Corbie and Auxerre, men of the early Middle Ages made their first attempts to grapple with abstract problems by the exercise of reason. I have presented evidence to suggest that philosophy is a term which can properly be used of some part of these thinkers' activity. The imposition of theological interests on logical texts led them to ask questions about the fundamental constitution of reality, and to give answers which were consistent with Christian dogma but not in any simple way derived from it.

The period of philosophy I have studied is thus one of beginnings. It is characterized not by the perfected clarity of its arguments, nor by the coherence of its systems, but rather by a tentativeness in reasoning that can approach dullness, or alternatively, by a premature brilliance which often conceals deep intellectual confusion. Moreover, much of the substance of early medieval philosophy lay in a tradition of teaching, learning and discussion in schools and monasteries: the evidence for this tradition is various in kind, and requires extensive analysis before it may be fully interpreted. The history of philosophy in this period therefore demands considerable patience of both its writers and readers. But it offers rich rewards, in the fascination of the material discovered, and in the light which it throws on the development of philosophy throughout the Middle Ages.

In some respects, the philosophy of the late eighth to early tenth centuries presents an impressive uniformity. The texts which formed the basis for philosophical study remained much the same. Chief among them was the *Categoriae Decem*. Put into circulation by Alcuin, it was known to Ratramnus of Corbie, used extensively by John Scottus, and glossed thoroughly by the next generation of thinkers. Porphyry's introduction (*Isagoge*) to the *Categories* also enjoyed great popularity throughout the early medieval period, and the corpus of other logical texts and commentaries did not vary greatly. Boethius's *Opuscula Sacra* played a major role in suggesting how concepts learnt from the *Categoriae Decem* should be understood. The *Opuscula Sacra* were used in Alcuin's Circle, by Ratramnus, Eriugena and the scholars of Corbie. The scholars of Charlemagne's court appear also to have used certain other philosophical texts, such as Calcidius's translation of Plato's *Timaeus* along with his commentary, and Boethius's *De consolatione philosophiae*. Even in the use of a writer like Augustine, who enjoyed enormous influence throughout the Middle Ages and the Renaissance, the early medieval period shows a particular consistency. For at no other time did Augustine's works, especially his *De Trinitate*, figure so prominently in the context of *philosophical* discussion.

Consistency in sources was accompanied by a more fundamental uniformity. Throughout the early medieval period a single group of problems was at the centre of philosophical debate. These problems were raised by Aristotle's theory of the Categories, and, especially, by the first of these Categories, *usia*. They included questions about the problem of Universals, because a decision on the ontological status of species and genera determined the role which the Categories, considered as classes of the greatest generality, would play in an explanation of the universe. *Usia*, treated as a *genus generalissimum* having real existence, could be used both to forge links and to point contrasts between God and his creation. A group of subsidiary problems, concerning the relationship of the soul to God, was linked to these central themes.

Despite this consistency, an examination of the methods of study and the type of conclusions reached shows that there was considerable change between the late eighth and the early tenth centuries. In the Circle of Alcuin, philosophical texts were studied, it seems, by excerption and compilation. Although the philosophy of these years shows far greater originality than scholars have generally allowed, it is very closely based on acquired material; and a thinker's views can often only be discovered by a careful examination of how he changes sources which he uses extensively and directly. The philosophers who lived under Charles the Bald showed far greater daring. Ratramnus considered the problem of Universals in length and detail. He did not go far beyond Boethius, his main source; but he explained Boethius's doctrines in his own words. John Scottus's *Periphyseon* is a vast treatise, original in its conception, theological in its overall bearing but containing extensive discussion of the problems of essence, the Categories and the Universals. The fifty years which followed Eriugena's lifetime did not see the composition of any treatise of comparable scope. Rather, the detailed study of texts such as the *Categoriae Decem* and the *Opuscula Sacra* by glossing became the normal method of philosophical discussion. Such glossing provided a way of understanding the exact meaning of an authoritative text, but it did not exclude original thinking.

The conclusions of philosophical discussion are never amenable to brief summary: so frequently, it is *how* a thinker reaches a certain position, rather than the position itself, which is of importance. Nevertheless, a few general remarks about the theories of essence and the Universals in the early Middle Ages may be made without undue distortion.

The ontology of the School of Alcuin, so far as it can be discerned, was a mixture between Aristotle's theory in the *Categories*, whereby *usia* was simply the individual of such-and-such a kind, and a theory of participation, derived from Boethius and Augustine, which made *usia* that on which everything depended in order to exist. Aristotle's theory may only have been understood in part, but it does not seem to have been misunderstood. In the work of John Scottus and his close followers, Aristotelian ontology was submerged beneath a weight of extravagant metaphysical theories. An ontology of participation was put forward, in a variety of different forms. But there was also posited a 'negative ontology' – based on the idea of negative theology – by which not-being was given a higher value than any type of existence and even, paradoxically, predicated of *usia* itself. These theories retained their popularity for only a short period after Eriugena's lifetime. A study of the various glossed manuscripts of the *Categoriae Decem* suggests that, as the tenth century drew on, and during the eleventh century, thinkers lost interest in John Scottus's more personal ideas, and turned their attention increasingly to Aristotle's doctrine.

In the early Middle Ages, the solutions to the problem of Universals were, by and large, realist. Genera and species were held to have a real existence, apart from the minds of men who perceived them. Characteristic of Eriugena and his followers is what I have called 'hyper-Realism', a theory which conflates individuals with their species and genera. The nominalism which some historians have detected in early medieval thought is almost entirely an illusion, based on the misinterpretation of a few imprecise words or phrases. But there were thinkers, such as Ratramnus of Corbie, who were willing to proclaim that species and genera had no real existence.

Most discussions of philosophy in the early Middle Ages give a good deal of space to the thought of John Scottus. Mine has been no exception. But the bearing of my remarks has been to suggest that Eriugena was far more a man of his time than has been believed. I have argued for this position from two directions. On the one hand, I have tried to show that John shared his contemporaries' interest in the problems of essence, the Categories and the Universals; that he examined these problems in terms of the philosophical tradition he inherited; and that his solutions, elaborate and impressive though they are, suffer from the confusions and contradictions so common in his time. On the other hand, I have assembled evidence to show that Eriugena worked with colleagues and pupils; that his writings were studied in his lifetime and beyond; and that his ideas and ways of thought were popular in a certain milieu. Ninth-century philosophy cannot be understood apart from the work of John Scottus: Eriugena's thought cannot be comprehended apart from the philosophy of the ninth century.

How much did the philosophy of the late eighth to early tenth centuries contribute to the thought of the period which followed? A thorough answer to this question would demand a book to itself. I shall limit myself to sketching a few ways in which this question might be made more specific, and to indicating what sort of research might give some of the answers.

The glossing of texts was the most important method of studying philosophy by the end of the ninth century. This method retained most of its importance, at least until the mid-twelfth century. And two of the texts which were heavily glossed in the late ninth or early tenth centuries – Martianus Capella's *De nuptiis* and Boethius's *Opuscula*

Sacra – received fresh commentaries in the twelfth century. How much did these commentaries owe to their early medieval counterparts? The investigation needed to give a thorough answer to this question would not limit itself to determining how much was taken over verbatim from early medieval glosses: it would also examine the debts which twelfth-century commentators owed to their predecessors in ideas and method. The most important philosophical text for the ninth century, the *Categoriae Decem*, was, however, ignored by commentators in the twelfth century. The reasons for this neglect have already been outlined. An increasing interest in the technicalities of Aristotelian logic led scholars to search for more accurate versions of Aristotle's *Categories*. How much did twelfth-century commentary on Boethius's translation of the *Categories* owe to the ninth-century tradition of *philosophical* glosses to the *Categoriae Decem*? And to what extent did a growing concern for formal logic push philosophical discussion out of commentaries on logical works and into independent works of philosophy?

The traditional view of Eriugena's influence has been that, neglected in his lifetime, the Irishman's works played an important part in the philosophy of the twelfth century. I have argued that the first aspect of this picture, John's neglect by his contemporaries, is very far from the truth: is the second aspect any truer? Eriugena's work was certainly known by some philosophers of the twelfth or early thirteenth centuries: Honorius Augustodunensis, Alan of Lille, Hugh of St Victor, and the author of the *Liber de causis primis et secundis*, to name but a few. Yet real proof that John's distinctive ideas had any influence on the most exciting thinkers of the age, such as William of Conches, Thierry of Chartres or Gilbert Porreta, has never been furnished. Careful research in this area is required.

Finally, and very briefly: I have argued that the central theme of early medieval philosophy was not the problem of Universals, but a complex of problems, at the centre of which stands the concept of *usia* or essence. Was this theme also predominant in eleventh- and twelfth-century thought? In my Introduction, I referred to two articles by Gilson, in which he argued the importance of essence as a theme in the work of Augustine and Aquinas. Did the problem of essence equally occupy the attention of the philosophers who lived in the nine hundred years which separated these two great minds?

TEXTS FROM THE CIRCLE OF ALCUIN

THE FORTUNE OF THE MUNICH PASSAGES

The fortune of the Munich Passages in the Middle Ages was of two markedly different kinds: for the *dicta Albini* and, to a much lesser extent, the *dicta Candidi*, a wide and various diffusion; for the other passages, a limited and specialized readership. This pattern emerges most clearly from the list of surviving manuscripts of the Passages which I have compiled (see below, pp. 149–51). In the following paragraphs, I will summarize the results of this survey.

To deal with the fortune of the Passages besides the two *dicta* first. Besides *V*, no Carolingian manuscript of the Munich Passages complete or nearly so survives, although an epistolary version of the *dicta Candidi*, written between 801 and 805, does append Passage I.[1] Benedict of Aniane, who, like Candidus, helped Alcuin in opposing the adoptionist heresy, borrows a number of passages in his *Munimenta fidei*, where they stand side by side with material from Augustine's *De Trinitate*, one of their main sources.[2] Two later manuscripts contain a substantial selection of the Passages. *B*, which dates from the second half of the ninth century, contains all the Passages except for the *dicta Albini*, x and xi: it is almost certainly a copy of a schoolbook from the milieu of Candidus himself.[3] *P* is complete, except for the *dicta Albini* and Passage vi. The manuscript dates from the first half of the tenth century and was probably produced in the School of Auxerre. The Passages follow without break on a florilegium from John Scottus's *Periphyseon*. This is a remarkable testament to the cultural continuity between the various Schools – of Alcuin, of John Scottus, of Auxerre – which have formed the main subjects of this whole study.[4] In general, therefore, the diffusion for the Munich

---

[1] See above, p. 41.   [2] See above, pp. 36–7.   [3] See above, pp. 55–7.
[4] See above, pp. 41 and 103ff., and below, p. 178, for *P*.

Passages as a whole was small. This may be explained in part by their sophistication for their time, which limited their interest to the most intellectually advanced circles; and in part by the fact that their function as an introduction to the Categories was taken over by the glosses to the *Categoriae Decem*, which became widespread from the beginning of the tenth century onwards (See Chapter 5).

By contrast, the *dicta Albini* enjoyed an immediate popularity, and one that was surprisingly enduring. I have already listed the early quotations from the work and the manuscripts in which it appears separately, in the course of discussing the integrity of the Munich Passages. Paulinus of Aquileia, Hrabanus Maurus and an anonymous missionary to the Slavs all make use of the *dicta*;[5] and it is also quoted in the *Libri Carolini* (see above, pp. 34–36), and in a work closely associated with Alcuin himself, the *Disputationes per Interrogationes et Responsiones*.[6] Of these early texts, only one, a dialectical corpus belonging to Leidrad of Lyon, contains material close to the concerns of the Munich Passages as a whole.

A tenth-century manuscript, *Wien 458*, contains both the *dicta Albini* and the closely related *dicta Candidi*. In the twelfth century these two passages enjoyed a certain joint popularity in a composite version which must have been the work of some logically minded scholar who came across them together as they are preserved in the Vienna manuscript. In this version, the *dicta Candidi* is sandwiched between the *dicta Albini*'s section on Man's image of God and Alcuin's concluding section on Man's Godlikeness. A twelfth-century manuscript, *BN 1941*, preserves this version complete. The text appears among Sentences compiled in the School of Anselm of Laon, without, however, its final section on Man's likeness to his maker.[7] And the extracts in Alcher of Clairvaux's compilation *De spiritu et anima* must also derive from this version.[8] There are a few unimportant

---

[5] See above p. 42, n. 57, 58 and 59.

[6] *MPL* 101, 1097–144, 1100D–1103A; for the authorship of this work (perhaps Alcuin's) see Manitius, op. cit., p. 281.

[7] Ed. O. Lottin, *Psychologie et morale aux XIIe et XIIIe siècles* v (Gembloux, 1959), pp. 248–50, no. 313 (= ms. *Douai 371* ff.32r–33v). The origin of this piece, unknown to its editor, was first pointed out by Mathon, op. cit., p. 221.

[8] *MPL* 40, 779–832, 805–6. Although the quotations are mainly from the *dicta Albini*, the beginning of the *dicta Candidi*, 'Et ideo mihi juste videtur dictum nostrum interiorem hominem esse imaginem Dei', is quoted between the end of Alcuin's section on Man's image of God and the beginning of his discussion of Godlikeness, so indicating that the

additions to the text in the Paris manuscript, and just one which deserves mention, since it illustrates a point of theological importance. Candidus had written, 'anima semper est, et scit, et scire uult';[9] but the implication here, that each human soul exists eternally in its individual form, had become heterodox by the twelfth century.[10] Both the compiler of the Paris manuscript and the author of the *Sentences* try to get round this problem by changing the text so as to posit an unspecific form of eternal pre-existence. The former puts: 'semper est, priusquam esse ceperit et scit';[11] and the latter: 'est ex quo esse cepit, et scit'.[12] The *dicta Albini*, uncombined with the *dicta Candidi*, also enjoyed a certain diffusion in the twelfth century, as exemplified by its use in the *Decreti* of Ivo of Chartres[13] and its presence in a manuscript of this century now in Berlin (*Deutsche Stadtsbibliothek 181*).

Manuscripts of the *dicta Albini* from the ninth, tenth and twelfth centuries had, for the most part, contained no acknowledgement of its authorship, the rare exceptions being *V* and the Vienna and Berlin manuscripts. By contrast, its popularity from the thirteenth to the fifteenth centuries, which far eclipses that of earlier periods, is linked to its widespread attribution to Augustine. The *dicta Albini* appears in three thirteenth-, five fourteenth- and no less than ten fifteenth-century manuscripts. Frequently it is considered to be a sermon (*sermo*); occasionally it is called a *tractatus* or a *liber*.[14] The most common title is 'qualiter homo factus est ad imaginem et similitudinem Dei'.[15] Almost all the manuscripts are now preserved in English collections, and six of them, at the very least, formed part of medieval English libraries.[16] Another mark of the popularity of the *dicta Albini*, in the guise of a sermon of St Augustine's, is its translation in this form into Middle English, of which four manuscripts survive. This pseudonymous popularity was not, however, entirely limited to

composite version must have been used. For the attribution of the *Liber de spiritu et anima*, see the article on Alcher of Clairvaux by P. Fournier in *Dictionnaire d'Histoire et de Géographie Ecclésiastique* II, 14–15.

[9] Cf. above, p. 47.
[10] Cf. T. Gregory, *Anima Mundi* (Firenze, 1955), p. 164.
[11] f.83ra.   [12] Ed. cit., l.90.
[13] *MPL* 161, 47–1022, 967B–969B = Pars XVII, cap. I.
[14] As in mss., 19 and 20 (numbers refer to list of mss. below, pp. 149–51).
[15] Mss. 19, 20, No. 25 has the title, 'Augustini de dignitate naturae hominum'.
[16] Nos. 12, 13, 16, 19, 25, 26. For details of these medieval collections, I have used N. Ker, *Medieval Libraries of Great Britain* (2nd edn, London, 1964).

England. Two fifteenth-century manuscripts of it survive in Continental collections:[17] they show no trace of an English origin. In both it is attributed to Augustine, as it is in an entry in the late fifteenth-century library catalogue of the monastery of St Aegidia at Nuremberg.

How did the attribution to Augustine arise in the first place? It is impossible to be sure. Perhaps a faded or partially erased title allowed the letters *ALBINI* to be read as *AVGVSTINI*. But, since the early diffusion of the work was mainly anonymous, it is more probable that a scholar, noticing the parallels between the section on God's image in Man and the *De Trinitate* of Augustine, decided that the *dicta*, too, must have been a work of Augustine's. The popularity of Alcuin's work under the name of Augustine is not without a certain irony, given the markedly un-Augustinian treatment of Man's God-likeness displayed in the final paragraph. But, beneath the irony, there lies an imputed tribute to Alcuin's didactic skills. Only the few who took the trouble to read the *De Trinitate* fully and profoundly could grasp the moral implications of Augustine, which Alcuin, at the cost of distorting the thought of Augustine, made open and direct. Augustine, who knew well how to judge the capabilities of his audience, may have been disparaging if he had had to pass judgement on Alcuin as a philosopher; but he would have praised him as a homilist.

In a few cases the *dicta Albini* is found in late medieval continental manuscripts as an anonymous work: in a thirteenth-century manuscript from Tegernsee (*München clm 19135*), a mid-fifteenth-century manuscript also from Tegernsee (*München clm 18639*), and, possibly, in two references in the late fifteenth-century catalogue of the Charterhouse at Salvatorberg. The oddest appearance of the *dicta* is in a manuscript from Amorbach, datable to 1456/7, *Würzburg Universitätsbibliothek M. ch. q. 159*, in which it is attributed to Ambrose and given the following heading: 'Incipit liber IV. de officiis beati Ambrosii episcopi tractatus, qualiter homo ad imaginem et similitudinem indiuiduae trinitatis sit factus.' The attribution of the *dicta* to Ambrose is also put forward by Trithemius. In his *De scriptoribus ecclesiasticis* (1494), he lists the *De dignitate conditionis humanae* as a separate work between Ambrose's *Hexaemeron* and his *De Paradiso*.

[17] Nos. 20 and 24.

The early publishing history of the *dicta Albini* and the *dicta Candidi* reflects the manuscript tradition, except that the attribution to Ambrose plays a more important part than might have been expected. The composite version of the *dicta Candidi* and the *dicta Albini* appears in the earliest editions of the works of Ambrose, placed, as in Trithemius's catalogue, between the *Hexaemeron* and the *De Paradiso*.[18] But even a fifteenth-century editor was not convinced by this attribution, describing the work as one 'qui Sancto Ambrosio auctori a quibusdam ascribitur';[19] and the Maurists, yet more critical, relegated the piece to an appendix.[20] The late medieval attribution of the *dicta Albini* to Augustine led to its inclusion among that Father's works, under the title *De creatione primi hominis*.[21] Its authenticity was not accepted, however, by Erasmus, or by the editors of the 1586 Louvain edition; and the Maurists realized that the piece was to be found elsewhere, although they did not trace it back to Alcuin.[22] This task was left to Alcuin's first editor, Duchesne;[23] but he did not recognize in the *dicta Albini*, which he printed simply and correctly as a work of Alcuin's, the by then discredited Augustinian and Ambrosian pseudepigraph.

[18] Ed. Amerbach (Basel, 1492) I, G2vb–G3vb; ed. Basel, 1506 I, ff.102v–103v; ed. Paris, 1529, f.246r–v; ed. Erasmus (Basel ap. Froben, 1538), II, pp. 88–9.

[19] Ed. of 1492, f.G2vb, and in all the other editions cited. Here, also, should be mentioned the latest of the manuscripts (31), written by a Dutch scribe in an accomplished humanist script for the Dean of Windsor. It contains the same composite version of the *dicta Candidi* and the *dicta Albini* as the early printed editions, and the same title, which mentions the authorship of Ambrose without fully accepting it. This manuscript, which was far more of a calligraphic showpiece than anything else, most probably copied the text of the two *dicta* from a printed book.

[20] Thus it appears in the *Patrologia Latina*, 17, 1105–7.

[21] Ed. J. Amerbach (Basel, 1505–6), pars x, f.2r; ed. Erasmus (Basel ap. Froben, 1529) IX, pp. 810–11; ed. monks of Louvain (Paris, 1586), IX, p. 452ff.

[22] Thus it appears only in part in *MPL* 40, 1213–14, with a note indicating that the complete text is to be found elsewhere.

[23] See above, p. 32, n. 10.

A LIST OF SURVIVING MANUSCRIPTS
CONTAINING THE MUNICH PASSAGES

(Roman numerals refer to the numbers of passages in the edition below)

DATE	MANUSCRIPT	PROVENANCE	CONTENTS	ATTRIBUTIONS
1. c. 800	*München clm 6407* (*V*)	Freising (written at Verona)	I–XV	VII to Alcuin VIII to Candidus
2. a. 818	*Roma Bibl. Padri Maristi, A.II.1* (*L*)	Lyon	VII	anon.
3. s. viii–ix/ s. ix in.	*Vaticanus Pal. lat. 1719* (*Pal.*)	Lorsch	VII	anon.
4. 835–870	*Würzburg Theol. fol. 56* (*W*)	Würzburg	VIII (in letter form) & I	anon.
5. s. ix²	*München clm 18961* (*B*)	Tegernsee	I–VI, VIII, IX, XII–XV	anon. but for VIII see text.
6. s. x¹	*Paris BN 13953* (*P*)	Corbie	I–V, VIII–XV	VIII to Candidus
7. s. x	*Wien 458*	Salzburg	VII, VIII	VII to Alcuin (?)
8. s. xii	*Berlin Deutsche Stadtsbibliothek 181*	S. Denys, Reims	VII (+ ?)	Alcuin
9. s. xii–xiii	*Paris BN 1941*		VII + VIII composite version	anon.
10. s. xiii	*Cambridge Univ. Lib. Ee.2.33*		VII	Augustine
11. s. xiii	*München clm 19135*	Tegernsee	VII (+ ?)	anon.
12. s. xiii	*Worcester Cathedral*	Worcester	VIII* (+ ?)	Augustine
13. s. xiii ex./ s. xiv	*Cambridge St John's Coll. 47*	Lincoln Franciscan Convent	VII	Augustine
14. s. xiv in.	*Oxford Bodleian Barlow 21*	written in England	VII	Augustine
15. s. xiv	*Cambridge UL Hh.1.4*		VII	Augustine
16. s. xiv	*Cambridge UL Ii.3.7*	Norwich	VII	Augustine
17. s. xiv	*Cambridge UL Ii.4.23*		VII	Augustine
18. s. xv in.	*Cambridge Peterhouse 203*		VII	Augustine

DATE	MANUSCRIPT	PROVENANCE	CONTENTS	ATTRIBUTIONS
19. s. xv	*Cambridge Corpus Christi Coll. 194*	London, Hospital of B.V.M. without Bishopgate	VII	Augustine
20. s. xv	*Bruxelles Bibl. Royale 1134*		VII (+ ?)	Augustine
21. s. xv	*Cambridge UL Gg.1.32*		VII	Augustine
22. s. xv	*Cambridge UL Hh.4.13*		VII	Augustine
23. s. xv	*Lincoln Cath. 210*		VII (+ ?)	Augustine
24. s. xv	*München clm 6947*	Fürstenfeld	VII★★	Augustine
25. s. xiii ex./ xv	*Oxford Christchurch 91*	Church of Holy Cross, Crediton, Devon.	VII	Augustine
26. s. xv	*Oxford Merton Coll 50*	Merton Coll.	VII	Augustine
27. s. xv	*Worcester Cathedral F 114*		VII★ (+ ?)	Augustine
28. c. 1450	*München clm 18639*	Tegernsee	VII	anon.
29. 1456/7	*Würzburg Universitätsbibliothek M.ch.q. 159*	Amorbach	VII (+ ?)	Ambrose
30. s. xv²	*Oxford Bodleian Misc. 117*		VII	Augustine
31. 1504	*Oxford Bodleian Douce 110*	Windsor	VII + VIII composite version	Ambrose (see text)

Other manuscripts mentioned in medieval library catalogues

32. (?) Salvatorberg, Charterhouse s. xv ex. catalogue: 'Descripcio pulcherrima dignitatis humanae' = VII (+ ?) (cf. P. Lehmann, *Mittelalterliche Bibliothekskataloge Deutschlands und der Schweiz*, II. p. 417:10–11)

33. (?) ibid. 'De ymagine Dei in anima humana unde homo excitatur ad devocionem et Dei amorem' = VII (+ ?) (ibid., II, p. 321:6–8)

34. St Ägidien monastery, Nürnberg s. xv ex. catalogue: Augustinus de dignitate conditionis humanae 'Tanta dignitas' = VII (+ ?) (ibid. III–iii, p. 479:30–1)

Texts from the circle of Alcuin

Manuscripts of the English translation of the dicta Albini
(All attributed to Augustine)

35–38. *Cambridge UL Ii.6.39* (s. xiv); *Ii.6.55* (s. xv); *London British Library Harley 2330*; *Oxford All Souls 24*. cf. P. S. Joliffe, *A Check-List of Middle English Prose Writings of Spiritual Guidance* (Toronto, 1974), pp. 74–5.

* In a version combined with another ps-Augustinian sermon, 'Resurrectio et clarificatio Domini nostri Jesu Christi . . .' = no. 252 (*MPL* 39, 2210–2212).
** Combined with other material to form a longer work.
+? A manuscript which I have not checked in person and which might contain the combined version of VII and VIII; in the case of those manuscripts where the work is attributed to Augustine, this is, however very unlikely.

THE MUNICH PASSAGES

SIGLA

V	München clm 6407
L	Roma Bibl. Padri Maristi A.II.1
B	München clm 18961
Pal	Vaticanus Palatinus lat. 1719
P	Paris BN 13953
E	Wien 966 (from *MGH Epp.* IV, pp. 488–9)
W	Würzburg Theol. fol. 56 (from ibid. V, pp. 615–16)
C	Vaticanus lat. 7207 (from *MGH Legum: III Concilia 2 suppl.* pp. 22–3)

* The uncorrected version of any manuscript
corr The corrector of any manuscript

PRINCIPLES OF EDITION

V, although certainly not the original copy of the collection of passages, presents by far the best testimony to it. I have therefore in general followed *V*'s readings, except where they are obviously corrupt. In such cases I have taken alternative readings from some other manuscript(s); only very rarely, where no manuscript gives an acceptable reading, have I introduced a conjectural emendation. In the case of the *dicta Albini* (VII), however, which may have originated separately from the other passages, and for which *L* and *C* have an authority equal to *V*'s, I have chosen more freely from the readings presented by the various manuscripts. All variations from the text of *V* are italicized. The orthography is strictly that of the text of *V*; punctuation and capitalization are my own.

In listing parallels here and in the other texts, I employ the following conventions:

'=' indicates a verbal parallel to the text; a reference given without preliminary sign indicates a close parallel, short of verbal identity; 'cf.' indicates an interesting possible source, analogue or parallel, which, however, diverges in detail or terminology from the passage of the text in question.

I.   DE DECEM CATHEGORIIS AVGVSTINI

'Usia' graece quod est latine 'substantia' siue 'essentia', hoc est Deus.[a][1]

Qualitas:	Deus autem sine qualitate bonus.
Quantitas:	Sine quantitate magnus.
Ad aliquid:	Sine indigentia creator.
Situs:	Sine situ praesens.
Habitus:	Sine habitu omnia continens.
Locus:	Sine loco ubique totus.
Tempus:	Sine tempore sempiternus.
Agere:	Sine sui mutacione mutabilia faciens.
Pati:	Et nihil paciens.[2]

Haec novem sunt omnibus substantiis uel essentiis accidentia[3] excepta illa una uera et aeterna substantia, quae Deus est, cui nihil accidit, quia[b], quod[c] est, a seipso et in seipso[d] est.[1] Decima autem, hoc est substantia siue[e] / essentia, 'omnis creatura' dicitur, ex quo[f] creatura est et quamdiu in sua natura persistit.

I (Hauréau no. 2; *V*ff.93v–94r; *B* f.39r; *P* f.42ra–b; *W*ff.34v–35r) (*a*) *W om.* Usia ... Deus (*b*) *W om.* quia (*c*) *corrB adds above line* id est Deus (*d*) *W* ipso (*e*) *W* si(*f*) *B* et quoniam; *corrB adds above the line* uel quod.

(1) cf. Augustine, *De Trinitate* v 2 (*CC* 50: p. 207:1–2): 'Est (*sc.* Deus) tamen sine dubitatione substantia vel si melius hoc appellatur essentia . . .'; and cf. Alcuin, *De fide S. Trinitatis* I 15 (*MPL* 101: 22C–24B, esp. 22D–23A): 'Proprie Deus dicitur substantia una, summa et ineffabilis, quae semper idem est quod est: qua nihil accidens vel recidens inesse poterit, quae semper est quod est, quia semper immutabilis.' (2) = Augustine, *De Trinitate* v 1 (ed. cit., p. 207: 40–44, 'sine qualitate . . . nihilque patientem') (3) cf. ibid. v 2 (ed. cit., p. 208:7–9): 'Sed aliae quae dicuntur essentiae sive substantiae capiunt accidentia quibus in eis fiat vel magna vel quantacumque mutatio.'

II.   QVOMODO SANCTA ET SEMPITERNA ATQVE
INCOMMVTABILIS[a] TRINITAS FACILLIME POSSIT[b]
INTELLEGI

Sumus enim, et esse nos nouimus, et nostrum esse ac nosse amamus.
Nam esse, nosse atque amare tria sunt; et haec tria sibimet inseparabiliter iuncta, unam[c] efficiunt in anima racionali personam. Quod,
qui[d] se nouit, facillime agnoscit. Creator autem omnipotentissimus,
qui solus incommutabiliter est, incommutabiliter[e] nouit atque amat.[1]
Quem ueram essentiam, ueram sapientiam, ueram caritatem, Patrem
et Filium et Spiritum Sanctum, unum Deum in tribus personis, confitemur. Animae, quam ad suam fecit imaginem, esse nosse atque
amare dedit; atque ita per haec corpori mouendo[f] ac regendo contemperauit,[2] ut sicut ipse est inlocaliter in tota uniuersitate quam
fecit, sic illa inlocaliter sit[g] in toto corpore quod sibi subditum[h] regit[j].[3]

III.   QVO ARGVMENTVM COLLIGENDVM SIT DEVM ESSE

Tota rerum uniuersitas in tria genera diuiditur[a]: in unum quod est;
in aliud quod uiuit; in tertium quod intellegit. Quae inter se sicut
potentia sic etiam bonitate differunt.[b] Vt, uerbi gratia, sicut plus
potest bestia uiuens quam lapis non uiuens, ita plus potest homo
uiuens et intellegens quam bestia uiuens et non intellegens.[c1] Atque[d],
eodem ordine, sicut melius est id quod est atque uiuit quam id quod
est tantum sed non uiuit[e], ita melius est quod uiuit et intellegit quam
illud quod uiuit sed non intellegit. Imum enim bonitate atque potentia
in rerum naturis constitutum uidetur id quod est tantum, sed non
uiuit. Medium uero quod est atque uiuit. Summum autem quod est,
uiuit et intellegit.

Igitur, quia sic hac argumentatione colligitur id inter res cunctas
praecellit quod intellegit, homo, qui intellegit, intellectum suum

II   (Hauréau no. 10; *V* f.94r; *B* ff.40v–41r; *P* ff.42vb–43ra) (*a*) *B* INCOMMVTABILIS
SIT; *B om.* FACILLIME . . . INTELLEGI (*b*) *V* POSSI (*c*) *V* una (*d*) *P* quis (*e*) *In V*
incommutabiliter *is added in the bottom margin with a reference sign to the correct position*
(*f*) *V*★ mondo (*g*) *B om.* sit (*h*) *corrB adds* est (*j*) *B* regat.
(1) cf. Augustine, *Confessiones* (ed. P. Knoell, p. 342:23–343:4) (2) cf. Claudianus
Mamertus, *De statu animae* I 14 (*CSEL* 11: p. 59:5–7) (3) cf. Passage VII, p. 159 below.

III   (Hauréau no. 12; *V* ff.94v–95r; *B* ff.41r–42r; *P* ff.43rb–va) (*a*) *V*★ diuitur (*b*) *V*★ differ
(*c*) *B om.* quam . . . non intellegens (*d*) *P* adque (*e*) *P* nou͂

1) Augustine, *De libero arbitrio* II 22 (*CSEL* 74: p. 42:24–7).

conetur intellegere et ipsius intellectus potentiam examinare, quae-
ratque si ipse, qui ob hoc melior et poten/tior est ceteris rebus (quia
intellegit), omnipotens esse – hoc est, quaecumque uult, facere possit.
Quod si inuenerit (sicut utique, si querit, inuenire poterit) se non
omnia, quae uult, posse – hoc est non ubi*f* et in quo uult perpetuo*g*
permanere (uellet enim si posset corpus sibi coniunctum in bona
ualitudine uigens semper amministrare ac regere, sed non potest),
sciat*h* ergo sibi superiorem melioremque praesidere potentiam, quae
illum in hoc regimine corporis, quamdiu uult, permanere*j* permittit,
et quando uult, dimittere facit. Et ipsam potentiam omnipotentem,
omnibus quae sunt, uiuunt et intellegunt dominantem, Deum esse
non dubitet.[2]

IV.   INTERROGATIO, RESPONSIO*a*

IN.*b*   Tu qui*c* dicis te scire uelle*d* si Deus sit*e*, dic*f* mihi quid putas
        esse Deum*g*, si est.

RE.   Bonum quo nihil melius et potentiam*h* qua nihil potentius.[1]

IN.   Si inuenerimus*j* tale aliquid, quod ita sit bonum atque potens
       ut eo nihil melius nihilque potentius ualeat inueniri, dubit-
       abisne id Deum / esse*k*?[2]

RE.   Minime dubitabo.

IN.   Ergo adgrediamur*m*: aderit ille quem quaerimus. Primoque*n*
       omnium, dic*o* mihi si scias te esse et ex quibus constes.

RE.   Non solum me esse scio, sed etiam ex anima et corpore con-
       stare firmissime teneo.

IN.   Bene tenes. Sed num illos uulgatissimos corporis sensus
       habere te nosti?[3]

RE.   Et illos me habere noui.

IN.   Quid putas ad eorum officia pertinere?

III (*f*) *corrB adds* uult (*g*) *P om.* perpetuo (*h*) *B* scit (*j*) *B om.* permanere
     (2) Compare Passage IV *passim.*
IV   (Extracts in Grünwald, *Geschichte der Gottesbeweise*, pp. 18–24; *V* ff.95r–98r; *B* ff.42r–
     46r; *P* ff.44ra–45ra) (*a*) *so V; V*P* INTERROGATOR, RESPONSOR; *B*
     INTERROGATOR AC RESPONSOR (*b*) *P om.* IN (*c*) *P* quod (*d*) *P* uelle scire
     (*e*) *V** sct(*f*) *so BP; V* di (*g*) *P* Deum esse (*h*) *B* potentia (*j*) *P* inuerimus (*k*) *P* esse Deum
     (*m*) *B* adgrediamur ergo (*n*) *B* primo (*o*) *P* dic̄
     (1) cf. Augustine, *De libero arbitrio* II 54 (ed. cit., p. 51:20–1). 'Non enim mihi placet
     deum appellare quo mea ratio est inferior, sed quo est nullus superior.' (2) cf. ibid., I 74
     (ed. cit., p. 22:15–18): '*A* . . . Quare illud restat ut respondeas, si potest, utrum tibi
     uideatur rationali et sapienti mente quicquam esse praestantius. *E.* Nihil praeter deum
     arbitror.' (3) ibid., II 25 (ed. cit., p. 43:11–12).

RE. Quaecumque corporea.[4] Iamdudum enim didici[p] non alia per eos sensus quam corporea posse sentiri.

IN. Quid tibi melius uidetur atque potentius: quo sentit aliquid an quod[q] sentitur?

RE.[r] Longe melius est longeque[s] potentius quo sentitur aliquid quam illud sit quod sentit[t].

IN.[u] Vnde hoc accidere putas[v]?

RE.[w] Ex naturali rerum[x] ordine. Quia[y] quod sentit[z] est tantum, sed non uiuit: quo[a] autem sentitur non solum est sed etiam uiuit. Omne siquidem quod uiuit iure illi praeponitur quod non uiuit, quia quod non uiuit ab eo quod uiuit mouetur et regitur. / Semper ergo melius et potentius esse debet id quod regit illo[b] quod regitur.

IN.[c] Si melius et potentius est[d] id quod[e] *sentit*[f] illo quod[g] sentitur[h], meliores et potentiores sunt sensus tui, per quos sentis corporea, quam ipsa corporea[j] quae per eos sentiuntur.[5]

RE.[k] Vtique meliores atque potentiores.

IN.[m] Quid igitur: ipsos sensus, quando tam potentes sunt ut corporeas sentiant, putasne seipsos posse sentire et sua quemque[n] offitia discernere?[6]

RE. Nequaquam puto. Scio quippe illos habere sibi presidentem iudicem, interiorem uidelicet sensum,[7] ad cuius iudicium cuncta quae sentiunt referunt[o]. Qui, per eorum officia sensibilia cognoscens, de his prout potest opinando iudicat ipsorumque sensuum ministeria discriminat[p].

IN. Quid[q] de hoc sensu tibi uidetur? Num melior et potentior est his quibus praesidet?

RE. Melior omni*no*[r] atque potentior. Non solum enim de his quae per sensus[s] agnoscit, sed etiam de ipsis sensi-

IV   (p) *P* iam enim dudum didici (q) *P*★ quo (r) *P om.* RE (s) *P* lonque (t) *V*★*BP* sentitur (u) *P* RE (v) *P* accidet reputas; *P*★ accidit reputas (w) *P* IN (x) *B om.* rerum (y) *P om.* quia (z) *BP* sentitur (a) *P* quod (b) *B* quam illud (c) *P* RE (d) *B* Si melius est et potentius (e) *P* quo (f) *so B*; *VP* sentitur (g) *P* quo (h) *so P*; *VB* sentit (j) *P om.* quam ipsa corporea (k) *P* IN (m) *P om.* IN (n) *B* quaeque illorum (o) *B* referuntur (p) *V*★ discrinat (q) *B* quod (r) *so BP*; *V* omnium (s) *P* sensum

(4) ibid., (ll. 14–17) (5) cf. ibid., II 46–7 (ed. cit., p. 49:18–22): 'non te credo inventuram regulam qua fidere possimus omne sentiens melius esse quam id quod ab eo sentitur ... Hoc enim falsum est ...' (6) cf. ibid., II 26 (ed. cit., p. 44:8–10): 'Quid igitur ad quemque sensum pertineat et quid inter se vel omnes vel quidam eorum communiter habeant, num possumus ullo eorum sensu diiudicare?' (7) ibid. (l. 11): 'Nullo modo, sed quodam interiore ista diiudicantur.'

Appendix 1

bus eorum ministeria cognoscendo ac distinguendo iudicat. /

IN.   Quid[t] igitur: numquid[u] non hic sensus est ratio qua bestiae
carent?[8]

RE.   Minime. Nam ratione cognoscimus hunc sensum non esse
rationem, eumque bestiis aeque[v] ac nobis[w] inesse compre-
hendimus.[9] Hoc etenim sensu bestiae ea quae[x] per corporis
sensus capiunt, uel appetunt delectatae et adsumunt, uel
offensae deuitant et respuunt.[10] Ratio uero est illud principale
animi nostri, quo ueritatis compotes efficimur, quo scientiam
adipiscimur. Quicquid enim scimus, ratione comprehensum
tenemus.[11] Neque aliud est scire quam rei[y] cuiuslibet noticiam
per rationem in ueritatis luce[z] comprehendere. Ipsa autem[a]
ratio ita illi interiori sensui praeposita est, ut quaecumque per
corpus sensa[b] ac per ipsius officium ad eam delata fuerint,
facta secum rerum examinatione, absque falsitate diiudicet.[12]
Quae diiudicatio intellectus uocatur, quo in natura hominis
nihil melius aut potentius ualet inueniri.[13] Quia, sicut in
rerum naturis illud est praestantius quod uiuit quam illud
quod est[c] tantum et non uiuit, / sic illud quod intellegit longe[d]
prestantius est illi quod uiuit sed non intellegit. Et, si bene con-
sideres, tota rerum uniuersitas in haec tria genera diuiditur: in
hoc quod est, et quod uiuit, quodque intellegit[e].

IN.   Adsentior[f]; uideturque mihi sicut ratiocinando probatum est.
Si illud est in rerum natura melius atque potentius, quod
intellegit, quod[g] ratio[h], qua[j] quaelibet res intellegit[k], longe[m]
omnibus quae in rerum natura sunt antecellat.

RE.   Hoc mihi uerissimum esse uidetur.

IN.   Queso ergo te, si inuenerimus aliquid quod huic rationi multo

IV   (t) B★ quod (u) P num quod (v) so B; VP aequae (w) P in nobis (x) P aequae (y) P re
(z) P in luce ueritatis (a) V★om. autem (b) B sensu (c) In V est *is above line over an erasure*
(d) P om. sic . . . longe (e) so VPB★; corrB intellegitur(f) B assentio (g) V★ quo (h) corrB
adds est (j) corrB adds ratione (k) so VPB★; corrB intellegitur (m) B et omnibus
(8) 'Num . . . carent' = ibid., l. 12. (9) ibid., II 27 (ed. cit., p. 44:15–17). (10) ibid.,
(ll. 17–23): 'Namque aliud est quo uidet bestia et aliud quo ea quae uidendo
sentit uel uitat uel appetit. Ille enim sensus in oculis est, ille autem in ipsa intus anima,
quo non solum ea quae audiuntur quaeque ceteris capiuntur corporis sensibus, uel
adpetunt animalia delectata et adsumunt uel offensa deuitant et respuunt.' (11) 'Quicquid
. . . tenemus' = ibid., II 29 (p. 45:2–3) (12) cf. ibid., II 36 (ed. cit., p. 46:22–25) (13)
ibid., II 52 (ed. cit., p. 51:3–7): 'ea [natura] quae simul et est et uiuit et intellegit, sicut in
homine mens rationalis: num arbitrabis in nobis . . . aliquid inuenire posse praestantius
quam hoc quod in his tribus tertio loco posuimus?'

melius atque potentius dominetur quam ipsa ratio sibi subiectis sensibus[n], dubitabisne hoc Deum esse?[14]

RE.   Non equidem dubitauerim. Sed quomodo id inuenire possimus nondum uideo.

IN.[o]   Videbis, si tibi[p] adesse uolueris[q].

RE.[r]   Volo quidem et adsum.

IN.[s]   Vtere igitur ratione tua, et ipsius rationis uoluntatem atque potentiam diligenter intuere[t], et si aliquid sit quod ipsa ratio uelit, sed[u] efficere non possit[v], examina. Si enim hoc[w] inueneris, noueris oportet esse / potentiam quam ipsam rationem coerceat et omnipotentem fieri non permittat. Esset autem omnipotens, si quaecumque uellet posset efficere. Si uero uult aliquid, sed quod uult efficere non ualet, profecta potentia est, cui ita ipsa ratio subiecta est, ut non quaecumque cupit, sed quaecumque debet, ualeat efficere.

RE.[x]   Iam aduerto quo ista tendant, et ea uera esse confiteor. Vult siquidem anima, cuius optimum est ratio qua intellegit, in regimine sui corporis atque in amministratione[y] sensibilium perseuerare, sed lege[z] quadam atque potentia[a] ineffabili prohibente non sinitur[b]. Cogiturque tale[c] aliquid pati, quod non pateretur si posset quaecumque uellet[d].[15]

IN.[e]   Bene aduertisti. Num igitur, cum ratione, qua in rerum naturis nihil melius nihilque potentius, inuenire potuimus potentiam superiorem – inuenimus[f] ipsum quod a nobis inuentum est, optimo[g] melius, potentissimo potentius – dubitandum est Deum esse?

RE.   Nequaquam mihi uidetur de hoc dubitandum.[h]

IN.   Esse igitur credis, quod ita potens esse / confiteris?

RE.   Credo firmissime. Non enim posset si non esset.

IN.   Ergo confectum[j] est Deum esse.

RE.   Ita est.[k]

IV   (n) *corrB adds here* RESPONSOR (o) *corrB* RE (p) *P* si ubi (q) *P* uoluerit (r) *corrB* IN (s) *corrB* RE (t) *P* intuere diligenter (u) *V* se. (v) *P* non uelit possit (w) *B* haec (x) *corrB* IN (y) *P adds* sui corporis atque in amministratione (z) *P* legem (a) *P* potentiam (b) *P* sinetur (c) *P* talia (d) *B om.* cogiturque . . . uellet (e) *corrB* RE (f) *so VPB★*; corr.B inuenerimus (g) *P* op (h) *P om.* dubitandum (j) *so BP*; *V* confactum (k) *corrB adds* INT
(14) ibid., II 54 (ed. cit., p. 51:15–17): 'Qui si aliquid invenire potuerimus quod non solum esse non dubites, sed etiam ipsa nostra ratione praestantius, dubitabisne illud quidquid est deum dicere?' (15) cf. Alcuin *De animae ratione* (MPL 101, 644AB) '[anima] non habens in se potestatem exeundi de carne, et redeundi iterum in eam, sed ejus arbitrio qui fecit eam carnique immisit. Exiet enim, quamvis nolens, praesentandus judicio Dei.'

Appendix 1

V. VTRVM SECVNDVM TEMPVS AN SECVNDVM EXCELLENTIAM DEVS[a] ANTE TEMPORA

Non secundum tempus sed secundum excellentiam Deus ante tempora. Non enim secundum tempus ante tempora: alioquin incipit[b] tempore precedere tempora. Et non iam[e] praecedit tempora, quia[d] tempore illa praecedit.[1]

VI.   DE LOCO DEI[a]

Deus non alicubi est. Quod alicubi est continetur loco[b]; quod continetur loco corpus est. Deus autem non est corpus; non igitur alicubi[c] est. Et tamen quia est[d], in loco non est: in illo sunt potius omnia quam[e] ipse alicubi.[1]

VII.   DICTA ALBINI[a] DE IMAGINE DEI[b]

'Faciamus hominem ad imaginem et similitudinem nostram'.[1] Tanta dignitas humanae conditionis esse cognoscitur, ut non solo iubentis sermone, sicut alia sex dierum opera, sed consilio sancte Trinitatis et opere maiestatis diuinae creatus sit[e] homo.[2] / Vt ex primae conditionis honore intellegeret quantum deberet suo conditori, dum tantum in condicione[d] mox dignitatis priuilegium prestitit ei conditor: ut tanto ardentius amaret conditorem, quanto mirabilius se ab eo esse[e] conditum intellegeret. Nec ab hoc solum, quod consilio sanctae Trinitatis

V   (Hauréau no. 4; V f.98r; B ff.40r–v; P f.42va) (a) corrB adds est (b) corrB adds id est Deus (c) P ita (d) B qui.
   (1) Augustine Confessiones XI, 13, 16 (ed. cit., p. 274:20–3): 'Nec tu tempore tempora praecedis: alioquin non omnia tempora praecederes. sed praecedis omnia praeterita celsitudine semper praesentis aeternitatis et superas omnia futura . . .'

VI   (V f.98r; B f.40r) (a) Added on right of line with ref. sign (b) B loco continetur (c) V★ acubi (d) B adds et (e) corrB adds id est sit
   (1) entire passage = Augustine, De diuersis quaestionibus XX (CC 44A, p. 25).

VII   (For details of editions, see Chapter 2, n. 10; V ff.98r–100v; C ff.18v–19v; L ff.106v–107r; Pal ff.46v–49r; E among ff.1r–5v) (a) V★ ALIBI (b) LPal om. title (c) so LPal; V est (d) so LPal; L★ tantum in condieone; V tantum condicionem (e) L se habeo esse
   (1) = Genesis 1 26 (2) cf. Ambrose, Hexaemeron VI, vii, 40–1 (CSEL 32: pp. 231:5–233:14); Augustine, De Genesi ad litteram III, 19 (CSEL 28, pp. 85:16–86:4); Bede In Genesim I (CC 118A: p. 25:746–54); Alcuin, Adversus Felicem I 10 (MPL 101, 135D); and esp.? Alcuin, Interrogationes et responsiones in Genesim no. 36 (MPL 100, 520B): Inter. Quare de solo homine dictum est: Faciamus hominem; de aliis autem creaturis legitur: Dixit Deus? Resp. Vt videlicet, quae rationabilis creatura condebatur, cum consilio facta videretur, et ut ejus nobilitas ostenderetur.

sic excellenter a[f] Conditori conditus est, sed etiam quod ad imaginem et similitudinem suam ipse creator omnium eum creauit, quod nulli alii[g] ex creaturis donauit.

Quae imago diligentius[h] ex interioris hominis nobilitate est consideranda. Primo quidem, ut[i], sicuti Deus unus semper ubique totus est,[3] omnia uiuificans, mouens et gubernans (sicut Apostolus confirmat quod 'in eo uiuimus, mouemus et sumus'[4]), sic anima in suo corpore ubique tota uiget, uiuificans *illud*[j] mouens et gubernans. Nec enim in maioribus corporis sui membris maior et in minoribus minor, sed in minimis tota et in maximis tota.[5] Et haec est imago unitatis omnipotentis / Dei quam anima habet in se.

Quae quoque[k] qu*a*ndam[m] sanctae Trinitatis habet imaginem. Primo, in eo quia, sicut Deus est, uiuit et sapit, ita[n] anima secundum suum modum[o] est, uiuit et sapit.[6] Est quoque alia trinitas in ea, quae[p] ad imaginem sui conditoris, perfectae quidem et summe Trinitatis, quae est in[q] Patre, Filio et Spiritu Sancto, condita est.[r] Et licet unius sit illa naturae, tres tamen in se dignitates habet[s], id est, intellectum, uoluntatem, memoriam.[7] Quod idem, licet aliis uerbis, in Euangelio designatur dum dicitur: 'Diligis[t] dominum Deum tuum ex toto corde tuo et ex tota anima tua et ex tota mente[u] tua'[8], id est ex toto intellectu et ex tota uoluntate et ex tota memoria.[9] Iam, sicut ex Patre generatur Filius, ex Patre Filioque procedit Spiritus Sanctus, ita ex intellectu generatur uoluntas et ex his item ambobus[v] procedit memoria, sicut facile a quolibet intelligi potest. Nec enim anima[w]

VII   (*f*) *V has an erasure after* a (*g*) *so* LPal; *V* alio (*h*) *C begins here thus:* Imago ergo Dei (*i*) LPal quod (*j*) *V* eum (*k*) *In C* quoque *is expunctuated* (*m*) *VL* quondam (*n*) *C* ita et anima (*o*) *V has an erasure after* modum (*p*) *E begins here thus:* Est anima imago et similitudo Dei, non tamen pars Dei, quia ad imaginem ... (*q*) LPal ex (*r*) *C om.* est (*s*) *E habet* dignitates (*t*) *so* VLPalE; *C* (*following Vulgate*) diliges (*u*) *E* menta (*v*) *E* ambobis (*w*) *E* animam (3) *cf.* Passage I, p. 152 above; *for the history of this phrase, see* M. Frickel, *Deus totus ubique simul* (Freiburg, 1956) (4) *Actus* XVII 28 (5) Claudianus Mamertus, *De statu animae* III 2 (ed. cit., p. 155:9–13): 'sicut deus ubique totus in uniuersitate, ita haec [*sc.* anima] ubique tota inuenitur in corpore, et sicut deus nequaquam minore sui parte minorem mundi partem replet, maiore maiorem, sed totus in parte, totus in toto est, ita et haec non pro parte sui est in parte corporis.'; *and cf.* Augustine, *De Trinitate* VI, vi, 8 (ed. cit., p. 237:20–25), *De immortalitate animae* xvi (*MPL* 32, 1034), *Contra epistolam Manichaei* xvi (*MPL* 42, 185); *and cf.* Alcuin *De animae ratione* viii (*MPL* 101, 643 A) *and* ibid. 10 (644 A) (6) Cf. Passages III, p. 153 *and* IV, pp. 155ff. above (7) *cf.* Augustine, *De Trinitate* x, xi, 17 (ed. cit., p. 329:1ff.) *and Contra sermonem Arianorum* xvi (*MPL* 42, 695–6); *and* Alcuin, *De animae ratione* (*MPL* 101, 641C) (8) *Matthaeus* XXII, 37 (9) *cf.* Claudianus Mamertus, op. cit. II 5 (ed. cit., pp. 117:18–118:10, esp. p. 118:5–10); *and* Alcuin *De virtutibus et vitiis* iii (*MPL* 101, 615D): 'Quod uero ait: "Ex toto corde ... mente", id est, toto intellectu, tota uoluntate et ex omni memoria Deum esse diligendum'.

perfecta potest esse[x] sine his tribus, nec horum trium / unum aliquod, quantum ad suam pertinet beatitudinem, sine aliis[y] duobus integrum constat. Et sicut Deus Pater, Deus Filius[z], Deus Spiritus Sanctus est, non tamen tres dii[a] sunt sed unus Deus tres habens personas, ita et anima intellectus, anima uoluntas, anima memoria, non tamen *animae*[b] tres in uno corpore sed una anima tres habens dignitates.[10] Atque in his tribus eius imaginem mirabiliter gerit in sua natura noster[c] interior homo.[d] Ex quibus, quasi[e] excellentioribus animae[f] dignitatibus, iubemur diligere conditorem, ut quantum intellegatur, diligatur, et quantum diligatur[g], semper in memoria habeatur.[11] Nec solus sufficit de eo intellectus, nisi fiat in amore eius uoluntas. Immo nec haec duo sufficiunt, nisi memoria addatur, qua semper in mente intellegentis et diligentis maneat Deus.[h] Vt, sicut nullum potest esse[j] momentum quo homo non utatur uel fruatur Dei bonitate et misericordia[k], ita nullum debeat esse[m] momentum / quo presentem eum[n] non habeat memoria[o]. Et haec de imagine habeto.

Nunc uero de similitudine aliqua intellege, quae[p] in moribus cernenda est.[q][12] Vt sicut Deus[r] creator, qui hominem ad similitudinem suam creauit, est caritas, est bonus[s] et iustus, paciens atque mitis, mundus et misericors, et cetera uirtutum sanctarum insignia quae de Deo[t] leguntur, ita homo creatus est ut caritatem haberet[u], ut[v] bonus esset[w] et iustus, ut patiens atque mitis, mundus et misericors[x] foret. Quas[y] uirtutes, quanto plus quisque in seipso habet, tanto proprius[z] est Deo, et maiorem sui conditoris gerit similitudinem[a].[13] Si uero

VII (x) C perfecta esse potest (y) E aliis his duobus (z) E Deus Filius est (a) C di (b) so CLPalE; V om. animae (c) E natura naturaliter (d) C *breaks off temporarily here* (e) E ceu (f) E om. animae (g) E *adds* eo amplior sit voluntas eum diligendi, et quanto maiori voluntate diligatur, eo magis (h) E om. Nec solus . . . maneat Deus *and adds* ita dumtaxat (j) E fore (k) V mã (m) E esse debet (n) E Deum (o) E habeat in memoria (p) E om. Et haec . . . quae *and adds* Similitudo in memoria (q) C *recommences thus* Similitudo uero in moribus cernenda est . . . (r) V* om. Deus (s) C bonitas (t) E eo (u) E ut haberet caritatem (v) C et; E om. ut (w) E esset bonus (x) E *finishes here* (y) V qua (z) V* prous (a) C *finishes here*

(10) Augustine, *De Trinitate* x, xi, 18 (ed. cit., p. 330:29–31): 'Haec igitur tria, memoria, intellegentia, uoluntas, quoniam non sunt tres uitae sed una uita, nec tres mentes, sed una mens, consequenter utique nec tres substantiae sed una substantia.'; and Alcuin, *De animae ratione* (MPL 101, 641CD) (11) cf. Alcuin, ibid., 639B: 'Quantum enim quisque Deum agnoscit, in tantum diligit; qui minus agnoscit, minus diligit.' (12) Gennadius of Marseilles, *Liber ecclesiasticorum dogmatum* 54 (ed. C. H. Turner, *Journal of Theological Studies*, 7, 1906, p. 99): 'libere confitemur imaginem in aeternitate, similitudinem in moribus inueniri.' (13) cf. Alcuin, *De animae ratione* 9 (MPL 101, 643BC): 'Beatitudo scilicet animae est Deum habere in se. Quomodo habere? id est, justam esse, quia Deus justus est; et misericordem esse, quia Deus misericors est; et bonam esse, quia Deus bonus est; et sanctam esse, quia Deus sanctus est; et charitatem habere, quia 'Deus

(quod absit!) aliquis per deuia uiciorum et diuorcio criminum ab hac nobilissima sui conditoris similitudine degener oberrat, tunc fiet de eo quod scriptum est: 'Et homo, cum in honore esset, non intellexit, comparatus est iumentis insipientibus: similis factus est illis'.[14]

Quae[b] maior honor potuit homini[c] esse, quam ad similitudinem sui factoris conderetur, et eisdem uirtutis uestimentis / ornaretur quibus et conditor, de quo legitur: 'Dominus regnauit decore indutus',[15] id est omnium uirtutum splendore et totius bonitatis decore ornatus? Vel quod maius hominis potest esse dedecus aut infelicior miseria, quam ut, hac similitudine gloria sui conditoris amissa, ad informem et inrationabilem brutorum iumentorum delabatur similitudinem?

Quapropter, quisque diligentius attendat primae conditionis suae excellentiam, et uenerandam sanctae Trinitatis in seipso imaginem agnoscat, honoremque similitudinis diuinae, ad[d] quem creatus est, nobilitate morum, exercitio[e] uirtutum, dignitate meritorum habere contendat. Vt, quando appareat, qualis sit, tunc similis ei appareat[f], qui se mirabiliter ad similitudinem suam in primo Adam condidit, mirabiliusque in secundo reformauit.

VIII. DICTA CANDIDI PRESBITERI DE IMAGINE DEI[a]

Iuste mihi uidetur dictum interiorem hominem imaginem esse Dei[b]. Anima enim nominatur totus interior homo, qua[c] uiuificatur, regitur, / continetur lutea illa massa humectata sucis[d], ne arefacta[e] dissoluatur[f]. Deus dicitur uis illa ineffabiliter magna et innumerabiliter sapiens et incomparabiliter suauis[g], ex qua et per quam et qua sunt[h] omnia quae

VII (b) *so VLPal* (c) *V* * *homine* (d) *VL at* (e) *L* exaercitio; *Pal* execratio (!) (f) *L* * *om.* qualis . . . appareat; *in L this passage is added in the hand of Leidrad in the bottom margin with a reference sign to its correct position.*

charitas est'. Qui plurimum haec in se habet, majorem in se similitudinem Dei habet et imaginem . . .'; and cf. Ambrose, *De fuga saeculi* 4, 17 (*MPL* 14, 578C): 'Hoc est igitur similem esse Dei, habere justitiam, habere sapientiam, et in virtute esse perfectum. Deus enim est sine peccato. Et ideo, qui peccatum fugit, ad imaginem est Dei'; and Ambrose, *De bono mortis* 5, 17 (*MPL* 14, 548 CD); and Leo the Great *Sermo* 20, 2 (*MPL* 54, 189C) (14) *Psalmus* XLIX 12; cf. Augustine, *De Trinitate* XII, xi, 16 (ed. cit., p. 370:1ff., esp. ll.13–15) and Claudianus Mamertus, op. cit. I 24 (ed. cit., p. 85:15–18) and Alcuin, *De animae ratione* (*MPL* 101, 643D) (15) *Psalmus* XCIII 1.

VIII (Hauréau no. 1; *V*ff.100v–102v; *B*ff.33r–35v; *P*ff.41vb–42va; *W* ff.33v–34v) (a) *W om.* title; *B* ITEM EIVSDEM DE IMAGINE DEI (b) *P* imaginem Dei esse (c) *P* quia (d) *W om.* sucis (e) *lacuna in P between* ne *and* arefacta (f) *B* * disoluator (g) *P om.* incomparabiliter suauis (h) *For* ex . . . sunt *P has* et insunt

sunt.[j1] Omnia dico ipsam uniuersitatem, quae est totum, quod aliud est quam[k] ipse qui[m] fecit et non est[n] factus. Sed ipse est[o] ex quo, et qui ex eo, et quo: quod ipse Deus ex quo est 'Pater' dicitur a nobis, pauperibus sensu pauperioribus uerbis[p]; quod qui ex eo 'Filius' dicitur; quod quo 'Spiritus Sanctus'. Ideo[q] autem dicitur Deus 'Pater', quia ipse est[r] ex quo, et[s] Sapientia est qua[t] ordinantur omnia, et Dilectio qua se uolunt omnia ita manere ut ordinata sunt. Ex quo ergo, et qui ex eo, et quo se diligunt. Ipsa duo tria sunt, et illa tria ideo unum; quia sic sunt ex uno illa duo, ut tamen ab[u] ipso[v] non sint separata, sed et ex ipso sunt, quia non a se, et in ipso, quia non separata. Et ipsum ipsa quod ipse; et ipsum ipse quod ipsa; / et non ipsa ipsa qui ipse[w], et non ipsa ipse[x] quae ipsa. Vis ista Deus est, et ipse Deus tria est[y]. Et unumquodque[z] horum trium Deus est, et omnia tria illa[a] non dii sed Deus est.

Ad imaginem ergo suam conditor fecit animam hominis, quae tota dicitur anima. Non autem aliud significo hominis quam animam, cum mentem[b2] dico; sed propter aliud animam, et propter aliud[c] mentem. Nam totum quod uiuit hominis anima est; cum autem anima[d] in se agit se et ex se et per se solam, mens dici solet.[e] Sensus uero, ad[f] sua ministeria implens, consuetius[g] anima dicitur. Mens ergo[h] scire gignit[3] et amat scire quod scit.[4] Non illud scire dico quod repente scitur res aliqua quae ante[j] nesciri putebatur, sed illud unde et aliquid et[k] omne quicquid scitur uel nescitur sciri potest. Illud ergo scire mens gignit et, cum genitum est, scientia[m] potest dici[n]. Sunt ergo iam duo: mens et quod ipsa mens scit. Restat tertium utrisque commune. Omnis mens, quicquid scit[o], amat scire. Amor non minus / quam inter duos[p] est[q] – amantem et quod amatur: unus est ergo

VIII   (*j*) *B adds* reguntur omnia quae sunt, continentur omnia quae sunt (*k*) *B* quia (*m*) *V*★ *om·* qui (*n*) *P om.* est (*o*) *V*★ e (*p*) *P adds* uerbum (*q*) *P* inde (*r*) *V*★ e (*s*) *B om.* et (*t*) *P* quia (*u*) *P* ut tamen ut ab (*v*) *B om.* ab ipso (*w*) *P* quia sae (*x*) *P* ipsae (*y*) *V*★ e (*z*) *B* unum quod (*a*) *P W* illa tria (*b*) *V* mente; *B* dico mentem (*c*) *B* propter illud (*d*) *B om.* anima (*e*) *B* solet dici (*f*) *B om.* ad (*g*) *P* consuetiuus (*h*) *B* sensus uero (*j*) *B* autem (*k*) *W adds and then deletes an* et (*m*) *B above line* uel m (*n*) *W* dici potest (*o*) *V*★ *om.* scit (*p*) *W* duo *with superscript* s (*q*) *V*★ e

(1) cf. *Libri Carolini* IV 13 (*MGH Legum* sec. III: *Concilia* II, suppl.: p. 194:14): 'Deus ex quo omnia, per quem omnia, in quo omnia, dicente Apostolo: "Quoniam ex ipso et per ipsum et in ipso sunt omnia."' (2) cf. Alcuin, *De animae ratione* 5 (*MPL* 101, 641A): 'Est quoque anima imagine et similitudine sui conditoris in principali sui parte, quae mens dicitur, excellenter nobilitata' (3) cf. Augustine, *De Trinitate* IX, viii, 13; IX, xii, 17; XIV, vi, 8 (ed. cit., pp. 304:12–305:14; 308:2–3; 432:50–54) (4) cf. ibid., IX, iii, 3–iv, 7 (ed. cit., pp. 295:1ff., esp. p. 297:1–5)

amborum amor^r qui et tertius est^s.[5] Non autem potest^t negari hoc totum unam^u esse animam, et unam animam haec tria esse; sicut enim haec tria uere una anima sunt^v, sic non minus^w uere una anima est hoc unum et hoc alterum et hoc tertium.[4]

Comparet igitur se haec creatura tam eminens creatori suo supereminenti sibi (excepto hoc, et multum supra^x se amoto, quod omnis bonitas et omne bonum et omnis bonit*atis*^{y} et boni dulcedo creatori a seipso est: creaturae uero non solum quod est, sed etiam quod talis est, ab alio est non a se. Et ipse quod est semper est[6] – licet et ipsa anima quodam modo suo^y* incommutabilis est, nam^z semper^a anima est, et scit et scire uult.) Conparet ergo, ut dixi, se anima eo modo quo potest creatori suo^b. Dicatur 'mens'^{c} Pater, quia gignit scire; dicatur 'scire' Filius, quia ex alio est, et non est aliud quam^d ipsum quod ipse est, ex quo est; dicatur 'amor' Spiritus sanctus, quia amborum est eorum qui se amant.[7] Vnde in nostris Scripturis saepius 'amor', id est caritas quae in Deo est erga nos et quae a nobis est in Deum, Spiritus ipse^e appellatur^f.

IX.   PROPTER QVID^a HOMO FACTVS EST

Factus^b scilicet ad se et Deum cognoscendum; quia^c aliter beatus esse non potest nisi se ac bonum suum agnouerit.^{d} Bonum autem hominis non aliud quam Deus est.[1] Deum uero cognoscere sine sui cognitione

VIII   (r) *W adds and then deletes an* et (s) *P om.* unus . . . tertius est (t) *P has a space of about three letters after* negari (u) *W*★ unum (v) *For* una anima sunt, *P has* una amans (w) *B om.* minus (x) *B super* (y) *so B; V W P* bonitas (y★) *W*★ sua (z) *W* nan (a) *P om.* semper (b) *V has* potest creatori suo *above an erasure* (c) *B om.* mens (d) *B* quia (e) *B om.* ipse (f) *P* appellatus.

    (5) *ibid.*, VIII, x, 14 (ed. cit., pp. 290:2–291:6): 'Amor autem alicuius amantis est, et amore aliquid amatur. Ecce tria sunt, amans et quod amatur et amor. Quid est ergo amor nisi quaedam uita duo aliqua copulans uel copulari appetens, amantem scilicet et quod amatur?' (6) cf. Boethius, *De Trinitate* IV (ed. Rand, p. 18:31–6): 'Sed distat, quoniam homo non integre ipsum homo est ac per hoc nec substantia; quod enim est, aliis debet quae non sunt homo. Deus uero hoc ipsum deus est; nihil enim aliud est nisi quod est, ac per hoc ipsum deus est.' (7) cf. Augustine, *De Trinitate* IX, xii, 18 (ed. cit., p. 310:75–80): 'Et est quaedam imago trinitatis, ipsa mens et notitia eius, quod est proles eius ac de se ipsa uerbum eius, et amor tertius, et haec tria unum atque una substantia. Nec minor proles dum tantam se nouit mens quanta est, nec minor amor dum tantum se diligit quantum nouit et quanta est.'

IX   (Hauréau no. 9; *V* f.102v; *B* f.46v; *P* f.42 vb) (a) *V*★ QVOD; *B om.* QVID; *corrB* QVOD (b) *B adds* est (c) *V* qui (d) *B* cognouerit

    (1) cf. Augustine, *De libero arbitrio* III 128 (ed. cit., p. 121:11–12): 'omne bonum aut deus aut ex deo'.

non potest. Sicut enim qui non amat imaginem Dei, Deum non amare conuincitur, sic, qui non agnoscit imaginem Dei, Deum utique non agnoscere probatur. Cognito autem Dei uita aeterna est, sicut ipse Dominus in Euangelio: 'Haec est', ait, 'uita aeterna, ut cognoscant[e] te[f] solum uerum Deum et quem misisti[g] Iesum Christum.'[2]

X. QVEMADMODVM PROBARI POSSIT ANIMAM[a] ESSE
INLOCALE[b]

Quae superius 'esse', 'nosse' atque 'amare' nuncupaui, 'memoriam', 'consilium' et 'uoluntatem'[c] non incongrue appellare possum; quia non est aliud memoria quam ipsa mentis[d] essentia, nec aliud consilium quam notio uel sapientia, nec uoluntas aliud / quam amor.[1] Dicat qui uelit si memoriam, consilium et uoluntatem putet esse corporea aut corporeo receptaculo posse concludi. Verbi gratia, ut utre, sacco, olla uel pyxide, uel alio quolibet uase, quo aer uel aqua uel quodlibet[e] corporeum contineri[f] potest. Quod[g] si illa corporea non esse, neque huiusmodi receptaculis, id est corporeis, includi posse concesserit, concedat necesse est, neque localia esse neque localibus contineri receptaculis. Quia idem est[h] locale quod corporeum, idemque corporeum quod locale. Omne quippe corpus in loco et omnis locus in corpore; et ideo omne locale corporeum esse conuincitur. Quod si memoria, consilium et uoluntas incorporea, proindeque inlocalia sunt[j]. Anima, quae his tribus constat, ut una anima sit, utique inlocalis est.

XI. SI[a] POSSIT VERVM ESSE SINE VERITATE[1]

Potestne aliquid uerum esse sine ueritate? Estne corpus uerum annon?[2] Si uerum est, ueritate uerum est. Ergo corpus ueritatis capax[b] est.

IX (e) *V* cognoscat (f) *P omits* te (g) *V*★ misti
(2) *Johannes* XVII, 3.
X (Hauréau no. 11; *V* f.102v–103r; *P* f.43ra–b) (a) *P om.* ANIMAM (b) PINLOCALI-
TER (c) *In V* –riam . . . uo- *is written above an erasure* (d) *P* menti (e) *V* quolibet (f) *P*
continere (g) *V*★ Quo (h) *P* i. (= id est) (j) *P* sit.
(1) cf. Augustine, *De Trinitate* XIV, vi, 8 (ed. cit., p. 432:34–54).
XI (Hauréau no. 3; *V* ff.103r–v; *P* f.42rb–va) (a) *V*★ *om.* SI (b) *V*★ pax
(1) Augustine, *Soliloquia* II 15 (*MPL* 32, 898): 'Nihil autem uerum sit sine ueritate'
(2) ibid., II 17 (*MPL* 32, 900): 'R. Opinor ergo, ueritatem corpus esse aliquod credis.
A. Nullo modo.'

Potestne corpus aliud / aliquid capere preter corpus? Si corpus ueritatis capax est, ergo ueritas corpus est. Deus ueritas est, ergo Deus corpus est. Nihil uerum nisi immortale; nec capit ueritatem, nisi quod uerum est. Corpus igitur non est immortale, ac perinde nec uerum.[3] Ergo non est capax ueritatis. Si corpus non capit ueritatem, ergo ueritas non est corpus.[e] /

XII.   QVOMODO QVIDQVE[a] SIT

Omne quod est, aut in seipso[b] est, aut subiectum, aut in subiecto. In seipso[c] est Deus; subiectum est in rebus incorporeis animus; in subiecto sapientia. In corporeis uero subiectum est corpus, et color corporis in subiecto.[1]

XIII.   QVID SIT SVBSTANTIA[a]

[b]Substantia est quod[c] neque in subiecto est neque de subiecto praedicatur. Substantia est Plato uel Cicero. In subiecto est caluus uel crispus. De subiecto praedicatio est, ut scribit uel disputat. Et ideo substantia non est in subiecto, neque de subiecto, sed potius subiectum, quia in illa sunt alia, non illa in aliis uel de aliis.[1]

XI   (c) *In V there follows (f.103v–104r)* SANCTI AVGVSTINI EX LIBRO SOLILOQVIORVM (= MPL *32, 886: Si manebit semper mundus iste ... Nullo modo igitur occidit ueritas*)
     (3) cf. ibid. (MPL *32, 901*): 'Nam si et in corpore, quod satis certum est recipere interitum, tale uerum inuenerimus, quale est in disciplinis, non continuo erit disputandi disciplina veritas, qua omnes verae sunt disciplinae.'
XII (Hauréau no. 5; *V* f.104r; *B* f.39v; *P* f.42va) (a) *P* QVIDQVID; *B* QVID (b) *B* semetipso (c) *V** ipso
     (1) Claudianus Mamertus, op. cit., III 3 (ed. cit., p. 157:14–17): 'omne quod est, ut breuiter dicamus, aut in se aut subiectum aut in subiecto est. in se est deus, in rebus corporalibus subiectum est corpus et color corporis in subiecto, in incorporeis animus et disciplina ...'
XIII (Hauréau no. 6; *V* f.104r; *B* ff.39r–v; *P* f.42va) (a) *B* DE SVBSTANTIA (b) *B adds* Quid est substantia? (c) *P* quae
     (1) cf. Boethius, *In Categorias Aristotelis* I (MPL *64*, 182D): 'Recte igitur quod prius subjectum est, hoc substantia principaliter appellatur. Maxime autem substantia prima dicitur, idcirco quod quae maxime subjecta est rebus aliis, ea maxime substantia dici potest: maxime autem subjecta est prima substantia; omnia enim de primis substantiis dicuntur, aut primis substantiis insunt ...; and cf. *Categoriae*, trsl. Boethius v (ed. Minio-Paluello, p. 7:10–12): 'Substantia autem est, quae proprie et principaliter et maxime dicitur, quae neque de subiecto praedicatur neque in subiecto est, ut aliqui homo vel aliqui equus'; and cf. Cassiodore, *Institutiones* II, iii, 10 (ed. Mynors, p. 113: 20–3).

Appendix 1

XIV.   DE LOCO

Locus est incorporea capacitas qua extremitates corporum ambiuntur et qua corpus a corpore seiungitur.[1]

XV.   DE TEMPORE

/Tempus est cuiuscumque*a* motus, ex quo incipit usque*b* finem sine interuallo, protractio.*c* Motus uero *tam*^d incorporearum quam corporearum rerum est, quo tempus efficitur.[1] Incorporearum, sicut est animorum*e* in cogitando; corporearum*f* autem, in translatione et circumlatione. Translatione, ut de loco in*g* locum; circumlatione*h*: uolubilitas mundi.

TEXTS FROM MÜNCHEN CLM 18961

A.   ITEM EIVSDEM

Tria ergo sunt a creatura in una deitate intelligenda: qui dat, et per quem dat, et quod datur. Dat Deus per Verbum agnitionem sui, et agniti dilectionem. Scit ipse se et diligit se, sed haec in se agit. Totus Deus fecit creaturam se scire et diligere; sed haec iam sunt quasi Verbum Dei genitum et dilectio procedens: quod tamen Verbum etiam genitum in genitore manet, et dilectio ibi, unde semper procedit, semper inesse non desinit.[1]

XIV   (Hauréau no. 7; *V* f.104r; *B* f.39v; *P* f.42va–b)
      (1) cf. *Categoriae Decem* 78 (ed. Minio-Paluello, p. 150:16–17): 'Locus . . . corpus quodcumque circumdat et corporis partibus occupatur . . .'

XV   (Hauréau no. 8; *V* ff.104r–v; *B* ff.39v–40r; *P* f.42vb) (*a*) *P adds* est (*b*) *B adds* ad (*c*) *P* protracto; *B interualli* protractione (*d*) *V omits* tam (*e*) *corr B adds* id est tempus rei (*f*) *P* corperearum (*g*) *B* ad (*h*) *B adds* ut est
      (1) cf. ibid., 73 (ed. cit., p. 149:18–21): 'Tempus quoque mensurae subicitur; nam cum movetur aliquid, ipso motu necesse est et temporis habere mensuram cum dicimus "primo" vel "secundo" vel "tertio anno pervenit", et "mense" vel "die" vel "hora" vel "momento".'

A   (Ineichen-Eder no. 10)
      (1) Cf. *dicta Candidi* (no. VIII), above pp. 161–3.

B. ITEM EIVSDEM

... Nulla unitas est in qua trinitas ⟨*non*[a]⟩ inueniatur./ Unitas numeri sic trina inueniatur, quia ex ipsa numerare incipimus, per ipsum numeramus, in ipsa numerum finimus. Et est ipsum quod in numeris dicitur 'unum' – sicut quidam sapiens dixit – Dei uestigium humanae menti impressum, per quod a[b] diligenter considerantibus Deum esse intelligi potest. Deus uero ita unus est ut in eo perfectissima Trinitas inueniatur: Pater et Filius et Spiritus Sanctus. In rebus corporeis trinitas est altitudo, longitudo, latitudo. In corporeis iterum prefatus numerus, mensura et pondus. Corporea sunt quattuor elementa: ignis, aer, aqua et terra; et omnia que ex[c] eis consistant. Et haec ex nihilo facta sunt. Incorporea sunt ea quae spiritualia dicuntur, ut sunt angelici spiritus et humanae animae / et quae ex anima procedunt – amor, memoria, cogitatio – et creator omnium.

C. ARGVMENTVM CVIVSDAM PLATONICI DE MVNDI OPIFICE INVENIENDO

Mundus ordinatissime compositus est. Ordo autem sine armonia esse non potest. Armonia demum analogie comes est. Analogia item cum ratione, at ratio comes indiuidua prouidentiae. Prouidentia uero nulla sine intellectu; neque intellectus sine / mente.[1] Mens ergo Dei, quae sola uere intelligens est, prouida dicitur.[2] Rationabiliter elimentorum congruentias coaptando huius immensi corporis, quod mundus sensibilis dicitur, composuit.

D. INTERPRETATIO ARMONIE ET ANALOGIAE

'Armonia' grece, latine 'modulata coniunctio' dicitur;[1] quae interuallorum quae ordinantur rerum, per numeros quantitate comprae-

---

B (Ineichen-Eder no. 11 – extract) (*a*) *ms. omits* non (*b*) *ms.* ā (*c*) ex *corrected from* in.
C (Ineichen-Eder no. 14)
    (1) *Ordo* . . . *mente* = Calcidius, *Commentarius in Timaeum* II, 304 (ed. J. Waszynk (revised edn), London, 1975), pp. 305:21–306:2. (2) cf. ibid., II, 268 (ed. cit., p. 273:11): 'prouida mens dei . . .'
D (Ineichen-Eder no. 15)
    (1) cf. *Glossarium* '*Abstrusa*' (*Glossaria Latina* III (Paris, 1926), p. 12, AR 35): 'armonia: ex multis vocabulis (vocibus?) modulatio apta'.

hensa, conuenienta quaeque coaptat et coniungit. Sine qua nullum esse ordinem ratio manifestissima demonstrat. 'Analogia' grece, latine 'proportio' dicitur;[2] quae extremitates uel terminos rerum coniungendarum, rata dimensione comparando, considerat. Ipse autem ordo, qui per haec duo constare dinoscitur, nihil aliud / esse uidetur quam rerum suis locis positarum apta et rationi conueniens dispositio.[3] Rationem autem his esse coniunctam, uel potius haec ex ratione procedere, ipsa quae de his fit ratiocinatio declarat. Prouidentiam uero rationi esse coniunctam cuilibet facile patet, qui se considerare uult, ratione non uti, nisi cum motu prouidentiae fuerit excitatus. Prouidentiam uero sine intellectu non esse manifestius est quam ut expositione indigeat. Similiter et caetera.

TEXTS FROM BRITISH LIBRARY HARLEY 3034

DESCRIPTION

1. f.1r–10r   'De ecclesia Esedoris' (extracts from Isidore *Etymologiae* VIII and *De Officiis* I).*
2. f.10v–58r   Augustine *Enchiridion*.
3. f.58r–61r   'PRAEDICATIO DE NATALI DOMINI', incip. 'Scire debetis fratres dilectissimi . . .'
4. f.61r–63r   Sermon. Incip. 'Fratres mei, sciendum est nobis . . .'
5. f.63r–65v   Sermon. Incip. 'Audite fratres uerba domini et intellegite . . .'
6. f.65v–66v   Passage on the number three. (Text in full below.)
7. f.66v   (in a s. xii hand) *probatio pennae* in Old High German; cf. H. Thoma, 'Altdeutsches aus Londoner Handschriften', *Beiträge zur Geschichte der deutschen Sprache und Literatur*, 73, 1951, pp. 197–271; especially pp. 265–7).
8. f.66v–96v   Account of the Passion. Incip. 'Notum est nobis . . .' (= Candidus *De Passione Domini* – MPL 106, 58–102).
9. f.96v   'Benediccio Palmarum'.

   * I owe the identification of this piece to the article of Thoma's cited in 7.

TEXT OF 6

Omnia tribus constant: esse, posse, uelle; sed de esse sunt posse et uelle: unum horum gignitur, alterum procedit ex ambobus. Quia

D   (2) cf. Isidore *Etymologiae* I, 28, I (ed. W. M. Lindsay (Oxford, 1911)): 'Analogia Graece, Latine similium conparatio sive proportio nominatur'. (3) cf. Augustine, *De musica* VI, 17, 57 (*MPL* 32, 1192): 'Unde corrationalitas quaedam (ita enim malui analogiam vocare), ut quam rationem habet longitudo ad impertilem notam, eamdem latitudo ad longitudinem et ad latitudinem habeat altitudo?'

ideo uult quisque quia est et potest. Nam posse semper natum est: semel enim potens, semper posse. Quicquid immutabile est non desinit. Velle autem semper quidem in mutabili*a* est. Sed, quoties hoc sit quod uolitur, procedit, et in sensibilibus quidem facilis intellectus est. Si quis uero forte scire cupiat in insensibilibus, quomodo ibi posse uel uelle dicendum sit – nam de esse forte non dubitet – sciat potestatem*b*, utputa arboris huius dicere, quod inde possit hoc uel illud fieri etiam si non / fiat; uelle, quod cedit adoperanti, id est facilem se praebet ad opus. Nam cum uideo arborem, statim sentio uel a me uel ab*c* aliquo sciri quod inde possit – uerbi gratia, uirga fieri manualis. Cum uero mihi incipienti succidere cedit ad hoc quod uolo, quoddam eius uelle est; sicut et cum non cedit, id est cum hoc non fit quod uolo, quasi nolle est. Sed eius posse et uelle alius utitur nimirum, quia omnia quae facta sunt, sicut omnia inrationabilia, propter hominem; homo uero et angeli propter Deum.

Item omnia constant*d* tribus: principio, medio, fine. Principium est unum, medium duo, finis*e* tres. Ab uno per medium ad finem perue- nitur. Vnum ideo medium non est, quia non habet principium ante se a quo per se ueniatur ad finem. Duo ideo finis non est, quia non habet medium alterum per quod ueniatur ad se. Tertium ideo medium non est, quia non habet in illa prima trina perfectione alterum finem ad quem per se ueniatur. Ergo et medium, id est duo, principium est, quia et medio caret et fine. Finis enim, ut dixi, est ad quem per medium uenitur. Non tamen sic dico duo principium esse ut duo principia dicam. Si enim et alterum unum ponerem, duo principia essent. Nunc autem, cum duo dicam, illud ipsum primum unum facio gignere. Et, cum gignit, ipsum quod gignitur idem est quod est hoc quod genuit. Quid enim est duo nisi unum et quod ex uno est? Duo igitur sunt unum et quod ex uno.¹ Tres quid sunt nisi tria unum et unum tria? Et hoc ideo principium quia prima perfectio est ex uno et duobus ueniens: unum primum*f* gignens, duo primo*g* genitus, tres prima perfectio gignentis et geniti.

Ideo non solum unum, quia non esset gignens nisi generaret. Ideo non sola duo, quia non aliter fieri potest nisi unum et duo aliquid sint.

(a) *ih* inmutabili (*a* means 'a' expunctuated, etc.) (b) potestatem *the* (c) ab *written above the line* (d) constat *with* n *added* (e) fines *corrected to* finis (f) primu*s with abbreviation for* m *added* (g) primi*s with* o *added*

(1) For *Item omnia constant* up to here, cf. Augustine, *De musica* I 12 (*MPL* 32, 1095–7)

Sunt ergo tria. Non sunt autem tria nisi iungas unum et duo. Nam unum per se et duo per se non sunt tria; si iungis, tria sunt. Et ipsa eorum iunctio, quasi amor quidam, facit / ea duo secum tria esse. Fitque mirabiliter: si in unum sunt, tria sunt; si tria diuisa sunt, non sunt tria. Et, si sic dici queat[h], si unum sunt, tria sunt; si tres sunt, tria non sunt. Unum enim, cum gignit ipsum quod est, gignit duo. Autem[i] considera quid sint, scilicet duo unum aequalia. Non potest hoc unum plus unum esse quam illud unum. Aequalis ergo[j] potentiae duo unum sunt. Vide ergo quod omnis perfectio trinitas est, immo haec sola: primo, medio, fine stare omnia. Et primum non esse sine medio et fine; et medium non esse sine primo et fine[k], et finem[m] non esse sine primo et medio. Et uno dicto, omnia dicta; et omnibus dictis, unam perfectionem dictam.

(h) queat (i) *Read* Nunc autem? (j) ego *with* r *added* (k) sine primo et medio non esse *with* et fine *added in the bottom margin and linked by a reference sign* (m) ms. fine

Appendix 2

A *PERIPHYSEON* FLORLEGIUM
FROM *PARIS BN 13953*

I quote the shorter extracts in full; for longer passages, I give the opening and closing words and indicate, in brackets, the contents of the passage. References are to the pages and lines of Sheldon-Williams's edition of the *Periphyseon*, Book I. I have provided a more detailed summary and discussion of this material in 'A Florilegium from the "Periphyseon"', *Recherches de théologie ancienne et médiévale*, 47, 1980, pp. 271–7.

I. (f.45ra) Ipse namque essentia est omnium qui solus uere est; ut ait Dyonisius Ariopagita: esse, inquit, omnium est super-esse diunitatis. (38:25–7)

II. Angelus est essentialis motus intellectualis circa Dominum rerumque causas. (40:32–3)

III. Qui uocat ea quae non sunt tamquam ea quae sunt. Hoc est, eos qui in primo homine perditi sunt et ad quandam in-subsistentiam ceciderunt, Deus Pater, per fidem in Filium suum uocat, ut sint sicuti hi qui iam in Christo renati sunt. (44:18–21)

IV. Teophania: incomprehensibilis intellectualis naturae quae-dam diuina apparitio. (cf. 46:17–18)

V. Deus ANARXOS ... (f.45rb) ... stabilitatem quaerentia. (God as the beginning, middle and end of all things) (58:22–9)

VI. IN(terrogatio). Primum si uidetur ... ita currendo fiunt omnia. (Dual etymology of θεός from θέω and θεωρῶ) (60:10–32)

VII. De essentia ergo dicitur ... (f.45vb) ... Nam luci obstant. (God's indescribability by any quality which has an opposite) (76:31–78:22)

VIII. Theologia: diuine essentiae inuestigatio. (84:33)

IX. Corpus est compositio quaedam ... (f.46ra) ... per corporales sensus infixa. (Definitions of *corpus, spiritus* and *forma*) (110:11–22)

X. Grammatica est articulatae uocis custos ... (f.46rb) ... temporibus inuestigans disciplina. (Definitions of the Seven Liberal Arts) (110:32–112:12)

XI. Si aliud est corpus et aliud est locus, sequitur ut locus non sit corpus. Aer autem istius corporalis atque uisibilis mundi quarta pars est; locus igitur non est. (112:26–8)

XII. Si mundus iste inuisibilis (*sic*) corpus est, sequitur necessario ut et partes eius non sint corpora; at, si corpora sunt, quantitatis non localitatis generi subiugatur (*sic*). Sunt autem corpora: loca igitur non sunt. (118:21–4)

XIII. Menica membranula cerebri foras funditur ... sentientis infigitur. (Definitions of *uisus* and *uisio*) (124:1–9)

XIV. Locus est ipse extra uniuersitatem ambitus, uel ipsa extra uniuersitatem positio, uel finis comprehendens, in quo comprehenditur comprehensum. (126:13–15)

XV. Quod enim de solo Melchisidech ... (f.46va) ... sola lux regnat. (The condition of humanity after the return of all things to God) (128:18–32)

XVI. Si rationalis anima incorporea est (unde nullus sapiens dubitat) necessario quicquid in ea intellegitur incorporeum esse manifestum est. Et locus in anima intellegitur, sicut prius dictum est. Incorporalis igitur est. (134:13–16)

XVII. Energia: operatio anime. (cf. 136:20)

XVIII. Omne corpus ... (f.46vb) ... mortale conceditur esse. (Corruptible body contrasted with incorruptible essence) (142:39–144:5)

XIX. Energia, hoc est essentia, uirtus, operatio naturalis. (144:21–2)

Appendix 3

GLOSSES TO THE *CATEGORIAE DECEM*

PREFACE

Tables 1 and 2 (below, pp. 182–3 and 184) present some detailed evidence for my discussion of 'standard', 'eccentric' and Eriugena-inspired glosses in Chapter 5 (above, pp. 121–3). Table 1 records the results of a study of the glosses to a selection of lemmata in the various early medieval manuscripts of the *Categoriae Decem*.[1] These glosses correspond only in part to those edited below: for the sake of the completeness of the survey, I wished to include certain rather dull or derivative glosses which are, nevertheless, included in most manuscripts (e.g. those to 137:14, 137:17–18); and the many important glosses unique to *M*, *G* and/or *H* are considered not here, but in Table 2.

The symbols used in the tables represent most of the characteristic features of the transmission of early medieval glosses. It will be seen that for each lemma there is a standard gloss ('x'), which occurs in more or less the same form in a considerable number of manuscripts. Table 1 illustrates how no standard gloss is included in every manuscript; and how no one manuscript has every standard gloss. Occasionally, one or more manuscripts will contain a gloss which is recognizably derived from the standard gloss but varies from it more than superficially ('x var'); whilst it is very common for one or more manuscripts to omit phrases or sentences from the standard gloss ('x

---

[1] I have been unable to see, or obtain microfilm of, one early medieval manuscript mentioned in the *Aristoteles Latinus* list as containing some glosses to its text of the *Categoriae Decem*: *Vercelli Bibl. archiv. S. Eusebii 138* (s. ix). *Berlin (DDR) Staatsbibliothek Phillipps 176* (Fleury) (s. x) was kindly made available to me in microfilm. But either the poor quality of the film, or the decrepit state of the manuscript, rendered many of the glosses illegible, and I felt it wisest to omit the manuscript from my comparative tables. From what I have been able to discern, the Berlin manuscript contains a rather less full selection of standard glosses than *A*, *C* or *W*; little eccentric material, but a number of shortened versions of standard glosses (e.g. at 137:23, 156:17–18, 173:5–6), which sometimes amount to no more than the briefest interlinear notes (e.g. to NATVRA, Alcuin's prologue, 135:13).

abb'). Equally, one or more manuscripts sometimes add a usually short additional element to the beginning, middle or end of a gloss ('x + e', 'x + f'); and occasionally such an element is abbreviated in one of the manuscripts in which it appears ('x + e abb'). Often the arrangement of elements (that is, the main gloss and the additional element(s)) varies from one manuscript to another ('tr'). Sometimes the standard gloss will be found in some manuscript(s) in drastically shortened versions ('sh'; 'sh¹, sh²' denote different shortened versions). Sometimes one or more manuscripts will contain an 'eccentric' gloss completely different from the standard gloss to the lemma in question ('a', 'b'). A few manuscripts contain merely the briefest interlinear glosses in place of some of the standard glosses ('il').

In all the manuscripts except one (*Paris BN 13953*) the glosses are not written out continuously, but appear as interlinear or marginal annotations to a text of the *Categoriae Decem*. In *H* some glosses are also added on inserted strips of parchment. Normally, the glosses are keyed to lemmata in the text by a system of reference signs, letters or numbers; but sometimes the references become displaced through mechanical error, and occasionally the system of reference is abandoned entirely. Elements which form a single gloss in some manuscripts ('x + e') may be split into two separate glosses in other manuscripts ('x/e'), perhaps keyed to two separate, contiguous lemmata. Some manuscripts may contain two separate glosses which belong to the same lemma (e.g. 'x/a', 'a/x+e'). In a few cases, the same gloss is keyed to quite different lemmata, at different points in the text: for example, the various glosses on *locus* are found in some manuscripts by the passage dealing with place in the section *De quantitate*, and in others by the section *De ubi et quando*. Even where the text of the *Categoriae Decem* is complete, a manuscript may contain glosses only to parts of it (blank = no text/ no glosses to the text at this point).

Table 2 records the occurrences of definitely or probably Eriugena-inspired glosses. It will be seen that *M* has by far the richest collection of these; and also, that where an Eriugena-inspired gloss is standard, often it will not be found in *M*. This table may suggest that *M* and *G* have less in common than is the case, since they share a certain amount of non-Eriugenian material not found elsewhere (e.g. Gloss xv).

The tables do not record the many variations in matters of detail between the text of the same gloss from one manuscript to another. Nor, except for two illustrations (Glosses I and XI), have I reproduced anything approximating to a full collation of the different manuscripts of the glosses. A look at these illustrations, which fully exemplify what I have found in the case of every gloss, may indicate why I have made this decision. In copying glosses, scribes and scholars did not show the same respect for accuracy of detail that, for the most part, they demonstrated towards literary texts. Changes in word order or the substitution for a word of its synonym are so common that one is forced to conclude that scribes would copy the substance of a gloss, but not necessarily its precise form. In no case have I found the evidence of textual collation such as to enable me to trace the textual relations between the glosses in one manuscript and another: the tradition is too fluid, too subject to the whim of the individual scholar or copyist. An editor who gave full collations of glosses belonging to a tradition like this would be indulging in textual criticism for its own sake. My collation of Gloss XI gives an example of the textual relations between glosses found only in *M*, *G* and *H*. It suggests, like all my collations of these three manuscripts, that, whilst the text in *M* may be better than that in *G* or *H*, it is not the original from which *G* and *H* are copied. The glosses which these three manuscripts, or two of them, share, derive from a common source, most probably indirectly.

The different manuscripts of the *Categoriae Decem* and their individual selections of glosses give a picture of the development of logical studies from the ninth to the twelfth century.[2]

I have suggested above that *M*, which contains some of the most fascinating, and most thoroughly Eriugenian of the glosses, was produced at Auxerre, perhaps under Heiric's direction. Like *M*, *G* contains the *Categoriae Decem* along with its glosses and nothing else besides a short preface, copied from the *Periphyseon*, which emphasizes the Eriugenian connections of both manuscripts. The text of *G*

---

[2] The following account is based on a personal examination of the manuscripts in the original or on microfilm; and aided by the descriptions – to which the reader is referred for full details of the contents of each codex – in the *Aristoteles Latinus: Codices* volumes. I have not, however, examined *L* in microfilm or in the original; but I am greatly indebted to Professor B. Bischoff and Mr David Ganz for making available to me excellent transcripts of the *Categoriae Decem* glosses in that manuscript.

and the *Periphyseon* extract are written in a mid-ninth-century hand from Sankt Gall;[3] and the glosses were mostly added, I believe, at the same place at much the same time.[4] *G* is remarkable not only for the Eriugenian material which it shares with *M* and *H*, but also for a number of unique glosses. Those on philosophical subjects show, in general, a steadier, less metaphysical approach than is found in *M* or *H*. A considerable part of this additional material is scholarly rather than philosophical: a division of the sciences; a note on Greek etymologies; anecdotal comment on some Greek philosophers.[5] The glossator of *G*'s scholarly interest extended to the text of the *Categories*: he appears to know the 'editio boetianis ... quae est uerbum e uerbo' (probably the composite translation, based on the lemmata of Boethius's commentary), which, he notices, differs greatly at one point from the *Categoriae Decem*.[6]

H is a complex, fascinating manuscript, which merits a full study.[7] The *Categoriae Decem* forms just a small part of an extensive collection of logical material, to which glosses and notes of all kinds have been added. Among these are glosses to Augustine's *De dialectica* which show the influence of John Scottus,[8] and glosses to Porphyry's *Isagoge*, one of which mentions the *Periphyseon*.[9] Eriugena is recalled on two other occasions in this manuscript: a poem of his is quoted;[10] and a computistical table is attributed to 'Aldelmus, frater Iohannis Scotti'.[11] The collection of Eriugena-inspired glosses in *H* is second only to *M*'s; and *H* also contains a very full set of standard glosses.

[3] Cf. A. Bruckner, *Scriptoria Medii Aevi Helvetica* III (Graf, 1938), p. 90. The *Periphyseon* passage (p. 84:16–26), was printed from *G* by M. Esposito in *Proceedings of the Royal Irish Academy*, 28C, 1910, p. 74.

[4] Only for one of two hands which gloss less frequently than the main glossing-hand, is Bruckner's identification with Ekkehart IV at all plausible: cf. Bruckner, op. cit., p. 46, n. 239; and compare his plate XVI, annotations in right margin and at the top of the left margin (= *G*, p. 32) with his plate XXXIX (= *Sankt Gallen 393*, p. 33).

[5] On pp. 24, 42 and 37 respectively.

[6] p. 33, referring to p. 153:22ff.

[7] This much-discussed manuscript has never been fully described. The best available description is provided by C. H. Beeson in 'The authorship of "Quid sit ceroma"', in *Studies in Honour of E. K. Rand*, ed. L. W. Jones (New York, 1938), pp. 1–7. I have transcribed and studied a great deal of material from this manuscript, and I hope to devote an article to it in the near future.

[8] Cf. Cousin, *Ouvrages inédits d'Abélard*, p. 619; and Hauréau, op. cit., I, pp. 186–7.

[9] Ed. Baeumker and Walterhausen.

[10] No. II pt. viii, ll.1 and 3 in Traube's edition (*MGH PLAC* III, p. 537) on f.23bis r.

[11] f.42r; cf. A. Van de Vyver, 'Hucbald de Saint-Amand, écolâtre, et l'invention du nombre d'or', esp. pp. 64–71.

The glosses to the *Categoriae Decem* are copied in a number of similar, contemporary hands. They were almost certainly entered in more than one stage, as two pieces of evidence illustrate. There is one lemma for which two glosses are found in a number of the manuscripts, the first an extract from Boethius, the second an extract from Alcuin:[12] although these two glosses are never found separately, the second is almost always marked 'Aliter', and presumably stood alone in some manuscript now lost. In *H* the first of these glosses is written in one hand; then, in another hand, there follows a shortened version of the second. Even clearer as evidence is Gloss VIa, where a note in *H* adds, in a different hand from that of the gloss, 'This gloss should not be accepted by us.' Courcelle has argued that the compilation of *H* took place in Auxerre under the aegis of Remigius.[13]

Leningrad F.V. Class. lat. 7 (L) and *Bern C 219 (B)* are the only two other manuscripts to date from the ninth or early tenth centuries. Otherwise they have little in common.[14] *L*, very probably from Corbie, contains an important collection of dialectical works, including one of the very rare early copies of the composite translation of the *Categories*. It includes a very good collection of the standard glosses to the *Categoriae Decem* and very little eccentric material. It is very close to *H* in its choice of glosses and in its readings, except that it omits the Eriugena-inspired material which *H* shares with *M* or *M* and *G*. *B* is a manuscript from Wales, to judge both from its script and a gloss probably in Welsh. If *B* is used as evidence of the Welsh roots of the English cultural renaissance at the turn of the tenth

---

12 PRIMO DE HIS QVAE SVNT (137:14). The first gloss is an extract from Boethius's first commentary on Aristotle's *De interpretatione* (ed. C. Meiser (Leipzig, 1877), p. 37:6–15, 22–7); the second is taken from Alcuin's *De dialectica* 3 (*MPL* 101, 956 AB).

13 See above, p. 122. However, some material cannot have been entered into the manuscript until the mid-tenth century. C. Jeudy ('Israel le grammarien et la tradition manuscrite du commentaire de Rémi d'Auxerre à l' "Ars Minor" de Donat', *Studi Medievali*, 3a Serie, 18,2, 1977 (A Gustavo Vinay), pp. 185–205, esp. pp. 204–5) has noticed that a passage written on f.44 mentions the name of Israel, an Irish grammarian active on the Continent in the middle of the tenth century. Many of the 'Icpa' glosses to the *Isagoge* are written in the hand which wrote this passage; and Miss Jeudy speculates that *Icpa* may be the first four letters of Israel's name, written in Greek script. I am very grateful to Professor Bernhard Bischoff for bringing this information to my notice.

14 *L* is from the ninth century (cf. *Aristoteles Latinus supplementa altera*, p. 173); for *B*, see W. M. Lindsay, *Early Welsh Script* (Oxford, 1912), pp. 22–6. Lindsay does not assign a date to this manuscript; but *B* shares certain features in its abbreviations with another Welsh manuscript, *Cambridge Corpus Christi College 153*, a copy of Martianus Capella. These features lead Lindsay to assign it a s. ix ex./x in. date; and so I would suggest the same for *B*; cf. ibid., p. 22.

century, then the picture which it supplies of the level of interest in logic is unflattering. Glosses appear only sporadically, and, when they do, they do not usually present the complete text of a standard gloss; more often, *B* substitutes a brief interlinear note, which paraphrases the pseudo-Augustinian text, rather than explaining or amplifying it. *Paris BN 13953* was probably produced at roughly the same time as *H*, and in the same milieu.[15] It is unique among surviving manuscripts in presenting the glosses to the *Categoriae Decem* as a continuous commentary; otherwise it is an unremarkable collection of standard glosses, with very little eccentric material.

Avranches 229 (A), *Cambridge Corpus Christi College 206 (C)*, *München clm 6373 (N)* and *Wien 843 (W)* all date from the tenth century; the provenance of *A* is Mont Saint-Michel; of *N*, Freising. Only *C* has the *Categoriae Decem* as part of a collection of dialectical works; the other three manuscripts contain just the pseudo-Augustinian text, accompanied by glosses and prefaced with Alcuin's dedicatory poem. In none of these manuscripts are the glosses written by the text-scribe; nor are they the work of a number of scribes, as in *M*, *G* and *H*. The impression, in each of these manuscripts, is of a group of glosses gathered from a single source and copied into the text by an expert scribe shortly after the production of the manuscript. *A*, *C*, *N* and *W* are also alike in presenting a generally good selection of standard glosses, whilst each of them has its own variants and eccentric glosses. *A* and *C* are particularly close in their variants and choice of glosses. *Orleans 263 (O)*, the other tenth-century manuscript, is very different. A collection of dialectical works written almost certainly at Fleury, it presents only a few of the standard glosses in their normal form. Otherwise, the standard glosses are reworked or abbreviated – the manuscript contains a large number of interlinear glosses – or else replaced by eccentric variants. The interest of the glossator appears to have been firmly directed towards the logical substance of the *Categoriae Decem* and away from any metaphysical or theological diversions.

The three substantial eleventh-century collections of glosses – *Paris BN 1750 (Q)*, *München clm 6367 (S)* from Freising, and *Vaticanus Reginensis 233 (R)* (written in France) – had their glosses copied integrally with their text. *Q* is a fragment and contains a fair selection

---

[15] See also above, pp. 103–5.

of standard glosses for the portion of the text it includes. It also has the peculiarity, which I have already mentioned, of containing one gloss of undoubtedly Eriugenian inspiration, not found elsewhere. *R* and *S* each contain a good selection of the standard glosses, with less eccentric material than in the tenth-century collections. It seems that the set of glosses to the *Categoriae Decem* was becoming standardized. *S*, however, is the only manuscript besides *H* to have a short treatise on place and a version of Augustine's doctrine on *similitudo*, *imago* and *aequalitas* following the pseudo-Augustinian text. To these two pieces, *S* adds a longer and more complicated discussion of time, which assembles some of the *Categoriae Decem* glosses found in this and other manuscripts on this subject, but goes far beyond them in the range and depth of its discussion.[16] The other eleventh-century manuscript, *Firenze Bibl. Laurenziana Gadd. plut. LXXXIX sup. 80*) (*F*), written by an Italian scribe, contains only a few standard glosses; its annotations are otherwise confined to simple interlinear notes. The manuscript is a collection of logical works, and contains some substantial glosses to Porphyry's *Isagoge* and to Boethius's second commentary on it.

Finally, there is a twelfth-century manuscript, *Vaticanus latinus 567* (*V*), the work of an Italian scribe, which contains a substantial collection of standard glosses which were written at the same time as the text. There are few eccentric glosses or unusual variants. The existence of this heavily glossed, carefully produced manuscript suggests that, in Italy at least, interest in the *Categoriae Decem* did not die out nearly so quickly as Minio-Paluello has suggested.[17]

---

[16] ff.17r–v. This passage probably dates from the eleventh century, and so I have not edited or discussed it here.

[17] See above, p. 17.

Appendix 3

M	Milano Ambrosiana B 71 sup.	s. ix^2
G	Sankt Gall 274	s. ix^2
H	Paris BN 12949	s. x in.
A	Avranches 229	s. x
B	Bern C 219	s. ix ex./ x in.
C	Corpus Christi College Cambridge 206	s. x
F	Firenze Laurenziana Gadd. pl. 89 sup. 80	s. xi
L	Leningrad F.V. Class. lat. 7	s. ix
N	München clm 6373	s. x
O	Orleans 263	s. x
P	Paris BN 13953	s. x^1
Q	Paris BN 1750	s. x ex./ xi in.
R	Vaticanus Reginensis lat. 233	s. xi
S	München 6367	s. xi
V	Vaticanus lat. 567	s. xii
W	Wien 843	s. x

Appendix 3

TABLE I

KEY

Symbols

x   the 'standard' form of a gloss

a, b   alternative glosses

–   no gloss

blank no glosses at all for this part of text/no text at this point

sh   a shortened form of the standard gloss (more drastically altered and cut than 'x abb')

il   a brief interlinear gloss

e, f an element, added at the beginning, in the middle or at the end, in some text(s) of the gloss

abb abbreviated (used of glosses or elements)

var varied (used of glosses or elements)

tr   transposed: the order of the elements is different

+   follows on without a break

/   forms a separate gloss

superscript arabic numerals distinguish different interlinear, shortened, abbreviated and varied glosses: e.g. 'abb[1], abb[2]'.

DETAILS OF SAMPLE-TEXTS

PAGE AND LINE NO.	LEMMA	NUMBER IN EDITION BELOW
Alcuin's Prologue	NATVRA	I
133:17	PER GRADVS, CVNCTA QVAE SVNT	—
134:19	VSIA	—
135:13	MENTE CONCEPTA SIGNARI	—
137:14	PRIMO DE HIS QVAE SVNT	—
137:17–18	SECVNDO, PERCIPIVNTUR	2
137:23	FANTASIAS	4 (and cf. 11)
140:2–3	IN PERMANENTE VSIA	3
140:17–18	NEC DE SVBIECTO	—
144:3	IDEM ANIMAL GENVS EST	6
145:28	VSIA	—
147:20	NEC IN SOLO	—
147:26–7	SIQVIDEM GENERALE EST	—
149:4[1]	beginning of DE QVANTITATE	7
149:4[2]	beginning of DE QVANTITATE	8
149:9	SI ERGO OMISSA LATITVDINE	—
152:19	NAM ET ANTIPODES NOSTRI	—
156:17–18	GRECI δύναμιν καὶ ἐνέργειαν VOCANT	9
167:23	HAEC CORPORATA ESSE	10
170:23	SIQVIDEM PRIVATIO	—
171:11–12	VIRTVTES MEDIAS ESSE	—
173:5–6	NATVRALITER SIMVL SVNT	—

TABLE I

	M	G	H	A	B	C	F	L	N	O	P	Q	R	S	V	W
NATVRA	sh	–	x/ e+a	a		x/ a	–		x tr abb				x tr	x	x abb	x tr
33:3	il		e	sh	x/ sh		x	x		x			x	x	x+e	x
33:17	il[1]	x	x	x	il[2]	x		x	x	x			x	x	x	x
34:19	sh	x	–	a	–	x	–	x	x	x var	–		x	x	il	x
35:13	il[1]	x	x	x	il[2]	x	il[3]	x	x	x			x	x	x	x
37:14	x+e	x	x+ eabb[1]	x	il[1]	x	il[2]	x+ eabb[2]	x+e	–	x+e		x+e	x	x+e	x+e
37:17-18	–	e+x	x	x	x	x	–	–	x	a	x		x+ f	x	x+ f	x+ f
37:23	e	x+e+f	x+e +fabb	x	–	x	–	–	x var	il	x		–	x	x var	x var
40:2-3	a	x abb[1] +e	x	x abb[2]	il	x	x abb[2]	x abb[3]	x	b	x		–	x	x abb[3]	x
40:17-18	x	–	x	sh	il[1]	x	–	x	x	x	x		–	x	il[2]	x
44:3	–	a/ x+e	a/x	x	–	x	a/ xabb	x	b	x			x	x	x	x
45:28	x	–	x	x	–	x	x	x+e	x	x	x		x+e	x	x+e	x+e/ a
47:20	x	–	x	–	–	–	x	x+e	x	x	–		x	–	x	x
47:26-7	–	–	x	–	–	–	x	x+e	–	–			x+e	–	–	x
49:4[1]	–	xabb	x	x	sh[1]	x	x	x abb	–	sh[2]			x	x	x	x
49:4[2]	x	–	–	sh	–	sh	–		x+e	–			x	x	x	e
49:9	–	–	x	sh[1]	sh[2]	sh[1]		x+e	x tr abb	–		a	x tr abb	x		x tr abb
52:19	–	x	x	il		x		x+e	–	sh			x		x+e	x
56:17-18*	–	x+e	x+ f	a			–	x+ f	x	xabb	x		x	x	x	
67:23	–	a	x	sh[1]		–	x	–	sh[2]	a			x	–	–	
70:23	–	–	x	sh	–	x	x	–	–				x	x	x	
71:11-12	–	–	x	–	–	sh	x	–					x	x	x	x
73:5-6	–	–	x	x	a	–	–		x var	a			x	x	x	

* For fuller details, see Passage ix below.

TABLE 2

Eriugena-inspired glosses in M, G, H and as Standard Glosses

NUMBER OF GLOSS IN EDITION BELOW	M	G	H	STANDARD
I	sh	–	x	x (for HAC see Table
IIIa	–	xabb	x	x (abb in ACFV)
IIIb	x	–	–	–
IV	–	x	x	x
XI	x	x	x	–
XII add el.	x	–	x	–
XIII	x	–	x	–
XIVa	x	–	–	–
XVI	x	–	–	–
XVII	x	–	–	–
XIX	x	–	–	–
XX	x	–	–	–
XXI	x	–	–	–
XXII	x	–	–	–
XXIII	x	–	–	–
XXIV	x			
XXX	–	–	–	– (Q only)
XXXI	–	–	x	– (HS only)

Probably Eriugena-inspired glosses:

	M	G	H	STANDARD
Va	x	–	x	x (abbRV)
Vb	–	xabb	–	AC (abb VW)
VII	–	xabb	x	x (abbBNQ)
VIIIa	x	–	–	x (N: x+e; W: e)

Symbols as in Table 1, except that 'x' means that a gloss is present, not that it is standard (except where 'x' appears in the Standard Glosses column).

PRINCIPLES OF EDITION

At the top of each gloss, I indicate: (line one) the lemma – where available, the page and line number of the lemma in *Aristoteles Latinus* I, 1–5; (line two) the manuscript(s) from which I have transcribed the text, followed by an asterisk, the other manuscripts in which this gloss occurs, the page/folio number of the gloss in the manuscript(s) from which I have transcribed it.

In general, I have chosen simply one manuscript in each case for the text of the gloss. I have emended only where the text is obviously corrupt, basing myself, wherever possible, on the readings of other manuscripts of the gloss. Such changes are italicized. I refer to manuscripts other than the main one being used in each case, where

(a) I emend; (b) their readings are of especial interest; (c) their versions of the glosses are abbreviated. The orthography is exactly that of the manuscript chosen in each case; the punctuation and capitalization are my own.

I. NATVRA (ALCUIN'S PROLOGUE)

(a) M f.36r*

Natura generale nomen est omnium rerum et earum quae sunt et earum quae non sunt.[1] Dicuntur autem ea esse quae sunt, ad quae nostri sensus penetrare possunt. Dicuntur autem ea non esse quae incapabilia sunt tam intellectuali quam rationali creaturae.[2]

*(b) Element I H*C*NR*S V*W* ff.24r/25r/1v/93r/1r*

Quicquid[a] est siue uisibile siue[b] inuisibile[c], sensibile[d] seu intelligibile[e], creans seu creatum[f3], natura dicitur. Ergo generale nomen est natura omnium rerum et earum[g] quae sunt et earum[h] quae non sunt.[1] Illa[j] autem non sunt[k] quae nec sentiri nec intellegi possunt – non quod non sunt, sed quod ita sunt[m] ut omnem cognitionem[n] corporis et mentis transcendant[o].[2] Deus itaque natura dicitur quod cuncta nasci faciat.[p]

Element II ibid. except V

Omnis creatura natura[q] uocatur eo quod nascatur[r].

Ib (Printed Hauréau p. 189 n. 2) (*a*) *R* Quicquid id; *W om.* quicquid (*b*) *W* siue eis (*c*) *R* inuisibile siue inuisibile (*d*) *V om.* sensibile (*e*) *W adds a word no longer legible* (*f*) *V* siue creans siue creatum (*g*) *C om.* et earum (*h*) *C* et illarum (*j*) *H is corrected to* ille (*k*) *For* illa . . . non sunt *C has* illarum non esse dicuntur (*m*) *C* sinit; *H* sint; *R* suit (*n*) *H** cognationem (*o*) *R* transcendent (*p*) (*N om.* Deus . . . nasci faciat); *R* faciat nasci; *V* nasci fecit; *W* nasci facit (*q*) *C* Creatura autem omnis (*r*) *W adds* per quod est

Arrangement of elements in (b):

V – I only; *HCS* I, II; *NRW* II, I

(1) John Scottus, *Periphyseon* (I, p. 36:5–7): 'primam summamque diuisi onem e sse in ea quae sunt et in ea quae non sunt, horum omnium generale uocabulum occurit quod . . . latine . . . "natura" uocitatur'. (2) ibid., p. 38:19–23: 'omnia quae corporeo sensui uel intelligentiae perceptioni succumbunt uere ac rationabiliter dici esse, ea uero quae per excellentiam suae naturae non solum sensum sed etiam omnem intellectum rationemque fugiunt iure uideri non esse . . .' (3) cf. ibid., p. 36:21–4

Appendix 3

(c) Element I H★ f.23bis

Decem Categoriarum ratio admiranda est, per quam praedicamenta tenent tam uisibilia quam inuisibilia, quia in Deo et angelis et in omnibus creaturis est substantiae [*sic*].

Element II H★A★C★ f.23bis/194r/24r

Natura generale nomen est omnium rerum[a] et earum quae uidentur et quae mortalibus latent. Naturam duobus dicimus modis[b], uel Dei essentiam[c] per quam cuncta procreantur; uel procreationem hominum ceterorumque[d] animalium quae gignunt et quae[e] gignuntur, id est[f] usia et eius accidentia nouem, quae sunt qualitas, ad aliquid, quantitas, situs, facere, pati, ubi, quando, habere[g], in omni re quae uidetur et tangi siue sentiri potest[h], et in omnibus creaturis est. In malo[j] non est, quia malum nihil est.[4] Non enim habet substantiam Deus, itaque[k] natura dicitur. Eo quod nasci[m] faciat creatura omnis, natura dicitur.[n] Deus nihilum, non quasi non sit aliquid[o], sed propter excellentiam ultra quam nihil est.

II.   SECVNDO: PERCIPIVNTVR EA QVORVM IMAGINES ANIMO VIDENDO FORMAMVS ET CONDIMVS (137:17–18)

(a) G★HABCNPRSVW p. 11

Exteriore itaque sensu ammonetur animus ad intellectum et excitatur primo. Postmodum uero uisa apud se per quasdam[a] imaginationes et phantasias recordatur et fingıt; sicque meditata, uerborum ministerio extrinsecus pandit. Cum multae igitur res et infinitae sint,[1] illarum solummodo cognitionem percipimus intellectu ad quas per exteriores sensus peruenitur ad interiores; quamuis quidam animus tantae subtilitatis sit ut eciam numquam uisa quodammodo inspiciat.

Ic (a) H artium (b) so H; A modis dicamus; C modis dicimus (c) A assenciam (d) H et
    ceterorum (e) H om. quae (f) A om. id est (g) AC om. quae sunt qualitas . . . habere
    (h) C post est (j) A in malum non est; C malum non est (k) H om. quae uidetur . . .
    itaque *and adds* omnis (m) H nascatur (n) H om. faciat . . . dicitur (o) H natura aliqua
    (4) A common Eriugenian theme: cf. J. G. Gruber, *Quid Scotus Erigena de
    Malo docuerit* (Halle, 1843).

IIa (a) G quosdam; H quasdam
IIa Arrangement of elements: G i+a; RV a+ii
II   (1) cf. Porphyry, *Isagoge* trsl. Boethius (ed. cit., p. 12:8–13): 'individua . . . quae
    sunt post specialissima infinita sunt. Quapropter usque ad specialissima a generalis-
    simis descendentem iubet Plato quiescere . . . infinita, inquit, relinquenda sunt,
    neque enim horum posse fieri disciplinam.'

Additional Elements

(i)   G* *p. 11*

Illos redarguit qui magnopere requirunt unde disputare uoluerit, cum mixtam disputationem faciat de tribus.

(ii)   R*VW *f.4v*

Verbi gratia, cum uidemus pedem hominis, extrinsecus cogitamus animo, que uidendo formamus quod intrinsecus lateat: neruos uidelicet medullamque intra ossa iacentem.

(b)   O*   *p. 40*

Ideo imagines dixit formari in animo, quia res ipsas non possumus in mente condere, sed similitudines rerum.

III.   IN PERMANENTE VSIA (140:2–3)

(a)   *Complete* HL*NPS W   *Incomplete* GACV   *f.37r*

In permanente usia, id est quae permanet dum mutantur eius accidentia. Sed melius permanentem usiam illam debemus accipere quae simpliciter ab esse uero, id est Deo, uenit. Illud enim esse, quod ita ab esse, id est Deo, uenit, sine corruptione durat et est semper. Quicquid enim essentialiter simplex creatum est perpetuo simpliciter perseuerat atque immutabiliter secundum sui essentiam manet, ut est anima uel elementa simplicia. Illud uero quod ex quattuor elementis est compactum perit et mutatur nec permanet. Ergo permanentem usiam ad illud esse retulit quod simplex creatum est et non ex partibus, et ideo simpliciter manet[a]. Vnde corpora licet resoluuntur, quae ex quattuor elementis *constant*[b], ipsa tamen elementa, quia simplex esse habent, nullo modo resoluuntur[c], sed ad TO ΠAN id est ad omne, reuertuntur:[1] terra scilicet ad terram, ignis ad ignem et cetera.

Additional element in G*   *p. 11*

his similia. Nam cum omnis res aut substantia sit aut accidens, et

---

IIIa (Printed Hauréau, p. 190 n. 1) (a) *AC end here; G adds* ut caelum (b) *L om.* constant
       (c) *GFV om.* sed . . . reuertuntur; *P* sed ad to – id est ad omne
III   (1) For the phrase τὸ πᾶν, cf. John Scottus, *Periphyseon* eg. 1, p. 98:18–20

substantiarum aliae sunt primae, aliae secundae, fit trina partitio. Ita ut omnis res aut accidens sit aut secunda substantia aut prima.

(b) M★ (*f.41r*)

Prima ocia est simplex ierarchiuum omonimum. Secunda, ut homo, deductiuum omonimum a primo ierarchiuo – – – augmentiuum superiorum duorum trionimum. Quarta, genus comprehensiuum quadrinomium trium superiorum. OCYA generalissima, – – collectiuum omonimum a primo ierarchico simplici processiuum. Ab hac generalissima usia componamus ordinem analiticum usque ad simplicissimam usiam. Genus processiuum bionimum ad comparationem generalissimae usiae. Animal, quae est tertia, intentiuum trionimum. Homo, quae quarta, descensiuum trionimum.[2] Iterum usia prima simplex continet – inter aliam ociam – generalissimam; haec tria, et est prima et nouissima, ut quod nouissima prima et omnia in prima et nouissima sine distinctione unum in prima quod in nouissima.[3] Prima simplex in qua omnia creata fuerunt secundum Euangelium: 'Quod factum est in ipso uita erat'.[4] Cum autem apparuerit, ecce iam in gradibus usque ad generalissimam usiam de simplici producta, in qua mouentur et sunt omnia.[5]

IV. FANTASIAS IMAGINES RERVM INSIDENTES ANIMO
(137:23) *cf.* NO. XI

G★HACNPSVW *p. 12*

'Fano' appareo. Fantasiae dicuntur propriae *apparitiones*[a] uel reuelationes mentis, et omnia[b] in humanis rebus. Theophaniae uero sunt in Deo et in diuinis rebus.[1] Fantasma autem delusio mentis uocatur.[c]

III   (2) cf. John Scottus, *Periphyseon* (esp. II pp. 6:26–8:17) (3) cf. *Matthaeus* XX, 16 'Sic erunt novissimi primi, et primi novissimi . . .' (4) *Johannes* I, 3–4 (5) cf. *Actus* XVII, 28: 'In ipso enim vivimus, et movemur, et sumus . . .'

IV   (*a*) G aparationes (*b*) HV et hoc (*c*) For delusio . . . uocatur NVW have sunt illusiones demonum
(1) cf. John Scottus, *Periphyseon* (I, p. 46:24–8): 'Non enim essentia diuina "deus" solummcdo dicitur, sed etiam modus ille, quo se quodam modo intellectuali et rationali creaturae, prout est capacitas uniuscuiusque, ostendit, "deus" saepe a sancta scriptura uocitatur. Qui modus a Grecis "theophania", hoc est dei apparitio, solet appellari.'

V.   ALIA SVNT EXTRA VSIAN (144:26–7)

(*a*) *M*HOWP   abbreviated RV   f.46r*

Omnis oysia in loco est, et locus extra usia est, quia tempus habet omnia.[a1] Sic et habitus extra usiam est, quia nullus se habet proprie.[2]

(*b*) *AC*   abbreviated in GVW   f.32v*

Locus est circumscriptio corporis,[3] que diuiditur in sex partes: sursum et deorsum; ante et post; dextra et sinistra.[a] Nec usia sine loco, nec locus sine usia, quia locus nihil aliud est nisi circumscriptio corporis.

VI.   IDEM ANIMAL GENVS EST (144:3)

(*a*) *G*HACNPRSVW   abbreviated L   p. 23*

In quantum OYCIA de animali praedicitur, animal species eius est. In quantum uero animal de homine dicitur, genus est, et homo species.[a] Dicit etiam Martianus, quod homo similiter et genus et species sit.[1] Genus quidem cum generaliter dicitur de omni homine, species autem cum cuiuslibet gentis homine praedicatur, ut homo grecus, homo ethiops, uel Africanus uel Romanus.[b2]

Additional element in G*

Nam species animalis homo est, disciplinae uero grammatica, quae omnino se discrepant.

Va   (*a*) *RV end here*
Vb   (*a*) *GVW end here; G and V continue with different material*
 V   (1) John Scottus, *Periphyseon* (I, p. 126:5–7): 'Omnium itaque existentium essentia localis atque temporalis est, atque ideo nisi in loco et tempore et sub loco et sub tempore nullo modo cognoscitur.' (2) cf. ibid., I, p. 104:19–21: 'Habitus quoque et extra OYCIAN et intra reperitur, ut armatum indutum secundum corpus dicimus.' (3) cf. *Categoriae Decem* 78 (ed. cit., p. 150:16–17): 'Locus . . . corpus quodcumque circumdat et corporis partibus occupatur . . .'; and John Scottus, *Periphyseon* I, ed. cit., p. 110:7–8.
VIa (*a*) *L finishes here* (*b*) *Added in H in a different hand*: Non est haec glossa a nobis recipienda
 VI   (1) Martianus Capella, *De nuptiis* IV (ed. Dick, p. 157:18–22): 'sed nonnumquam aliquae formae ita generi subiciuntur, ut etiam ipsae aliis sub se positis genus esse possint, ut hominum genus, quod animali forma est, barbaris et Romanis genus'. (2) cf. John Scottus, *Annotationes in Martianum* IV (ed. Lutz, p. 84:23–4): 'FORMAS Secundum Augustinum species differt a forma, nam forma potest fieri genus, species autem proprie individua intelligitur' (!)

(b) O* *p. 46*

Species est animal sub OYCIA et genus in animalibus omnibus dum ea comprehendit sub uno nomine.[3]

(c) G*HL *p. 20*

Posset aliquis dicere non esse hoc uerum. Nam de animali praedicatur genus: est enim animal genus. Non autem praedicatur genus de homine; neque enim homo genus est, sed species. Ac per hoc, inqu*ita*, non possunt praedicari de homine quaecumque praedicantur de animali. Sed huic occurrimus, dicentes genus non praedicari de animali secundum rem*b*, sed designatiuum nomen[4] esse animal*ise*, quo designatur animal de pluribus specie differentibus, dici. Nam neque rationem animal*isd* potest habere genus, cum dicitur animal est substantia animata et sensibilis. Similiter nec species dicitur de homine secundum id quod significat sed iuxta illud quod de numero differentibus praedicatur. Ideoque rectum esse dicitur quaecumque praedicantur de animali iuxta rem ipsam, quod subauditur eadem et de homine et de Cicerone praedicari posse. Verbi gratia, animal est corpus et substantia, sic et homo et Cicero corpus et substantia. Eodem modo communis est eorum ratio: ut est animal quod cybum capiat et reliqua; identidem de homine et Cicerone.

VII.   TO BEGINNING OF DE QVANTITATE (149:4ff.)

*H*ACLRSVW *abbreviated GN *shortened* BQ f.29*

Non corpus usie, sed quasi quoddam corpus trium mensurarum,[1] scilicet longitudinis, latitudinis et altitudinis, quae non sunt corpus quidem sed, corpori accidentes, mensuram ei tribuunt. Ergo non de

---

VIc   (Printed Hauréau, p. 192, n. 2) *(a) so HL;* G inquam *(b) H adds above line* id est substanciam *(c) so HL;* G animale *(d) so HL;* G animale
(3) Martianus Capella, op. cit., IV (ed. cit., p. 157:17–18): 'GENVS est multarum formarum per unum nomen complexio . . .' (4) cf. Boethius, Commentary on Aristotle's *De interpretatione,* editio prima (ed. C. Meiser (Leipzig, 1877) p. 48:4–6): 'nomen esse vocem secundum placitum designativam sine tempore, cuius partes nihil extra significent'.

VII   (1) cf. *Categoriae Decem* 72 (ed. cit., p. 149:14–17): 'Sin autem et altitudo fuerit mensurae sociata, corpus cuncta perficiunt; quod tamen non ita accipimus quemadmodum solemus accipere naturale, ne ad usian reverti videamur.'

corpore usiadis, sed de corpore mensure, nunc disputat[a]. Ac si dixisset, non de naturali quantitate, quae in ipsa usia uidetur, sed de ea quae in solis figuris geometricis cognoscitur[b].[2] In geometrica enim de corporibus incorporaliter disputamus et, ut iam dicam, ipsum corpus geometricum incorporale est. Ideoque longitudo, latitudo et altitudo eius incorporalia sunt. Incorporaliter corpus perfitiunt eius, et incorporaliter tractantur cum diuisio fit in eis.

VIII. TO BEGINNING OF DE QVANTITATE (149:4ff.)

(a) M*NQRSV f.49r

Quantum pro quantitate posuit, quia quantitas ipsa a qua omne quantum est[1] nec uideri neque augeri nec minui potest[a],[2] nec aliter hodie, aliter cras potest esse. Queritur etiam cur non quantum naturalium rerum in hoc loco posuit sed quantum geometricum. Ad quod respondendum, quia in solo illo inuenitur linea, id est longitudo per se, quia non potest in quanto naturali fieri.

Additional element

N*W f.14r

Inter quantitatem uero et quantum hoc interest, quia quantitas accidens est. Et longitudo et latitudo et altitudo quantitas est. Cum ergo fecerit corpus, quantum est. Quia dubium est, nisi addatur mensura, quantum sit illud corpus, ut bipedale, tripedale. Nam hoc a numero est. Numerus est collectio unitatum. Omnes figurae, cum per se in anima intelleguntur, incorporales sunt; cum autem corporibus adherent, tunc quasi corpus sunt atque diuisionem certam habent minime. Locus ut uidetur secundum istum corpus non est.[3] Tamen, quia in eo corpora diriguntur, ita pariter locus sicut corpus. Ipsa

---

VII (Printed in part by Barach, p. 18) (a) *B ends here; GN begin here; AQS are split into two glosses at this point* (b) *Q ends here*
(2) cf. John Scottus, *Periphyseon* I, p. 152:13–30
VIIIa (a) *M om.* potest
VIII (1) cf. John Scottus, *Periphyseon* I, ed. cit., p. 150:26ff. (containing quote from *Categoriae Decem*, ed. cit., p. 149:4–17) (2) cf. Boethius, *De arithmetica* I (ed. G. Friedlein, pp. 7:26–8:7) (3) cf. John Scottus, *Periphyseon* I, ed. cit., p. 118:5ff.

quadrata figura epiphania est. Ipsa autem linea uel lineae in medio positus communes termini sunt.

(b) $AC^\star$ f.36r

Quantum ad corpus pertinet geometricale; quantitas ad rem incorporalem.[1]

IX.   QVAS GRECI δύναμιν καὶ ἐνέργειαν VOCANT
                     (156:17–18)

Element i
$G^\star HALNQSVW$ *abbreviated* O   *p. 38*

Tria sunt in omni re: usia, dina*mis*[a], energia.[1] Usia quidem ipsum est esse. Dinamis uirtus et potentia naturalis, qui inest omni usyae, sicut etiam in ipsis cernitur elementis. Vtpote lapis difficile per naturalem potentiam secatur, nec facile redintegratur; aqua e contra facile quidem diuisionem recipit, nec minus integritatem e uestigio recipit. Energia tertio[b] sequitur, id est operatio, quia post scibile cui inest scientia, id est dinamis, ei subsequatur operatio, dum scientia ipsa percipitur ab aliquo.

Element ii
$G^\star HLNQSVW$ *abbreviated* O   *p. 38*

ΗΝΗΡΓΙΑΝ id est operationem; hinc et sinergus dicitur cooperator. Vnde etiam energumini uocantur, quibus fantasiae apparent per ludificamenta demonum.[c]

X.   HAEC CORPORATA ESSE (167:23)

(a) $G^\star Q$ *p. 53*

Inter corporeum et corporatum hoc distat, quod corporeum est quod constat ex corpore; corporatum est quod aliunde accipit corpus, ut

---

IX   (a) G *dinanis* (b) G *tertia* (c) G *adds* Inde ergastulum dicitur rerum custodia; HL *add*
uel quos etiam uariis fantasmatibus deludunt demones
Arrangement of elements: HLQVW i+ii GNOS i separate from ii.
(1) cf. ibid., ed. cit., p. 136:13ff.

angeli de puro ethere et demones de crasso aere corpora formant. Incorporatum uero dicitur quod corpori adiacet, ut est locus et tempus, quae in circumscriptione et in motu corporum cognoscuntur, sed tamen subtracto corpore non apparent.[1]

*(b) H*LS f.35v*

Inter corporeum et corporatum hoc distat: corporeum est quod constat corpore, sicut homo; corporatum uero est quod quando uult accipit corpus, et quando uult dimittit, sicut angelus.

(c) A f.222r*

Distat inter corporeum et incorporatum, quod corporeum quod adiacet corpori, corporatum ipsum corpus dicitur.

(d) O p. 67*

Corporatum est quod corpori iacet, ut locus et tempus. Corporeum est quod corpus habet.

XI. FANTASIAS IMAGINES RERVM INSIDENTES ANIMO (137:23) *cf.* NO. IV

*M*G*H f.39v/p. 12/f.25 ter v*

Priscianus ad Regem Osdroe[a] dixit quid inter 'fantaston' et 'fantasiam' et 'fantasma'[b]. Nascuntur[c] enim a uerbo 'ΦΑΝΩ'[c*], quod est appareo uel uideo. 'Fantaston'[d] est quod uidetur et de quo sensus formatur; fantasia imago in sensu formata; fantasma imago memoriae infixa[e].[1] Fantaston de[f] his quae sunt; fantasia de his[g] quae percipiuntur; fantasma de[h] his quae dicuntur. Et haec de uirgis Iacob intelleguntur.[k] Iunguntur[m] enim ista extasi, id est[n] excessui mentis,[2] et per hoc[p] et per[q]

X (1) cf. Claudianus Mamertus, *De statu animae* II 3 (ed. Engelbrecht, p. 105:21ff.)

XI *(a) so GH; read* Chosroem *(b)* Priscianus . . . fantasma *is lost in M because of trimming* *(c) M* nascunt *(c*) H* phano *(d) M* ΦΑΙ-ΘΑCΩΝ *(e) G* infixia *(f) M* est in *(g) M om.* de his *(h) M* in *(k) M* intelligenda sunt *(m) In M* iunguntur *follows a word* (quaerendum – ?) *which has been erased (n) GH om.* extasi id est *(p) M* haec; *H* h · *(q) H om.* et per

(1) cf. Priscianus Lyddus, *Solutiones ad Chosroem* (ed. J. Bywater, pp. 59:28–60:1): 'non enim alia quedam parte animalium est somnus, alia uero somniari, sed eadem, dum phantasia ex sensiua sit. est enim phantasia motus ex facto sensu secundum operationem. in somno uero phantasma somnium dicimus, apertum quia sensiuae quidem partis est somniari: illud itaque phantasticum est'. (2) cf. Jerome, *Hebraicae quaestiones in Genesim* II 21 (*CC* 72, p. 4:21–2): 'pro extasi, id est mentis excessu . . .'

extasin[r] raptus est Paulus ad tertium[s] caelum. Primum caelum est[t] quae sunt, id[u] est[v] corporale, id est[w] fantaston. Secundum caelum in his quae percipiuntur, id est[x] fantasia et est mentuale[y]. Tertium caelum[z] in his[a] quae dicuntur, id est[b] fantasma, hoc est intellectuale.[3] Propter[c] haec[d] in extasi inquit, 'siue in corpore siue extra corpus nescio[e]; Deus scit'[f].

[g]Imago Dei est[h] in forma ipsius Dei, quae est uera, pura et[j] simplex. Ab illius splendore, quasi in speculo, repercussa est nostra imago[k],[4] subtilitate quadam reuerberando, dicta[m] incomprehensibiliter et ineffabiliter.[5]

XII. SIMILITVDO EST VT 'HOMO PICTVS' ET 'VERVS'
(137:4–5)

M*GH f.39r

Quid similitudo sit dicendum Dei et hominis? Similitudo Dei generaliter in omnibus non est, sed solummodo in rationabilibus et intellectualibus naturis, quibus datum est et seipsas et Deum quantum possibile intelligere. Et ⟨non[a]⟩ mirum cum dicitur, 'Fecit Deus hominem ad imaginem et similitudinem suam'.[1] Similitudo est ut ouum gruis et gallinae, et similitudo hominis picti et ueri. Similia enim sunt, sed aequalia non sunt. Ita et anima imaginem et similitudinem Dei habet propter intellectum et inmortalitatem, sed non aequalitatem eius habet. Similiter de picto homine et uero: nomen aequale est sed diffinitio aequalis non est. † ductum ex uoluntate et industria et similitudine †[b2] Haec enim, industria et uoluntas, quattuor sibi dant genera: similitudinem, pro parte[c], ab uno, ad unum.[3] Similitudo est,

XI (r) *H* extasi (s) *M* in tertium (t) *M* Primum est caelum (u) *For* quae sunt id *H has* quasi (v) *For* quae sunt id est *G has* quod sit (w) *M om.* id est, *adds in* (x) *G om.* id est *adds in* (y) *For* id est . . . mentuale *M has* et est mentuale in fantasia (z) *H adds* id est (a) *M om.* caelum in his (b) *M* et est in (c) *M post;* GH p̄(d) *H* h · (e) *H* extra ne s. c. o. (f) *MH* sit (g) *This paragraph is separate in M but joined to the preceding in* GH (h) *GH om.* est (j) *M om.* et (k) *GH om.* imago (m) *so* GH; *M* deducta

(3) John Scottus, *Periphyseon* IV (818C): 'Tertium siquidem caelum, in quod raptus est Paulus, spirituale esse summi utriusque linguae auctores non dubitant, sed unanimiter affirmant, illud intellectuale uocantes.' (4) *II Ad Corinthios* XII 3 (5) cf. Gregory of Nyssa, *De hominis opificio* quoted at *Periphyseon* 789C

XII (a) *MGH om.* non (b) *Corrupt. For* aequalis . . . ductum est *G has* inaequalis est; *H om.* uero . . . ductum ex *and adds* de (c) *M* partem

(1) *Genesis* I 26 (2) cf. *Categoriae Decem* 18 (ed. cit., p. 136: 30ff.): 'Horum autem quae industria vel voluntate nascuntur quattuor sunt genera . . .'; and cf. Augustine, *De diuersis quaestionibus LXXXIII* no. 74 (ed. cit., pp. 213–14) (3) cf. *Categoriae Decem* ibid. (ed. cit., 137: 2ff.)

ut dixi, ouum gruis et gallinae, et Dei similitudo et animae, et picti et ueri hominis. Ecce in his similitudo, non aequalitas*ᵈ*. Aliud genus est pro parte, quod a summo principio Dei ineffabili part*e* qu*a*dam.*ᵉ*

Additional Element

*M*H   ibid.*

Eo pactum principium dicuntur, ut cor animalis, aquae fons*ᶠ*, principium coeli, principium terrae, et multa alia quae pro parte sui similitudini primi principii Dei nominis uidentur adiuncta. Ista enim haec adiuncta similitudo in solo Deo*ᵍ* – nomine similitudinis Dei – stat, non in natura. Tertium genus est ab uno, cum dicimus ab uno creatore creatura caelestis, creatura terrestris, et multae aliae. Vnde et ab uno Deo dicuntur dii, id est electi, et ab ipso ea quae per ipsum facta sunt, et in ipso iuuando dicitur*ʰ*. In ipso sunt omnia causaliter. In Deo facta sunt omnia; siue quando acceperunt formas et suum esse, in ipso sunt; quoniam omnia*ᵏ* in Deo Deus sunt.⁴ Quartum genus est ad unum, quod coniungit et facit unitatem, ut ille sol clarus. Et notandum quod illud genus quod dicitur ab uno profertur per ablatiuum; istud uero, uidelicet ad unum, per nominatiuum. Sicut enim adunant haec dicta in uno nomine quod est salubris,⁵ ita adunantur omnia in Deo; et diffunditur Deus per omnia ut ipse in omnibus sit omnia.⁴ Non enim aliud est creatura nisi Dei in seipso a seipso infinita coadunatio.

XII   (d) G ends here (e) so H; M partes quaedam (f) M fontis (g) so H; *reading in M not legible* (h) *so* H; *for* et in ipso iuuando dicitur M *has* et in ipso ea quae ipse est, hoc est sub ipso sunt, qua //// dicitur (k) H *om.* quoniam *and ends at* omnia.
Arrangement of elements: M Gloss + Additional element; H Gloss; Additional element keyed to 'ut, quo pacto . . .' (137:5–6).
(4) cf. *I Ad Corinthios* XII 6: 'Deus qui operatur omnia in omnibus . . .'; *Ad Ephesios* I 23: 'plenitudo eius qui omnia in omnibus adimpletur,'; and cf. John Scottus, *Periphyseon* e.g. III (683C): 'Et hoc manifestissime docet omnium reditus in causam, ex qua processerunt, quando omnia reuertentur in Deum, sicut aer in lucem, quando erit Deus omnia in omnibus.' (5) cf. *Categoriae Decem* 18 (ed. cit., p. 137:10–11): 'Ad unum est ut "illa potio salubris est", "ille medicus salubris", "ferramentum illud salubre" . . .'

XIII. COGITARI POTEST (134:19)

M★H f.37r

DE VSIA. Vsia extra quam nihil est continet superhumanum intellectum et – – – *ᵃ* in nihilo melius ponitur, quoniam ipsa ultra usian
nostram se dilatando porrigit, et facit ipsum Deum qui est ipse sibi et
suum ipse est quod sibi est esse.[1] Ideo ultra nihil est, et in nihilo est, et
ipsum nihil ueriorem reddit apud nos quam praedicatio aliqua.[2] Vnde
ultra omnia et supra et infra et extra et intra. Supra quod eminet;
infra quod sustinet; extra regit; intra continet. Et nec alius est infra
quam supra, nec alius est intra quam extra, sed unus idemque sibi
similis.[3] Non consimilis alicuius rei, nec particeps, nec communica-
bilis, sed speculum et caracter[4] et symbolicum.*ᵇ*

XIV. HOMO AB HVMANITATE (136:19)

(a)   M★ f.38v

In heronimis*ᵃ*, id est deductiuis nominibus, ponitur Deus, cum dicitur
Deus caeli, Deus terrae.[1] Tamen non ipsum faciunt quod sunt, nec
ipsa sunt quod ipse, sicuti hominem reddunt et denominantur, ut
'homo' ab humanitate, 'mortalis' et necessitate mortis, et cetera.
Sicut quaeruntur in rebus superioribus nomina rerum, ita in his
oportet, id est heronimis, originem nominum quaerere, unde distat
inter nomina rerum et originem nominum. Quaeritur in Deo origo

XIII (a) *Three words lost in M because of trimming; in H* lipidissimo in tactu (?) (b) *H om.*
et caracter et symbolicum
(1) cf. Boethius, *De Trinitate* IV (ed. Rand, p. 18:34–6): 'Deus vero hoc ipsum deus
est; nihil enim aliud est nisi quod est, ac per hoc ipsum deus est'. (2) cf. John Scottus,
Periphyseon III (681A): 'Dum ergo incomprehensibilis intelligitur, per excellentiam "nihilum" non immerito vocitatur (Deus)'. (3), Gregory the Great,
Moralia in Job II 8 (MPL 75, 565BD); cf. 'Dunchad' glosses to *De nuptiis* (ed.
Lutz, p. 11:29–32) and Remigius of Auxerre, Commentary to *De nuptiis* (ed.
Lutz, I, p. 204:25–9). (4) cf. John Scottus, *Periphyseon* IV, quoting from Gregory of
Nyssa, *De hominis opificio* (789B): 'Sic quidem dicimus similitudine principalis
exempli pulchritudinis animum ornari, veluti quoddam speculum charactere
apparentis in eo formatum . . .'
XIVa (a) a neologism based on the Gk. ἱερός+ὄνομα?
(1) cf. Isidore, *Etymologiae* I (ed. cit., viii, 5): 'Omnia autem pronomina aut
primogenia sunt aut deductiva . . . Reliqua autem deductiva dicuntur, quia ex istis
deducta atque conposita existunt, ut "quispiam", "aliquis", et reliqua.'

nominis: quur nuncupatur 'Theos'. Dicitur enim uidens, quod omnia uidet;[2] ut est, 'Vidit Deus cuncta quae fecerat et erant valde bona'.[3] Ideo ab illius nomine 'uidentia' possunt dici, quia inter sese non in una specie, nec in una forma ammiratur alia species aliam, sed in diuersis.

(*b*) G★ *p. 10*

'Homo' ab 'humo';[4] humanitas dicitur ipsa humi as*sumptio*[a]. Ponitur autem non numquam pro fragilitate, non numquam pro honestate.[5] Humanitas quoque est libertas, que grece dicitur philantropia, id est amor hominum. Homo ex diuersis subiectis: ex mortali et inmortali. Corpus eius, quod mortale est, ex ossibus et carnibus constat, diuidi- turque in quattuor elementis aliis.[6] Habet in se etiam aliquid ignis, aeris, aquae uel terrae.[7] Ratio terrae in carne est; humoris in sanguine; aeris in spiritu; ignis in calore.

XV.   *cf.* VINVM AVTEM VEL AQVAM SINE CADO IN QVO FVERIT (141:23)

MG★ *p. 19*

Ea uero quae sunt inuisibilia inuisibili re adhaerent, sicuti sapientia in anima, et faciunt ipsam sapientiam esse in anima, sicut dixit superius.[1] Digitum autem quem ait corporis esse partem, non est in subiecto sed de subiecto, id est de substantia corporis. Sic et uinum in cado non in subiecto esse sine subiecto, ut quidam male dicunt, quia uinum et aqua sine cado in quo fuerint possunt alio loco esse. Ideo duo *sunt*[a] subiecta, cadus unum, uinum alterum. Ecce uisibilia taliter segregan- tur. Inuisibilia faciunt ipsum esse quod ipsum inuisibile est. Vt ait Iohannes: 'Volo Pater ut sicut ego et tu unum sumus, ita et hi in nobis

---

XIVb (*a*) *ms.* asuptio
XIV (2) John Scottus, *Periphyseon* I, p. 60:19–22: 'Nam, cum a uerbo ΘΕΟΡΩ deducitur ΘΕΟC "uidens" interpretatur. Ipse enim omnia quae sunt in se ipso uidet dum nichil extra se ipsum aspiciat, quia nihil extra se ipsum est . . .'. (3) *Gen- esis* I 31 (4) Isidore, *Etymologiae* XI (ed. cit., 1, 4) '. . . proprie homo ab humo . . .' (5) cf. ibid., x (ed. cit., 116) (6) cf. ibid., XI (ed. cit., 1, 4–6) (7) On the theme of man as a microcosm, see Jeauneau, edition of Eriugena's Homily on the Prologue to *John*, appendice VII, pp. 336–8.
XV (*a*) so *M; G* duos subiecta
(1) *Categoriae Decem* 33 (ed. cit., p. 140:26–8)

unum sint'.[2] Bene addidit, 'in nobis', ut est sapientia in anima. Non ut una substantia sint,[3] ut Pater et Filius, sed in nos per gratiam illuminationis luceant in Patre et Filio uirtutibus, et sint in hoc quod lux uera est, id est Pater et Filius a quo ipsa in eis processit; et quae fecit iterum flecti in ipsa luce, quae est ipse Deus, remuneratione diuina. Et in alio loco: 'Ego sum uitis uera et uos palmites'.[4] Vt sapientia in anima, ita fructus in uite[b]. Similiter in Deo omnes uirtutes sanctorum, et gratia, et dilectio, et amor. Et cum de affectu uenerint ad habitum per disciplinam in ea parte qua uersatur, anima secundum rationem solidatur per uirtutem in habitu. Quoniam uirtus omnes partes animae complectitur: ex ipso habitu fiunt in Deo ipsum *quod*[c] Deus est.

XVI.   AEQVVM TAMEN (134:1)

M* f.36v

In uno equo uel in uno homine deputandi sunt omnes et qui sunt et qui fuerunt et erint. Quoniam ex uno sumptu primi hominis, et ex una compagine quattuor elementorum, ex uno seminis fluxu, ex una massa, ex una materia omnia animalia consistunt. Vnde unus dies, una nox, una terra, unum caelum, unus uirorum crescent ut herbarum in. . .[a]

XVII.   EX SVBIECTIS AGNOSCI (134:21)

M* f.37r

Subiectum principale omnium rerum est Theos et Theogoros[a].[1] Quoniam Theos 'uidens' dicitur, Theogoros 'currens': qui uidet

XV   (b) *so M; G* uitae (c) *so M; G* quia
   (2) *Johannes* XVII 21 (3) cf. Augustine, *Tractatus in Iohannem* 110 (*CC* 36, p. 622:11–20): 'Vbi diligenter aduertendum est non dixisse Dominum, ut omnes unum simus, sed: "Vt omnes unum sint, sicut tu, Pater, in me, et ego in te" (subintellegitur, unum sumus, quod apertius dicitur postea), quia et prius dixerat de discipulis qui cum illo erant; "Vt sint unum sicut et nos". Quamobrem ita est Pater in Filio, et Filius in Patre, ut unum sint, quia unius substantiae sunt, nos uero esse quidem in eis possumus, unum tamen cum eis esse non possumus, quia unius substantiae nos et ipsi non sumus, in quantum Filius cum Patre Deus est.' (4) *Johannes* XV 5

XVI   (a) *The rest of this gloss has been destroyed by trimming; the only words which survive are* esse his unitas et sic

XVII   (a) *'corrected' from* theodoros
   (1) cf. (?) pseudo-Dionysius, *De divinis nominibus* 2 (*MPG* 3, 637 B): 'περὶ μὲν τῆς θεογόνου θεότητος...'

omnia et percurrit omnia.² Hoc subiectum non suscipit accidentia,
nec de subiectum (*sic*) nec in subiectum (*sic*) ubi sunt accidentia.

XVIII.   *cf.* ET HIS SIMILIA αἰσθητά, ἄτομα (134:30)

M* f.35v

Queritur quur singularitas et quur numerus simplex et indiuisibilitas,
quod est athomum, dantur homini cum tactu corporali, qui est
uisibilis et dicitur 'esteta' et solummodo uiuaciter. In Deo solo com-
prehunduntur ineffabiliter, unde uocatur tetragrammaton, quod est
ineffabile. Ista accidentia sunt corpori et non reddunt eum quod est,
nec componunt, sed extra substantiam intelliguntur, et informi
materia sine motu quasi tunc proprie Dei: homini cum acciderit, tunc
accidentia. Et non sunt quod sunt, nec intelliguntur nisi in aliquid (*sic*)
quod procedit de nihilo. Nihil, namque, quod sunt tenebrae et
absentia uocis, aliquid significat.¹ Quia absentiam lucis in tenebris
significat – hoc est aliquid; et in silentio absentiam uocis.²

Animalis homo non percipit ea quae sunt Spiritus Dei. Vnus sonus
syllabarum, sed diuisus sensus et intellectus. Vt alias ait, 'Renouamini
spiritum mentis uestrae', secundum interiorem hominem qui
secundum Deum creatus est, 'et induite nouum hominem, qui
secundum Deum creatus est'.³ Ecce qui homo non homo, quia cor-
ruptibiliter est et ad nihilum redigitur. Interior homo est quod homo,
quia secundum Deum creatus est et in hoc permanet, et in ipso uiuit
et mouet et est.⁴ Viuit a primigenia uita,⁵ a qua deducitur secunda
ipsa. Mouet secretissimo motu et inmobili gratia diuina infusus ipse
iuxta quod gratiosus in eo esse habet et ab eo.⁶

XVII   (2) John Scottus, *Periphyseon* I (p. 60:16–25); cf. n. 62 to this edition.
XVIII   (1) cf. Fredegisus, *De substantia nihili* (*MGH Epp.* VI, p. 553:15 … 18): 'Item nihil
vox significativa est. Omnis autem significatio ad id quod significat refertur. Nihil
autem aliquid significat' (2) cf. Augustine, *De ciuitate Dei* XII 7 (*CC* 48, p. 363:6–9):
'si quisquam uelit uidere tenebras uel audire silentium … neque illud nisi per
oculos, neque hoc nisi per aures, non sane in specie, sed in speciei priuatione'; and
cf. John Scottus (?) Glosses to Boethius, *Opuscula Sacra*, ed. Rand, p. 60:4–7 (3) *Ad
Ephesios* IV, 23, 24 (4) cf. *Actus* XVII, 28 (5) cf. Augustine, *De ciuitate Dei*, XIX, 4c,
(ed. cit., p. 665:39–41) (6) cf. John Scottus, *Periphyseon* II (p. 100:16ff.).

XIX.   *cf.* OMONIMA.... SINONIMA VERO SVNT
(136:4–5 and ff.)

M* (*f.38r*)

Inter sinonima et omonima hoc differt: quod omonima in accidentiis,
ut crassus, tenuis. Et hoc distat, quod in primo gradu stant omonima;
et diuiduntur in praedicatione discretiue, ut est Ihesus, et alius Ihesus
et multi alii Ihesus. Ihesus Deus et homo, alii Ihesu (*sic*) non utrumque,
sed unus homo. Ob hoc, nec primus Ihesus quod alii Ihesu (*sic*), nec
ceteri quod primus; unde nec Ihesus est quod Ihesus et est quod
Ihesus. Eccce (*sic*) catafasin et apofasin,[1] quia et est quod est, quia est
uermis et non homo, quia sicut uermis ex ligno sine semine, sic
Christus ex uirgine sine semine.[2] Non est in hoc Ihesus, quia non ex
semine ut homo.

Sinonima sunt in tertio gradu. Extendunt in infinitum et faciunt
obscurum sensum et sunt in incertis causis et in generatione tem-
porum: ut animalia, ut homines – et habent communionem et con-
participationem cum homine praeter duo accidentia, risu et ratione.[3]
Et hoc nomen ponitur in eo sensu, uidelicet in operatione Dei, ut est,
'Qui uiuit in aeternum creauit simul omnia'.[4] Et quamuis dicat
'omnia', animalis nomen sequestratur et non sequestratur ab hoc.
Sequestratur ab his quae non mouentur nec uiuunt nec sentiunt; et
non sequestratur, quia in causis elementorum, ubi omnia sunt, intelliguntur. Vnde utrumque et sunt animalia, in hoc quod animantur, et
non sunt, cum adhuc non sunt producta de causis elementorum.[5]

XX.   POLIONIMA (136:16)

M* *f.38v*

Polionima in Deo haec sunt: deus, fons, principium, origo, rex,
creator increatus, dispositor, dispensator. Ista uestiunt eum et ornant.
Alia inpropria denudant, cum dicitur: agnus, bos, leo.[1]

XIX (1) cf. John Scottus, *Periphyseon* I (p. 80:20ff.) (2) cf. John Scottus, *Expositiones
super Ierarchiam Caelestem* II, 1076–85 (*CC* 31, p. 49) – quoted by Jeauneau in
'Quisquiliae', p. 122 (3) cf. *Categoriae Decem* 48 (ed. cit., p. 144:7–9); and John
Scottus, *Periphyseon* I (p. 40:31–2) (4) *Ecclesiastes* XVIII I (5) cf. Augustine, *De
Genesi ad litteram* IV 33 (*CSEL* 28, p. 133:11–19).
XX (1) cf. John Scottus, *Periphyseon* I (p. 74:1–15 and p. 194:1–29); and pseudo-
Dionysius *Caelestis Hierarchia* II (trsl. John Scottus, *MPL* 122, 1039C–1044B).

XXI. *cf.* SIQVIDEM ALIA SIT PARS CAPITIS ETC.
(139:16ff.)

M* f.40v

^aPars dicitur a toto ex quibus totum constat. Nullum enim elementum in sua singularitate potest et in natura sen*tiri*^b. Haec enim ideae uocantur, id est formae, quoniam ab aeterna forma fluxerunt. Et ideo nulla res moritur, sed desinit; et separantur a compaginatione elementa, et redeunt in proprium statum. Vnde dominus in Euangelio: 'Capillus de capite uestro non peribit';[1] id est, elementa non peribunt, unde restaurabuntur corpora et omnia in spirituali natura. Et tunc non fluent neque refluent sicuti modo, cum in Deo fuerint omnia et Deus in omnibus. Modo uero, si ultra fluxissent et in sese non refluxum haberent, omnia uiderentur, quaecumque sunt, perire.[2]

XXII.

M* (f.42r)

Subtilissime haec intendenda sunt et in Deo et in anima . . . pore in . . . . . – – – – – – ^a rerum quia in ipse et ex ipso et per ipsum sunt. Cum enim purgatur animus cuiuslibet sancti et inlumin*atur*^b – – – – – – ad ipsum per fantasiam et talem reddit ipsam scientiam . . . homine in quo in subiecto est in eo ipse Deo, qui^c uera sap*ientia*^d – – iustitia, temperantia et cetera. Post, ut euidentius elusceat, demus exemplum. Aer enim, cum inluminatur a sole, totus uidetur lux perfusus . . . . lucis et nihil discernitur ibi aliud nisi tota lux.[1] Simile et omnes uirtutes, cum inluminantur a subiecto, Deo, nihil aliud intellegitur, praeter quod ipsum est a quo inluminantur. Et ideo, quia diuerse sunt uirtutes quibus inluminantur homo a Deo, 'diuerse sunt mansiones', ut ait Euangelium, 'in domo Patris',[2] id est, diuersa remunerationum merita. Domus namque Patris est ipse Filius a quo per condescensionem humanitatis inluminantur corda † Filium †^e; et fiunt lux in

XXI (a) *Up to this point, the gloss is so badly damaged by trimming as to be incomprehensible*
(b) *ms.* senſ   (1) *Luca* XXI, 18 (2) cf. John Scottus, *Periphyseon* V, *passim.*

XXII (a) *In this badly damaged gloss, I use the symbol* – *to represent a word missing, and* . *to represent a letter missing.* (b) *ms.* inlumin.. (c) *ms.* qu. (d) *ms.* sap...... (e) *The text must be corrupt; before* Filium *a different hand has added above the line* d.e
(1) Maximus, *I Ambigua* vi. 3 quoted in John Scottus, *Periphyseon* I (e.g. p. 54:22–3) and elsewhere frequently. See n. 49 to ed. (2) *Johannes* XIV 2; cf. John Scottus, *Periphyseon* I (p. 52:1–8)

eo ipso et sunt quod ipsa lux uera.³ Sic intellegendum de anima et de corpore differenter. Sapientia in subiecto animae est. Cum autem per amorem studii ipse amor ab anima inluminatur, percipiendo ipsam, talem reddit amorem, qualis et anima est, a qua est et in qua est et ex qua est et in qua est (*sic*) et pro qua est et de qua est. Similiter de corpore.

XXIII.

M* f.42r

Etenim differentia inter usias et accidentia: usie uisibiles et intelleguntur sine accidentiis; accidentia uero non nisi animo colliguntur sine corpore. Sicuti triangulus non potest separari a singularitate sua nisi animo. Causa enim corporum sunt accidentia, et cum esse ceperit corpus, simul cum eo oriuntur. Sicuti anima sine corpore non oritur, et causa animae oritur corpus;¹ et cum desierint sinodalia accidentia, desinit corpus, ita ut inceptionem habuit simul cum his.

XXIV.

M* f.45v

Haec cathegoriae omnes in copulatione et in compositione orationum porrigunt se per multiplices intellectus, et, quodcumque uerbum ore prolatum fuerit, uariando per haec omnia discurrunt per infinitas locutiones uerborum; ut possumus aduertere hoc exemplo. 'Ego sum pastor bonus'¹ – intendendum quid pastor et quid ego, si est intra usiam, aut uera usia, aut summa usia. Vt enim Aristoteles et philosophi, usiam per seipsam diffinire et dicere quid sit nemo potest.² Pastor namque, cum dicitur quod est secunda usia, simplicem usiam

XXII (3) cf. *Johannes* 1 9.

XXIII (1) cf. John Scottus, *Periphyseon* II (p. 122:28ff.): 'Ex deo siquidem ad imaginem dei de nihilo facta est (anima), corpus uero suum ipsa creat, non tamen de nihilo sed de aliquo.'

XXIV (1) *Johannes* X 11 (2) cf. *Categoriae Decem* 57 (ed. cit., pp. 145:25–146:2): 'sed usian, quoniam secundum artem definiri non poterat . . . per partes eam uoluit definire, ut quid sit, non solum eius definitione, uerum partium quoque cognitione noscatur'; and cf. John Scottus, *Periphyseon* I (p. 38:27–30): 'Gregorius etiam theologus multis rationibus nullam substantiam seu essentiam siue uisibilis siue inuisibilis creaturae intellectu uel ratione comprehendi posse confirmat quid sit.'

desiderat, quae est Ihesus. De prima et secunda, nihil differunt, nisi tantummodo in natura, specie et in numero. Natura est uniuscuiusque rei specifica differentia.³ Species est numerorum unitas, numerus speciei pluralitas⁴ perspicue possumus aduertere, quia natura istius pastoris, qui in specie numerorum unitas est, in unitate bonitatis naturaliter a ceteris bonis pastoribus sequestratur qui accidentialiter, non essentialiter, boni sunt, cum dicitur, 'Ego sum pastor bonus.' Ecce singularis et unus pastor separatus et summus a ceteris imitatoribus et non imitatoribus: singulus in singulis et singuli in uno singulo, et singulus per omnes singulos et omnes per unum ipsum singulum qui est singulus singulorum, et singuli in unitate ipsius singuli pastoris. Vtrumque enim diximus: in hoc uero pastore naturam proprietatis suae et numerum per specie (*sic*) pluralitatem; in ceteris bonis imitatoribus et non imitatoribus quale sit.

XXV.   ELEMENTA ENIM QVIBVS (156:11)

G★ *p. 38*

Ylen Greci dicunt*ᵃ* rerum quandam primam materiam nullo modo prorsus*ᵇ* formatam, sed omnium corporalium formarum capacem.¹ Inde 'ylementa' dicuntur.² Sed quando elementa proprie proferuntur, quasi 'eluementa' dicuntur, quod inde eluentur corpora. Quando proprius proferuntur ⟨'elimenta'⟩*ᶜ* dicuntur, eo quod inde formantur; quia 'elimo' formo dicitur.³

XXVI.   BEFORE TEXT IN *A*★ *f.193v*

Numquam predicantur minora de maioribus, sed maiora de minoribus, et necesse est descendere per quasdam (*sic*) ad differentiam.

XXIV (3) Boethius, *Contra Eutychen* I (ed. cit., p. 80:57–8): 'natura est unam quamque rem informans specifica differentia' (4) John Scottus, *Periphyseon* I (p. 102:15–21)

XXV (*a*) ms. dicitur (*b*) ms. prossus (*c*) ms. *om.* elimenta
(1) Augustine, *Confessiones* XII vi 6 (ed. cit., p. 269:14–17); cf. John Scottus, *Periphyseon* I (168:16–21) (2) cf. Isidore, *Etymologiae* (ed. cit.) XIII iii 1 (3) cf. glosses to Bede's *De Natura Rerum* (CC 123A, p. 195 n. to l.2): 'Ylementum secundum Isidorum grecum est et sonat latine materies; yle enim grece, latine materies. Secundum autem Ambrosium, latinum nomen est et diriuatur ab eo quod est elimo, id est formo, et quod nos elimentum dicimus, Greci stochium.'

Appendix 3

Secundum affirmationem Augustini[1] actoritatemque (sic) Porphirii[2] OYCIA genus generalissimum.

XXVII. ET OMNIBVS NECESSARIAM (133:8)

C* f.24r

Necesse dicitur quod nec esse aliter potest. Quia solo uocabulo quod est 'usya' conclusit omnia quae est; quia, quod alii philosophi 'species' apellauerunt, ille uno uocabulo 'usian' apellauit.

XXVIII.

G* p. 37

Sed id falsum est.[1] Nam, sicut fuit scibile ab aeterno, ita etiam scientia eius – licet defuisset qui eam caperet – sicut arithmetica[a] et ceterae artes quae ab aeterno sunt. Circulus ergo semper fuit, licet scientia eius ignorata esset.

XXIX.

G* p. 37

Scientia est rerum quae sunt comprehensio ueritatis.[1] Et quicquid sibi animus figit, uel imaginatione repperit, cum in substantia atque ueritate constitutum non sit, illud posse sciri non dicitur. Atque ideo non est eorum scientia ulla, quae imaginatione sola subsistunt: ut, si quis chimeram uel centaurum animo finxerit, quia uera ratione nihil sunt, nec scientia aliqua poterit esse de eis.[a]

XXVI (1) *Categoriae Decem* 57 (ed. cit., p. 145:25-8) (2) Porphyry, *Isagoge* trsl. Boethius (ed. cit., p. 10:8-9): 'substantia quae cum suprema sit, eo quod nihil sit supra eam, genus est generalissimum . . .'; but cf. ibid., p. 12:2ff.

XXVIII (a) *ms.* arithmatica
(1) cf. *Categoriae Decem* 102 (ed. cit., 156:20-4): 'scibili enim [sive circulo] in ipso ortu naturae scientia sociata est; simul namque ut scibile esse coepit, habuit scientiam sui, sed necdum ἐνέργεια . . . monstratam. Non ergo tunc coepit esse scientia eius quando coepit operari, sed cum ipso scibili orta est, et operatio est postea consecuta'.

XXIX (a) This gloss continues on different matters.
(1) Boethius, *De institutione arithmeticae* I, I (ed. G. Friedlein (Leipzig, 1867) pp. 7:26-8:1): 'Est enim sapientia rerum, quae sunt suique inmutabilem substantiam sortiuntur, conprehensio veritatis.'

204

XXX.

Q* f.25r

Substantia non punitur per penas a Deo, quia deficere ob hoc uidere-
tur. Sed dolor et tristitia et amaritudo, quae a Deo nihil sunt, immagi-
nibus quibusdam impressae animo poenaliter afficiunt: ut sitis, quando
in homine non ipsa est natura, sed in ipsa ui naturae ipsius accidit et
recedit.[1] Quoniam sicut uita est Deus uiuentium, est mors morien-
tium. Non: ipse non est mors, sed est mors mortis,[2] id est ipsius rei
quae est ipsa mors.

XXXI. DE LOCO

H*S f.38r–v

Loci uocabulo multi exprimi solent. Nam et urbes et oppida et
castella locorum signo sepe exprimuntur. Partes etiam terrarum
locum dicuntur uerbi causa, ut Germania frigida loca, Libiaeque
calida loca sepe dicuntur. Sedilia quoque loca dici solent, sed et
uulgari more quarumque personarum sustentacio uel iactus seu etiam
subsidium quod adhibet inhabitacionis sepe loci nomine depromitur.
Sed haec, quia extendi et contrahi / ceterisque uarietatibus moueri
possunt, incorporalia esse nequeunt. Ac idcirco aut locus corporeus
est et haec dicta significans ab incorporali recedit: aut, si incorporeus –
quod satis considerantibus probabilius esse uidetur – ab his praefatis
remoueri necesse est.[1] Sed quia inter corporalia cetera hic locus
introductus esse cernitur, necessarium est ut et in corporali intelligentia depromatur. Locus igitur in corpore quidem percipitur, sed
corpus ipse esse minime credendum. Est ergo locus spatium quo
quodlibet corpus in sua latitudine, longitudine, altitudine tenere aut
occupare ualet.[2] Hoc autem spatium, sicut nec longitudo aut latitudo
extendi aut contrahi minime potest, sed in sua natura propria ui

XXX (1) cf. John Scottus, *De praedestinatione* xv–xviii (*CC c.m.* 50, pp. 86–118); *Periphyseon* V (925D ff.) (2) *Osea* XIII 14: 'ero mors tua, o mors, morsus tuus ero,
inferne . . .'; cf. John Scottus, *De praedestinatione* xviii (ed. cit., p. 113:96–7) and
Periphyseon V (924B, 927A).

XXXI (1) cf. *Categoriae Decem* 146 (ed. cit., p. 167:19–24); and John Scottus, *Periphyseon* I
(p. 110:6ff.) (2) cf. *Categoriae Decem* 71–8 (ed. cit., p. 149:4–150:19)

integrum ac inuiolatum permanet.[3] Notandum quoque est omne locatum, *quocumque locatum, loco quidem locatum est.* Non tamen locus est, quia locatum[a] uarietates patitur diversas. Locus huiusmodi semper incommutabilis est, et si locatum perierit locus integer permanebit. Locus autem quia semper huiusmodi est periri non potest.[4]

XXXI (*a*) *H om.* quocumque locatum . . . quia locatum
(3) cf. Boethius, *De arithmetica* I I (ed. cit., pp. 7:26–8:7), esp.: 'sed in propria semper vi suae se naturae subsidiis nixa custodiunt'. (4) cf. John Scottus, *Periphyseon* v (888A–890A, 970D).

BIBLIOGRAPHY

This bibliography comprises four sections. (A) is an index to the discussions of the various manuscripts mentioned in the course of this study. I have excluded Appendix I – where a whole group of manuscripts not used elsewhere is listed – from its scope. (B) lists the series and collections of articles which are cited by abbreviation throughout my work. (C) details the editions used of early medieval philosophical texts and the *most important* of their sources. (D) is a select list of the secondary material I have used: it contains only books and articles of direct relevance to the subject of this study, and works which are referred to frequently in my notes. A fuller listing of incidental bibliography will be found in the footnotes to each chapter.

(A) INDEX OF MANUSCRIPTS

Arabic numerals denote page numbers. Italicized numerals refer to the use of a manuscript in editing a text. Manuscripts which I have examined in person are marked with an asterisk; those which I have examined in facsimile or microfilm, by a double asterisk.

Firenze	Laurenziana	
	Gadd. pl. 89 sup. 80* 17, 179–80, 183–4	
Karlsruhe	Reichenau 172 16	
Laon	24 94	
	55* 95–6	
	81* 89, 92	
	444* 109–11	
Leningrad	F.V. class. lat. 7 16–17, 123, 132–4, 175, 177, 180, 183, 187, *189–93*	
Leiden	BPL 67 94, 96	
	BPL 88* 92–3, 118	
London	British Library	
Cotton	Tiberius A xv 38	
	Harley 2735* 122	
	Harley 3034* 57–9, 61, *168–70*	
Milano	Ambrosiana	
	B 71 sup.* 121–3, 125–6, 131, 133–8, 173–6, 180, 183, 185, *188, 191, 193–203*	
München	clm 6367* 123, 133–4, 178–80, 183–4, *185–6, 188–93, 205–6*	
	6373* 123, 129, 133–4, 178–80, 183, *185–92*	
	6374 18	
	6407* 32–3, 36–7, 40–1, 49, 151, *152–68*	
	14510* 59	
	18961* 40–1, 49, 55–7, 61, 151, *152–68*	
Orléans	263* 123, 138, 178, 180, 183, *187, 190, 192–3*	
Oxford	Bodleian	
	Auct. T.II.19* 117–18	
Paris	Bibliothèque Nationale	
	lat 614a* 3	
	1750* 121, 123, 132, 134, 137–8, 178–80, 183–4, *190–3, 205*	
	1764* 100	
	2164 38, 57	
	2853 64	
	10457* 3	
	10616* 3	
	12255* 100	
	12597 18	
	12598 18	
	12949* 17, 121–5, 129, 133–5, 173–7, 180, 183–4, *185–96, 205–6*	
	12960* 100–1, 117–19	
	12964* 98, 100–2	
	12965* 98, 100	

                    13345* 93
                    13908* 93, 96
                    13953* 32, 40–1, 103–4, 123, 151, *152–66, 171–2,*
                            174, 178, 180, 183, *186–9*
                    13955* 18
                    14065* 3
                    14088* 94
Paris   Bibliothèque Mazarine
                    561* 93–4, 100
Reims   875** 89–90, 92, 96–9, 113
Roma   Bibl. Padri Maristi
                    A.II.1* 17, 36, 42, 50, 52–3, 151, *158–61*
Sankt Gallen   48** 106–9
                    274** 121–3, 133–8, 173–6, 180, 183–4, *186–90, 192–5,*
                            197–8, 203
                    393   176
                    904   106
Valenciennes   167* 103–4
Vaticanus   lat   567* 123, 133–4, 179–80, 183–4, *185–92*
                    7207   151, *158–60*
                    Pal 1719* 36, 42, 151, *158–61*
                    Reg 233* 123, 129, 178–80, 183–4, *185–7, 189–91*
                    1332   18
Vercelli   Arch. Capit. S. Euseb.
                    138 16, 17, *173*
Wien   458 32, 145
                    843** 123, 129, 132–4, 173, 178, 180, 183–4, *185–92*
                    966 151, *158–60*
Würzburg   Theol. fol. 56 32, 41, 151, *152, 161–3*

(B) COLLECTIONS CITED IN ABBREVIATION

CC [c.m.]   *Corpus Christianorum [continuatio medieualis]*
CSEL   *Corpus Scriptorum Ecclesiasticorum Latinorum*
Dublin Conference   *The Mind of Eriugena,* ed. J. J. O'Meara and L. Bieler (Dublin,
       1973): Papers of a Colloquium, Dublin, 14–18 July 1970.
Freiburg Conference   Proceedings of a Colloquium, Freiburg August 1979, ed.
       W. Beierwaltes; publication forthcoming.
Laon Conference   *Jean Scot Erigène et l'histoire de la philosophie,* Actes du Colloque
       No. 561 du CNRS à Laon, du 7 au 12 juillet 1976, organisé par R. Roques
       (Paris, 1977).
MGH   *Monumenta Germaniae Historica*
MGH Epp.   *MGH Epistolae*

Bibliography

MGH PLAC MGH Poetae Latini Aevi Carolini
MPL J. P. Migne *Patrologia Latina*
MPG J. P. Migne *Patrologia Graeca*
Periphyseon Books I and II: Iohannis Scotti Eriugenae *Periphyseon* ed. I. P. Sheldon-
  Williams (Dublin, 1968, 1972) (= *Scriptores Latini Hiberniae* VII and IX; *Books
  III–V: MPL* 122
SC Sources Chrétiennes

(C) PRINTED PRIMARY SOURCES

Agobard of Lyon Letter to Fredegisus. *MGH Epp.* V, pp. 210–21.
Alcuin Opera. *MPL* 100–1.
Aristotle *Categories.* ed. L. Minio-Paluello (Oxford, 1949); trsl. in J. L. Ackrill,
  Aristotle's Categories and De Interpretatione (Oxford, 1963).
Augustine *Confessiones* ed. P. Knoell; rev. M. Skutella (Leipzig, 1934). *De diuersis
  quaestionibus LXXXIII* ed. A. Murzenbecher (Turnholt, 1975) (*CC* 44A). *De
  musica. MPL* 32, 1081–194. *De Trinitate* ed. W. J. Mountain and Fr Glorie
  (Turnholt, 1968) (*CC* 50). *De libero arbitrio,* ed. G. M. Green (Wien, 1956)
  (*CSEL* 74). *Soliloquia. MPL* 32, 869–904.
Boethius *Opuscula Sacra.* ed. E. K. Rand, (rev. edn. Cambridge Mass., 1973).
  Commentary to Aristotle's *Categories. MPL* 64, 159–294. Commentaries on
  Porphyry's *Isagoge* ed. G. Schepss and S. Brandt (Wien/Leipzig, 1906) (*CSEL*
  48).
Calcidius *In Timaeum.* ed. J. Waszink (rev. ed. London, 1975).
Cassiodorus *Institutiones.* ed. R. A. B. Mynors (Oxford, 1937).
Claudianus Mamertus *De statu animae.* ed. G. Engelbrecht (Wien, 1885) (*CSEL* 11).
'Dunchad' *Glossae in Martianum.* ed. C. Lutz (Lancaster, Pa., 1944).
Fredegisus of Tours *De substantia nihili et de tenebris. MGH Epp.* IV, pp. 552–5.
'Icpa' Glosses to Porphyry. ed. Cl. Baeumker and B. von Walterhausen, *Frühmit-
  telalterlichen Glossen des angeblichen Jepa zur Isagoge des Porphyrius* (Münster i.
  W., 1924) (*Beiträge z. Geschichte der Philosophie im Mittelalter* XXIV, 1).
Libri Carolini. ed. H. Bastgen *MGH Legum:* III Concilia II-suppl. (Hannover/
  Leipzig, 1924).
Martianus Capella *De nuptiis Philologiae et Mercurii.* ed. A. Dick (rev. ed., Stuttgart,
  1969).
Maximus the Confessor *Ambigua. MPG* 91, 1027–418.
Porphyry *Isagoge.* Trsl. Boethius: *Aristoteles Latinus* I, 6–7, ed. L. Minio-Paluello
  and B. G. Dodd (Bruges/Paris, 1966). English trsl.: *Porphyry the Phoenician –
  Isagoge* ed. E. W. Warren (Toronto, 1975).
Ps.-Augustine *Categoriae Decem.* ed. L. Minio-Paluello, *Aristoteles Latinus* I, 1–5
  (Bruges, 1961).
Ratramnus of Corbie *Liber de anima.* ed. D. C. Lambot (Namur, Lille, 1952)
  (*Analecta Mediaevalia Namurcensia* 2).
John Scottus (Eriugena) *Opera. MPL* 122. For *Periphyseon,* see section A above.
  Expositiones in Hierarchiam Caelestem, ed. J. Barbet (Turnholt, 1975) (*CC*

Bibliography

contin. med. 31). *Commentaire sur l'Evangile de Jean*, ed. E. Jeauneau (Paris, 1972) (*SC* 180). *Homélie sur le Prologue de Jean*, ed. É. Jeauneau (Paris, 1969) (*SC* 15). *Annotationes in Martianum*, ed. C. Lutz (Cambridge, Mass., 1939). *De diuina praedestinatione liber*, ed. G. Madec (Turnholt, 1978) [*CC c.m.* 50].

(D) SECONDARY WORKS

M. Ahner   *Fredegis von Tours* (Leipzig, 1878).

C. S. Barach   'Zur Geschichte der Nominalismus vor Roscellin' in *Kleine Philosophische Schriften* (Wien, 1878).

C. H. Beeson   'The authorship of "Quid sit ceroma"', *Studies in honour of E. K. Rand*, ed. L. W. Jones (New York, 1938), pp. 1–7.

B. Bischoff   *Die südostdeutschen Schreibschulen* (Leipzig, 1940). 'Irische Schreiber im Karolingerreich', *Laon Conference*, pp. 47–58.

B. Bischoff and É. Jeauneau   'Ein neuer Text aus der Gedankenwelt des Johannes Scottus', ibid., pp. 109–16.

T. A. M. Bishop   'Autographa of John the Scot', ibid., pp. 89–94.

G. Billanovich   'Dall'antica Ravenna alle biblioteche umanistiche', *Aevum*, 30, 1956, pp. 319–53.

M. Brennan   'A bibliography of publications in the field of Eriugenian Studies', *Studi Medievali*, 3a Serie, 18, 1, 1977, pp. 401–47.

H. J. Brosch   *Der Seinsbegriff bei Boethius* (Innsbruck, 1931) (*Philosophie und Grenzwissenschaften* IV, 1).

F. Brunhölzl   'Der Bildungsauftrage der Hofschule', *Karl der Grosse: Lebenswerk und Nachleben* II, ed. B. Bischoff (Düsseldorf, 1965), pp. 28–41.

M. Cappuyns   *Jean Scot Erigène: sa vie, son oeuvre, sa pensée* (Louvain/Paris, 1933). 'Note sur le problème de la vision béatifique au IXe siècle', *Recherches de théologie ancienne et médiévale*, 1, 1927, pp. 98–107. 'Le plus ancien commentaire des "Opuscula Sacra" et son origine', *Recherches de théologie ancienne et médiévale*, 3, 1931, pp. 237–72. 'Les "Bibli Vulfadi" et Jean Scot Erigène', *Recherches de théologie ancienne et médiévale*, 33, 1966, pp. 137–9.

J. J. Contreni   *The Cathedral School of Laon from 850 to 930: its manuscripts and masters* (München, 1978) (*Münchener Beiträge zur Mediävistik u. Renaissance-Forschung* 29). 'À propos de quelques manuscrits de l'école de Laon au IXe siècle: découvertes et problèmes', *Le Moyen Âge*, 78, 1972, pp. 5–39. 'Three carolingian texts attributed to Laon: Reconsiderations', *Studi Medievali*, 3a Serie, 17, 2, 1976, pp. 797–813. 'The Irish "Colony" at Laon during the time of John Scottus', *Laon Conference*, pp. 59–67.

P. Courcelle   *La Consolation de Philosophie dans la tradition littéraire* (Paris, 1967).

V. Cousin   *Ouvrages inédits d'Abélard* (Paris, 1836).

M. Cristiani   'Lo spazio e il tempo nell'opera dell'Eriugena', *Studi Medievali*, 3a Serie, 14, 1973, pp. 39–136.

M.-T. D'Alverny   'Les "Solutiones ad Chosroem" de Priscianus Lydus et Jean Scot', *Laon Conference*, pp. 145–60.

Bibliography

P. Delhaye *Une controverse sur l'âme universelle au IXe siècle* (Namur, Lille, 1950) (*Analecta Mediaevalia Namurcensia* 1).

J. Dräseke *Johannes Scottus Eriugena und dessen Gewährsmänner in seinem Werke De divisione naturae libri V* (Leipzig, 1902) (*Studien zur Geschichte der Theologie und Kirche* IX, 2).

J. A. Endres *Forschungen zur Geschichte der frühmittelalterlichen Philosophie* (Münster i. W., 1915) (*Beiträge z. Geschichte der Philosophie des Mittelalters* 17).

K. Eswein 'Die Wesenheit bei Johannes Scottus Eriugena', *Philosophisches Jahrbuch*, 43, 1930, pp 189–206.

É. Gilson 'Notes sur l'être et le temps chez Saint Augustin', *Recherches Augustiniennes* 2, 1962 = *Hommage au R. P. Fulbert Cayre*, pp. 205–23.

M. Grabmann *Die Geschichte der scholastischen Methode* I (Freiburg i. Breisgau, 1909).

T. Gregory 'Note sulla dottrina delle "teofanie" in Giovanni Scoto Eriugena', *Studi Medievali*, 3a Serie, 4, 1963, pp. 75–91.

P. Hadot 'Marius Victorinus et Alcuin', *Archives d'histoire doctrinale et littéraire du Moyen Âge*, 21, 1954, pp. 5–19. 'La distinction de l'être et de l'étant dans le "De Hebdomadibus" de Boèce', *Die Metaphysik im Mittelalter* = *Miscellanea Mediaevalia* II (Berlin, 1963), pp. 147–53.

B. Hauréau *Histoire de la Philosophie Scolastique* I (2nd edn, Paris, 1872).

W. Heil 'Der Adoptianismus, Alkuin und Spanien', *Karl der Grosse: Lebenswerk und Nachleben* II, ed. B. Bischoff (Düsseldorf, 1965), pp. 95–115.

S. Hellmann *Sedulius Scottus* (München, 1906) (*Quellen und Untersuchungen z. lateinischen Philologie des Mittelalters* hrsg. L. Traube, I, 1).

C. Ineichen-Eder 'Theologisches und philosophisches Lehrmaterial aus dem Alcuin-Kreise', *Deutsches Archiv für Erforschung des Mittelalters*, 34, 1978, pp. 192–201.

É. Jeauneau 'Dans le sillage de l'Érigène', *Studi Medievali*, 3a Serie, 11, 1970, pp. 937–55. 'Influences érigéniennes dans une homélie d'Héric d'Auxerre', *Dublin Conference*, pp. 114–24. 'L'Héritage de la philosophie antique durant le haut Moyen Âge', *Settimane di studio del centro italiano di studi sull'alto Medioevo*, XXII, (Spoleto, 1975), pp. 17–54. 'Quisquiliae e Mazarineo codice 561 depromptae', *Recherches de théologie ancienne et médiévale*, 45, 1978, pp. 79–129. *Quatre thèmes érigéniens* (Montreal, 1978).

L. Labowsky 'A new version of Scotus Eriugena's commentary on Martianus Capella', *Medieval and Renaissance Studies*, 1, 1943, pp. 187–93.

C. Leonardi 'I codici di Marziano Capella', *Aevum*, 33, 1959, pp. 443–89; 34, 1960, pp. 1–99 and 411–524. 'Glosse Eriugeniane a Marziano Capella in un Codice leidense', *Laon Conference*, pp. 171–82.

H. Liebeschütz 'Zur Geschichte der Erklärung des Martianus Capella bei Eriugena', *Philologus*, 104, 1960, pp. 127–37. 'The place of the Martianus *Glossae* in the development of Eriugena's thought', *Dublin Conference*, pp. 49–58.

W. M. Lindsay *Notae Latinae* (Cambridge, 1915).

A. C. Lloyd 'Neoplatonic and Aristotelian logic', *Phronesis*, I, pp. 55–72 and 146–60.

Bibliography

H. Löwe 'Zur Geschichte Wizos', *Deutsches Archiv für Erforschung des Mittelalters*, 6, 1943, pp. 363–73.

P. Lucentini 'La nuova edizione del "De divisione naturae (Periphyseon)" di Giovanni Scoto Eriugena', *Studi Medievali*, 3a Serie, 17, 1976, pp. 393–414.

P. Mandonnet 'Jean Scot Erigène et Jean le Sourd', *Revue Thomiste*, 5, 1897, pp. 383–94.

M. Manitius *Geschichte der lateinischen Literatur des Mittelalters* I (München, 1911).

G. Mathon *L'Anthropologie chrétienne en occident de Saint Augustin à Jean Scot Erigène* (Lille, 1964). 'Un florilège érigénien à l'abbaye de Saint Amand au temps d'Hucbald', *Recherches de théologie ancienne et médiévale*, 20, 1953, pp 302–11.

M. Miller 'Glossaire Grec-Latin de la Bibliothèque de Laon', *Notices et extraits des manuscrits de la Bibliothèque Nationale* . . ., 29, 2, pp. 1–230.

L. Minio-Paluello *Aristoteles Latinus: Codices supplementa altera* (Bruges/Paris, 1961). 'The text of the *Categoriae*: the Latin tradition', *The Classical Quarterly*, 39, 1945, pp. 63–74. 'Note sull'Aristotele latino medievale: xv – Dalle *Categoriae Decem* pseudo-Agostiniane (Temistiane) al testo vulgato aristotelico Boeziano', *Rivista di Filosofia Neoscolastica*, 54, 1962, pp. 137–47. *Opuscula: the Latin Aristotle* (Amsterdam, 1972) (containing reprints of the above two articles on pp. 28–39 and 448–58 respectively). 'Nuovi impulsi allo studio della logica: la seconda fase della riscoperta di Aristotele e di Boezio', *Settimane di studio del Centro Italiano di studi sull'alto medioevo*, 19, 1971, pp. 743–66.

C. Prantl *Geschichte der Logik im Abendland* I (Leipzig, 1855); II (Leipzig, 1861).

J. Préaux 'Le commentaire de Martin de Laon sur l'oeuvre de Martianus Capella', *Latomus*, 12, 1953, pp. 437–59.

R. Quadri *I Collectanea di Eirico di Auxerre* (Fribourg, 1966) (*Spicilegium Friburgense* 2).

E. K. Rand *Johannes Scottus* (München, 1906) (*Quellen und Untersuchungen zur lateinischen Philologie des Mittelalters*, hrsg. L. Traube I, 2). 'The supposed autographa of John the Scot', *University of California Publications in Classical Philology*, 5, 1920, pp. 135–41. 'How much of the *Annotationes in Marcianum* is the work of John the Scot?', *Transactions of the American Philological Association*, 71, 1940, pp. 501–23. 'The supposed commentary of John the Scot on the "Opuscula Sacra" of Boethius', *Hommage à* . . . *Maurice de Wulf* extracted from *Revue néoscolastique de philosophie*, 36, 1934, pp. 67–77.

J. Reiners *Der aristotelische Realismus in der Frühscholastik* (Aachen, 1907).

O. Richter 'Wizo und Bruun, zwei Gelehrte im Zeitalter Karls des Grossen', *Programm des städtischen Realgymnasiums zu Leipzig*, 1889–90, pp. 3–39.

M. Schmaus 'Das Fortwirken der Augustinischen Trinitätspsychologie bis zur karolingischen Zeit', *Vitae et veritati: Festgabe für Karl Adam* (Düsseldorf, 1956), pp. 44–56.

G. Schrimpf *Die Axiomenschrift des Boethius (De Hebdomadibus) als philosophisches Lehrbuch des Mittelalters* (Leiden, 1966) (*Studien zu Problemgeschichte der antiken und mittelalterlichen Philosophie* II). 'Zur Frage der Authentizität unserer Texte von Johannes Scottus' 'Annotationes in Martianum', *Dublin Conference*, pp. 125–39.

Bibliography

I. P. Sheldon-Williams 'Eriugena's Greek sources', ibid., pp. 1–15.

L. C. Stern 'Bemerkungen zu den Berner Glossen', *Zeitschrift für celtische Philologie*, 4, 1902–3, pp. 178–86.

B. Stock 'The philosophical anthropology of Johannes Scottus Eriugena', *Studi Medievali*, 3a serie, 8, 1967, pp. 1–57.

L. Traube 'O Roma nobilis', *Abhandlungen der phil.-phil. Klasse der bayerischen Akademie der Wissenschaften*, 19, 1891, pp. 299–395. 'Palaeographische Forschungen. v: Autographa des Iohannes Scottus', ibid., 26, 1., 1912.

F. Troncarelli 'Per una ricerca sui commenti altomedievali al *De Consolatione* di Boezio', *Miscellanea in memoria di Giorgio Cencetti* (Torino, 1973), pp. 363–80.

J. Trouillard 'Érigène et la théophanie créatrice', *Dublin Conference*, pp. 98–113.

M. M. Tweedale *Abailard on Universals* (Amsterdam/New York/Oxford, 1976).

A. Van de Vyver 'Les étapes du développement philosophique du haut Moyen Âge', *Revue belge de philologie et d'histoire*, 8, 1929, pp. 425–53. 'Hucbald de Saint-Amand, écolâtre, et l'invention du nombre d'or', *Mélanges Auguste Pelzer* (Louvain, 1947), pp. 61–79.

A. Wilmart 'La lettre philosophique d'Almanne et son contexte littéraire', *Archives d'histoire doctrinale et littéraire du Moyen Âge*, 3, 1928, pp. 285–320.

F. Zimmerman 'Candidus. Ein Beitrag zur Geschichte der Frühscholastik', *Divus Thomas = Jahrbuch für Philosophie und spekulative Theologie*, 3 Serie, 7, 1929, pp. 30–60.

INDEX

Numerals refer to page-numbers; where a numeral is italicized, the reference is to one of the texts edited, or its apparatus.

Index

Boethius, *cont.*

203; translations, 16, 17, 51, *165*, 176; *see also* Glosses to Boethius's *Opuscula Sacra*

Calcidius, 57, 140, *167*
Candidus Bruun, monk of Fulda, 33
Candidus Wizo, 31; *life of*, 38–40, 58–9; on Trinity, 56, 59–61, *166–70*; *dicta Candidi*, 32–3, 36–7, 41–3, 46–7, 55–6, 60, 65, 144–6, 148–51; **edited 161–3**; passages in Breton schoolbook, 55–7, 144: **edited, 166–8**; passage on number three, 55, 57–61: **edited, 168–70**
Cappuyns, M., 10, 112, 119
Cassiodore, 1, 2, 20, 38, 51, 94, *165*
cataphatic theology, 72, 83, 125, 135, *200*
Categoriae Decem, 16–18, 60, 101, 137, 140, *143*, *166*, *176*, *190–1*, *194–5*, *197*, 202, *204–205*; on essence, 20–3; on place and time, 21, 51, 84–6; peculiarities of, 20–1; use by Alcuin and his circle, 31, 51–2, 140; use by Heiric of Auxerie, 16, 122, *175*; use by John Scottus, 75, 140; use by Martin of Laon, 111; *see also* Glosses to *Categoriae Decem*
Categories, 4–6, 9, 14, 19–20, 22, 30, 46, 54, 56, 88, 104, 116, *146*; Augustine on, 28, 51, 72–3; Boethius on, 28; early medieval glosses on, 124–5, 138, *186*, *189–92*, 202; John Scottus on, 10, 67, 70–3, 78–9, 83, 86, 104, 138, 141–2; Munich Passages on, 50–5, 60, *152*
Charlemagne, 39; court and palace school of, 4, 30–2, 40, 61–2, 139–40
Charles the Bald, 61, 112, 139, 141; palace school of, 31, 109
Claudianus Mamertus, 38, 43, 52, *153*, *159*, *161*, *193*
conceptualism, 127–9, 131; *see also* nominalism
Contreni, J., 10, 94, 101, 109, 114, 119
Corbie, 100–1, 139–40
Courcelle, P., 122, *177*

D'Alverny, M.-T., 134
De dignitate conditionis humanae, 33, 147–8; *see also* Alcuin, *dicta Albini*; Candidus, *dicta Candidi*
De mirabilibus sacrae scripturae, 3
Dionysius the Areopagite, *see* pseudo-Dionysius
Disputationes per interrogationes et responsiones (attrib. to Alcuin), 145, *158*
δύναμις, *see* potentiality
Dunchad, 101, 118, *196*

Einhard, 33
ἐνέργεια, *see* operation
England, achievements of 7th and 8th centuries in, 3–4; Alcuin and, 4; Candidus and, 38; 10th-century renaissance in, 177–8
Erasmus, 148
Eriugena, *see* John Scottus
essence, 1, 4–6, 9, 29–30, 88, 116, 140–1, 143; Aristotle on, 13, 22, 86, 123; Augustine on, 28–9, 51, 74, 143; Boethius on, 22, 26–8, 52–3, 74; Candidus on, 59, *168–9*; *Categoriae Decem* on, 20–3; early medieval glosses on, 123–7, 132, 138, *185–92*, *196–8*, *202–5*; Gilson on, 11; John Scottus on, 9–10, 53, 71–5, 78–86, 99, 111, 113, 115, 123, 138, 141–2, *171*; Munich Passages on, 51, 55, *152–3*, *157*, *164–5*; Porphyry on, 22; pseudo-Dionysius on, 74–5, 78, *171* theoretical possibilities of, 14–15

Fleury, *178*
Florus of Lyon, 111
form, 26–7, 74, 89, 130, *195*, *197*, 201, *203*
Fredegisus, 31, 47, 62–6, *199*
Freeman, A., 35

Gennadius of Marseilles, 45–6, *160*
Gilbert Porreta, 143
Gilson, É., 11
Glossarium 'Abstrusa', *167*
Glosses, 89–94, 97, 115, 142; use as evidence, 8, 43, 101, 115–17, 121, 173–85; *see also* entries on individual sets of glosses which follow
Glosses to Boethius's *Opuscula Sacra*, 19, 116–117, 131, 141–2, *199*; authorship of, 119–120; essence in, 123–4, 138; Universals in, 130–1
Glosses to *Categoriae Decem*, 16–17, 116–17, 133–8, 141, 143, 145; authorship of, 121–3; Categories in, 125, 138, *186*, *189–92*, 202; essence in, 123–7, 132, 138, *185–92*, *196–8*, *202–5*; manuscripts of, 173–84; place and time in, 131–3, *179*, *189*, *191*, *193*, *205–6*; Universals in, 125–31, 136, *188–90*, *198*, *202–4*; **edited, 185–214**
Glosses to Martianus Capella's *De nuptiis*, 20, 93, 96, 101, 107–9, 131, *189*, *196*; authorship of, 116–18; essence in, 123–4, 138; Universals in, 129–30
Gottschalk, 106–7, 111
Grabmann, M., 30
Greek, 93–4, 96, 102, 104–5, 109–11, 114, 119, 137, 176
Gregory Nazianzen, 75, 94, 96

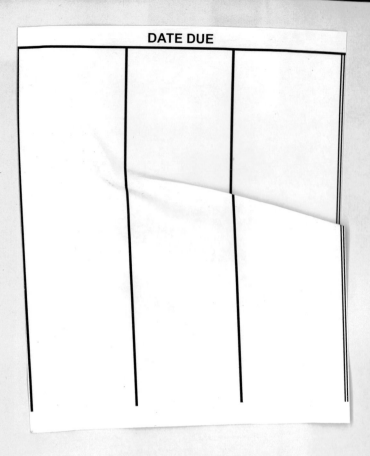

DATE DUE